Paranormal Technology

Understanding the Science of Ghost Hunting

David M. Rountree

iUniverse, Inc.
New York Bloomington

Paranormal Technology
Understanding the Science of Ghost Hunting

iUniverse books may be ordered through booksellers or by contacting:

iUniverse
1663 Liberty Drive
Bloomington, IN 47403
www.iuniverse.com
1-800-Authors (1-800-288-4677)

ISBN: 978-1-4502-5356-7 (pbk)
ISBN: 978-1-4502-5357-4 (ebk)

Printed in the United States of America

iUniverse rev. date: 8/19/2010

Dedication

I would like to dedicate this book to my lovely wife Laura, for without her support, neither my research nor this book would be possible. She was always there to give me a wise opinion, a direction to point my cameras, and a keen insight into the known as well as the unknown. She also generally tends to keep my feet firmly planted on the ground, and my attention focused on the tasks that matter most in life.

Epigraph

"Before God we are all equally wise - and equally foolish."
-Albert Einstein-

"A scientific truth does not triumph by convincing its opponents and making them see the light, but rather because its opponents eventually die and a new generation grows up that is familiar with it."
-Max Planck-

"Scientists willing to risk their reputations on higher dimensions soon found themselves ridiculed by the scientific community. Higher-dimensional space became the last refuge for mystics, cranks, and charlatans."
-Michio Kaku-

"I may not have gone where I intended to go, but I think I have ended up where I needed to be."
-Douglas Adams-

Somebody once asked Niels Bohr why he had a horseshoe hanging above the front door of his house."Surely you, a world famous physicist, can't really believe that hanging a horseshoe above your door brings you luck?".
"Of course not," Bohr replied, "but I have been reliably informed that it will bring me luck whether I believe in it or not."
-Neils Bohr-

"We have found a strange footprint on the shores of the unknown. We have devised profound theories, one after another, to account for its origins. At last, we have succeeded in reconstructing the creature that made the footprint. And lo! It is our own."
-Sir Arthur Eddington-

"ummm…that's weird…"
-David M. Rountree-

Contents

List of Illustrations

Foreword

The widespread public interest in Ghost Hunting today makes it easy to forget that not too long ago exploring the paranormal was "taboo". Just twenty years ago, the mere mention of the word, "ghost" sent shivers through a person's spine. A ghost encounter often doomed a person to keep silent about the experience for fear of being labeled "crazy". For those who dared to explore beyond the perceived boundaries of what was considered "normal", society reacted adversely to their endeavors.

However, during the last ten years, ghost hunting has changed in leaps and bounds. The popularity of television shows with paranormal themes has spawned tens of thousands of ghost hunting groups across America. Now, instead of running from ghosts, people are flocking to "haunted" locations to gather evidence of paranormal activity or to experience a chance encounter. Not only is it a new "sport" for some, but it is also serious research for others.

Ghost hunting groups believe they are already using a scientific approach to ghost hunting. However, the technology used to find evidence of spirit activity and the data recorded by investigative groups do not provide enough information to answer the paranormal puzzle or to get the scientific community interested in the data. Paranormal research has come a long way, but it is about to take a quantum leap forward in its evolutionary development.

With this book, ***Paranormal Technology: A Guide to Understanding the Science of Ghost Hunting,*** David Rountree, takes his place as a "paradigm pioneer" in real investigative ghost hunting. This is the first book to provide a scientific method for ghost hunting, which includes in-depth explanations of what the collected data means. ***Paranormal Technology*** offers new techniques, answers questions, and provides experiments, which will help bridge the gap between the paranormal and science.

Do you know how to tell the difference between chemical flaws in photographs and real paranormal evidence? Do you know what proves an orb is more than dust? Do you know under what circumstances is it better to use film or a digital camera to increase your chances of photographing a paranormal event? Can the theory of Parallel Universes help explain how paranormal activity interacts in our world? What types of data and methods will provide credibility for paranormal research in the eyes of scientists? These are just some of the questions answered in this book, which a ghost hunter or paranormal researcher at any level of experience could use to help analyze the collected data. For the serious paranormal investigator, this book will move you closer to finding the answers.

During the last twenty years, I have used my psychic ability in numerous ghost investigations with or without researchers. To be psychic was never enough for me. I had to understand the "gift" and then somehow correlate it to science. In every step of my psychic development, I sought to understand the ability as psychic impressions manifested in visions and feelings. Whether I was "seeing" into the future or receiving impressions in "haunted" situations, I scrutinized the psychic impressions for insights that could give me clues for any scientific proof of the sixth sense. ***Paranormal Technology: A Guide to Understanding the Science of Ghost Hunting*** not only provided me with breakthrough tools for investigating ghost phenomena but gave me some scientific insights which clarified how my psychic ability is possible.

The crowning glory of ghost hunting is not in our ability to collect data, but in our ability to understand the data. David Rountree expertly opens us up to that possibility.

Jane Doherty
Author, Awakening the Mystic Gift

Preface

"A man should look for what is, and not for what he thinks should be."
-Albert Einstein-

What is a ghost anyway? If you ask this question in paranormal circles, chances are you will get a lot of different answers. A quick internet search alone turns up hundreds of references from hundreds of resources. But no matter what answer you get, or what definition you choose, the common theme is a ghost is believed to be the physical manifestation of a dead person.

Unfortunately, the reality of the idea of the existence of a "ghost" is for the most part unproven scientifically. Since our beliefs and perceptions of ghosts are based loosely around folklore and not corroborative scientific research, many naturally explainable phenomena have been mistakenly labeled a "ghost". In fact, when we take the time to look deeper into the phenomenon of a haunting from a scientific perspective, a plethora of very real scientific possibilities emerge. While the following speculations may seem rather deep to some, they are based on sound scientific principles of physics. I will try to explain the concepts as simple as possible, but some technical jargon is required.

Possible scientific explanations of a "ghost" include:

Time anomalies – It is very possible that some "hauntings" are anomalies that have occurred in the fabric of space-time in such a fashion that when we enter the area of effect, we "witness" an event that has occurred at a previous time in history. This is a result of time being a landscape, not a flowing entity, and based on where you are physically located on that landscape determines the period of time you experience. Some theories, (most notably special and general relativity), point out that certain geometries of space-time, or specific types of motion in space, may possibly allow time travel into the past and future if this landscape is a reality. Generally speaking, in white papers physicists avoid using the terms "moving" or "traveling" through time as movement refers only to a change in spatial position as the time coordinate is varied, and instead discuss the concept of closed time-like curves, which are considered to be world lines that form closed loops in the space-time stew, allowing *objects* to return to their own past. Interestingly, there are solutions to the equations of general relativity that define space-times which contain closed time-like curves, but the physical plausibility of these solutions has yet to be proven. On the other hand, it may be that certain conditions may occur naturally that cause a spatial flux to occur creating a space-time "nodule" or bubble if you will, which would allow a witness, if contained within the area of effect, to experience events from another time. This would not necessarily break any rules of physics and may be a more plausible explanation for "ghosts".

Physicists assume that if one were to move away from the Earth at relativistic (near light) velocities and return, more time would have passed on Earth than for the traveler. It is therefore accepted that relativity allows "travel into the future". But, many in the scientific community believe that traveling back in time is highly unlikely. Any theory which would allow time travel would require that issues of causality (cause and effect and the resultant time-line alteration) be resolved. The classic example of a problem involving causality is the "grandfather paradox", in which if one were to go back in time and kill one's own grandfather before one's father was conceived, he would have never existed to kill his grandfather in the first place.

WARNING! Thinking about things like this can make your head ache. Not so fast though; some scientists believe that paradoxes can be avoided, either by appealing to the Novikov self-consistency principle (the Novikov consistency principle states that if an event exists that would give rise to a paradox, or to any "change" to the past whatsoever, then the probability of that event is zero) or to the notion of branching parallel universes (the casualty simply causes the creating of a new alternate universe in which the new series of events unfold). However, there is another possibility. What if instead of a corporeal body traveling back in time, we experience a glimpse back in time, which may encompass the environment as well as the witness' perception? Perhaps this has something to do with how psychics see things from the past or the future. Maybe they "glimpse" a notion in time.

Simply put, we may be witnessing an event unfold over and over again because of a condition which alters our perception when standing in a specific sphere of influence relating to an event that has occurred in the past. The big question is what the specific sphere of influence is, and what causes it?

Parallel dimensions, universes and worlds – This idea is getting a lot of juice now because of new developments in mathematical research at Oxford by Dr. David Deutsch who has demonstrated the mathematical reality of parallel universes, and researchers at other institutions such as Don Page, who is investigating the philosophical implications of quantum mechanical mathematics involved. Don has determined that quantum mechanics' equations imply that there are an infinite number of universes that are as real as the universe revealed by human perception. The universe, it appears, may not be alone.

So now we don't have to feel bad. TRYING to understand what lies behind the bizarre mathematics of quantum mechanics gives even physicists a splitting headache. I don't know about you but I certainly harbor some comfort from that!

A parallel universe or alternative reality per se is a self-contained separate reality that co-exists with our own. This concept is as old as man himself and is reflected in the practices of ancient cultures via shamanism and endures to this day. A related or connected grouping of parallel universes is called a multiverse, although this term has also been used to define the potential parallel universes that comprise physical reality. While the terms "parallel universe" and "alternative reality" are for the most part synonymous with one another and can be used interchangeably in most cases, the term "alternative reality" can also mean that the reality is a *variation* of our own. The term "parallel universe" on the other hand is more general, lacking any implications of a relationship or lack thereof with our own universe. For example, a universe where the very laws of nature are different, such as it has no relativistic limitations by our definition and the speed of light can be exceeded at will, without consequence, would qualify as a parallel universe but not an alternative reality.

Hugh Everett was an American physicist who first proposed the many-worlds interpretation (MWI) of quantum physics in his doctoral thesis back in 1957, as his "relative state" formulation. He left the field of research physics shortly after completing his Ph. D., discouraged at the lack of response to his theories from other physicists. He went on to pioneer the use of generalized Lagrange multipliers in operations research and applied this commercially as a defense analyst and a consultant, becoming a multi-millionaire. So while he was a success, he never fully covered from the ridicule he experienced as a doctoral student.

Proponents argue that MWI reconciles how we can perceive non-deterministic events (such as the random decay of a radioactive atom) with the deterministic equations of quantum physics. Prior to the postulation of many worlds our reality had been viewed from the perspective of a single "world-line". Many-worlds introduced it as a many-branched tree where every possible branch of history is realized.

Although several versions of MWI have been proposed since Hugh

Everett's original work, they all contain one key idea: the equations of physics that model the time evolution of systems without embedded observers are sufficient for modeling systems which do contain observers; (In simpler terms, if a tree falls in the forest and no one is there does it still make a sound? Absolutely!) In particular there is no observation-triggered wave function collapse which the Copenhagen interpretation proposes. Provided the theory is linear with respect to the wave function the exact form of the quantum dynamics modeled, be it the non-relativistic Schrödinger equation, relativistic quantum field theory or some form of quantum gravity or string theory, it will not alter the validity of MWI since MWI is a meta-theory applicable to all linear quantum theories, and there is no evidence of any non-linearity of the wave function in physics. MWI's main conclusion is that the universe (or multiverse in this context) is composed of a quantum superposition of very many, possibly infinitely many, increasingly divergent, non-communicating parallel universes or quantum worlds. Or perhaps, from our point of view, based on our paranormal experience, they do communicate.

The many-worlds interpretation shares many similarities with later, other "post-Everett" interpretations of quantum mechanics which also use decoherence to explain the process of measurement or wave function collapse. MWI treats the other histories or worlds as real since it regards the universal wave function as the "basic physical entity" or "the fundamental entity, obeying at all times a deterministic wave equation". The other decoherent interpretations, such as many histories, consistent histories, the Existential Interpretation etc, either regard the extra quantum worlds as metaphorical in some sense, or have no basis for their reality; it is often hard to distinguish between the different varieties, with some being more philosophical than scientific. MWI is distinguished by two outstanding qualities: it *assumes* realism, which it assigns to the wave function, and it has the minimal formal structure that is possible, rejecting all hidden variables, quantum potential, any form of a collapse postulate (i.e. Copenhagenism) or mental postulates (such as the many-minds interpretation makes). Eureka! A Quantum Occam's razor!

Many worlds is now considered a viable theory, rather than just an interpretation, by those who propose that many worlds can make testable predictions, (such as David Deutsch of Oxford University) or is falsifiable as Everett advocated or that all the other, non-MW interpretations are inconsistent, illogical or unscientific in their handling of measurements; Hugh took the stand that his interpretation was a meta-theory, since it made statements that included other interpretations of quantum theory and that it was the "only completely coherent approach to explaining both the contents of quantum mechanics and the appearance of the world". In my opinion, he was a genius.

While this may all seem Greek to most, parallel universes offer very real solutions for questions concerning paranormal phenomena. Allow me to sum up in plain English: Picture a clothesline outside in your yard that had five lines on it, all running parallel to each other (remember those?). Let's assume that our reality or universe is the center line, with two lines on either side of it. Now let's hang a bed sheet on each line, all parallel to each other. This would be a practical example of parallel universes. Under normal conditions, all five sheets hang independent of each other, and never touch. But under special conditions (i.e. the wind blows at a specific strength) the sheets undulate, flap and touch each other in various places. If the polarities and resonances are not at odds with each other, and no catastrophic effect occurs, then matter could transfer from one universe to the other, possible creating what would appear to be a paranormal event or in this case, different colored lint. Instead of creating a Big Bang, we may have what could be perceived as ghostly activity.

Or perhaps, when we die, our consciousness shifts to a higher frequency and we enter into a parallel universe, where from time to time, when conditions are right, we can interact with the former reality. The possibilities are many, and not impossible. We just need to establish how probable it is.

Wormholes - In physics, a wormhole is a hypothetical topological feature of space-time that is basically a 'shortcut' through space and time. A wormhole has at least two mouths, which are connected to a single throat or tube. If the wormhole is traversable, matter can 'travel' from one mouth to the other by passing through the throat. While there is no observational evidence for wormholes (yet, but more on this later), space-times containing wormholes are known to be valid solutions in general relativity.

The term wormhole was created by theoretical physicist John Wheeler in 1957. However, the idea of wormholes was invented already in 1921 by the German mathematician Hermann Weyl in connection with his analysis of mass in terms of electromagnetic field energy. I find the correlation between wormholes and electromagnetic fields compelling. It could possibly explain elevated EMF during a paranormal event.

The concept of an intra-universe (or multidimensional) wormhole is that it is a compact (relatively small) region of space-time whose boundary is topologically of little significance but whose interior is not simply connected. Formalizing this idea leads to definitions such as the following, taken from Matt Visser's Lorentzian Wormholes. Stand by for another headache:

"If a Minkowski space-time contains a compact region Ω, and if the topology of Ω is of the form $\Omega \sim R \times \Sigma$, where Σ is a three-manifold of nontrivial topology, whose boundary has topology of the form $d\Sigma \sim S2$, and if, furthermore, the hypersurfaces Σ are all space-like, then the region Ω contains a quasipermanent intra-universe wormhole".

OUCH!

Characterizing inter-universe wormholes is more difficult. For example, one can imagine a 'baby' universe connected to its 'parent' by a narrow 'umbilicus'. One might like to regard the umbilicus as the throat of a wormhole, but in this case the space-time is simply connected.

Intra-universe wormholes connect one location of a universe to another location of the same universe in the same present time or in the future or the past. A wormhole can also connect distant locations in the universe by creating a shortcut through space-time that would allow travel between them that is faster than it would take light to make the journey through normal space. Inter-universe wormholes connect one universe with another. But could a wormhole also connect two or more universes? Many physicists believe it can and does. In fact, a wormhole that connects different universes is called a Schwarzschild wormhole (named after the German Jewish physicist and astronomer Karl Schwarzschild).

Another application of a wormhole might be time travel. In that case, it is a shortcut from one point in space and time to another. In string theory, a wormhole has been envisioned to connect two D-branes, where the mouths are attached to the branes and are connected by a flux tube. Traversable wormholes are a special kind of Lorentzian wormholes which would allow a human or animal to travel from one side of the wormhole to the other. Could this explain Ghosts? Certainly, but it could also explain Bigfoot, Nessie, Mothman and even UFOs. Serguei Krasnikov suggested the term space-time shortcut as a more general term for traversable wormholes and propulsion systems like the Alcubierre drive and the Krasnikov tube when referenced to hyperfast interstellar travel.

It is universally regarded that (Lorentzian) wormholes are not excluded within the infrastructure of general relativity, but the physical plausibility or probability of these solutions is uncertain. It is also unknown whether universal theory, in other words a theory of quantum gravity, merging general relativity with quantum mechanics, would still allow them to exist. Most known solutions of general relativity, which allow for traversable wormholes, require the existence of exotic matter, a theoretical substance which has negative energy density. To date, no evidence of exotic matter has ever been found. But it is interesting to add that it has not been mathematically proven that this is an absolute requirement for traversable wormholes, nor has it been established that exotic matter cannot exist.

In other words, things could be coming through a wormhole, or "vortex, or "gate" and they may be quite different from our form of life. In reality there are many possible explanations for paranormal activity that may have everything or nothing to do with what we traditionally believe them to be.

This demonstrates another justification for this book. There is a real need for a broad spectrum of scientific research focused on the paranormal, and few serious scientists are involved in finding the answers. Since the empirical scientific community hasn't gotten on board with it, it is up to us to find the bait that will lure them in. You don't need a degree to make a discovery. All you need to know is where to look, and what to look with.

I have been "hunting ghosts" in one fashion or another since 1976. While my first encounter with a "haunted house" took place a few years earlier, in the summer of 1972, it wasn't until I left my tour of duty in the United States Air Force that I seriously began seeking answers to paranormal questions. Along the journey, I have used metaphysics, physics and finally quantum mechanics in the search for the truth. During the span of years, since I began my journey technology has grown by leaps and bounds. In 1976 there was no such thing as a personal computer, much less a laptop. There were no cell phones, flat screen TVs, cable television, or affordable hand held laboratory quality test instruments available to the public. It was a world of large bulky equipment, such as heavy reel to reel tape recorders, converted military surplus mine detectors, Civil Defense radiation detectors (I still own and use four of these units) and government surplus weather instruments. And yet using these crude (error tolerances of 5% were common in those days), incredibly non-portable technological tools, I captured evidence.

As the technology improved, and instrumentation became more accurate and compact, I added to my personal arsenal of measurement devices. Today this inventory ranges from a mechanic's stethoscope to a complete sensor driven data logging system. Equipment that produced results was kept, equipment that didn't was discarded. I searched for other parameters to look for and measure. I talked to some of the greatest minds in physics of my time about probabilities and possibilities. The result of all this is that in the course of my research, I debunked nearly 95% of all the cases I investigated. But the lingering 5% is the inspiration or grist if you will, for this book.

There are thousands of paranormal investigative groups around the United States, and hundreds of thousands around the world. When I started out there were perhaps twenty organizations worldwide and hunting for ghosts wasn't a cool thing to do. In fact, most folks thought I was somewhat insane. All that has changed, thankfully, since the advent of today's reality based TV shows focusing on aspects of paranormal phenomena. These programs have not only made ghost hunting a household term, it made the study of paranormal phenomena quite chic'. Unfortunately, while most of these televised groups proudly proclaim they employ the scientific method and employ technology to find evidence of "spirit" activity, few really understand what the scientific method is, and equally as unfortunate, this has trickled down to many of the current "ghost hunting" groups spawned by the popularity of these entertaining TV offerings.

Those who genuinely grasp the concept of the Scientific Method lack a clear understanding of what equipment should be used, how to employ it, and what the collected data is telling them. Hence we have another motivation for authoring this work on paranormal technology. While there are many books on ghost hunting published, there are preciously few that properly cover the technology employed in the research. Since there is no nationally regulating organization, no certification process, and no established scientifically recognized protocols for the study of paranormal phenomena, we have to rely on the protocols established by other disciplines of science. While I don't proclaim that this book is the end all and be all of paranormal investigative technology, it is certainly intended to be a vital reference work to build upon.

Scientific study is about sharing information, duplicating methods and recreating experiments in order to verify or discard beliefs and conclusions. This is my humble attempt to share with other researchers the lessons I have learned over the years, in the hopes I can help them avoid some of the mistakes I have made, and to help them move closer to finding the answers. For if the answers will be found, it will take all of us working together as a collective and sharing our information to uncover the secrets that have eluded us for so long, instead of hoggishly hoarding our findings for our own personal agendas. So relax, fasten your seat belt, and open your mind. You are in for a bumpy ride to discovery.

Acknowledgements

The author wishes to thank my wife Laura and my son Ian for putting up with me during this two year project. Additionally, thanks to the New Jersey Paranormal Resource Group, the New Jersey Ghost Hunters Society, the Garden State Ghost Hunters Society and last but not least the Scientific Paranormal Investigative Research Information Technology Laboratory for their support and input. Without their help and their work this book would have not been possible.

Special thanks to my friends Rosemary Ellen Guiley, Jeff Belanger, John Zaffis, Jane Doherty, Mark Ramsay, Kristian Tigersjal, Ingrid Irwin, and L'Aura Hladik. Also I would be remiss if I neglected to thank Brian Sandt for that steak dinner.

To my friend and colleague Stephen Rorke, for the encouragement and friendship that inspired me to dig deeper that I thought possible. To my friend and colleague Tim Clark for allowing me to realize I can make a difference, one persona at a time, and especially for talking his wife Denise into doing the cover design.

Finally, extra special thanks to John Keegan, for all those late night quantum conversations that started it all...

Introduction

There is an interesting white paper from The Journal of Parapsychology, Volume 67, from the spring of 2003. The title is Research Strategies for Enhancing Conceptual Development and Replicability, by Rex G. Stanford. He brings up some interesting concepts. In fact, he blew my mind. His opening sentence was;

"Some inconsistency of outcomes is not unique to any particular research field."

This is so true.

He goes on to say that the consistency with which inconsistency is found in many research domains is a major reason that meta-analysis has become something of a cottage industry. (In statistics, a meta-analysis combines the results of several studies that address a set of related research hypotheses. The first meta-analysis was performed by Karl Pearson in 1904, in an attempt to overcome the problem of reduced statistical power in studies with small sample sizes; analyzing the results from a group of studies can allow more accurate data analysis.)

What Rex is talking about here is that often, experiments are difficult to replicate to arrive at similar data. Often times the inconsistencies outweigh the consistencies. In the field of paranormal research, like in his area of research, PSI, the thing we can agree on the most is the inconsistency of the evidence we encounter. In a field where inconsistency is the constant, this offers a perplexing problem to the paranormal researcher.

What we MUST do, however, is focus on the consistencies that remain. I will try to explain why this is important, but it is not an easy task, and I may lose some of you, so bear with me. There can be many causes for experimental repetition failures. Cross studies and inconsistencies in situational variables may differentially affect data gathering, while environmental differences may affect phenomena measured, and so forth. Since we have little in the way of proof of what affects paranormal phenomena, it is difficult to exactly replicate any given experiment even when it IS done on the same premises in the same spot. Meaning, if I were to perform an ion bombardment experiment in New Jersey in a reportedly active house, and John Doe performed the same experiment in Seattle Washington in an abandoned factory, also reportedly active, chances are we will not yield an exact match in findings. That being the case, HOW do we establish any form of replicability in our research?

Let's take a different perspective for a moment. Let's assume that all effects have boundary conditions and that replication failure potentially can provide clues to those boundary conditions. Learning about those boundary conditions for effects is one of the most important tools for understanding the underlying causes of those effects. If we carefully examine replication failures they can provide a major direction for future work that can possibly identify boundary conditions, allowing us to glean some understanding into the replication failures, which in turn would enhance replication as well as support conceptual advance. "Whew that was a mouthful." I know this all sounds like mumbo jumbo to some of you, but in essence it means that there are interfaces between what we witness as unexplainable and what is explainable.

These interfaces are where the variables lie that tends to skew our methodology when it comes to replication. If we observe these interfaces, and even explore their nature, it is possible that we will find the answer to the effect we are observing. In other words we have to look beyond the effect to find the source. And the source may be an independent variable.

Replicability in this field is difficult at best; we are never in the same conditions in any situation and there are always variables that are different even if we were. Because of this, we must set aside inconsistencies and focus on the consistencies. The case of paranormal phenomena research is a very complex building of sorts, and we are just now laying the foundation. We are not sure what is important, and what isn't. However, by comparing consistencies, we will know what may be important. Do we lay the plumbing in before running the electrical wiring? It doesn't matter because we know we will need them both.

Consistencies are what will guide us and give us direction. So while I may have found that I had a green cloud in a room that I was investigating, and John Doe found a blue fog, then we must focus on the fact that we both experienced "colors" or "fog" in our experiment. The next logical step would be to determine why and what caused the fog or what determined the colors witnessed. That would make us focus both on specific atmospheric conditions, and on a particular wavelength of light involving the color. Our course of action would then be to measure in that band of frequencies in hopes of discovering a source. Does that make sense?

In the end the point is this. When you find a point of commonality, you must explore that point, and everything around that point, in an effort to identify what is at work to create the point. Now THAT is a lot of points.

As I stated in the Preface, my humble beginnings in the field of paranormal research began in 1976, long before it was the chic' thing to do as it is perceived today. The equipment was large and crude, comprised of government surplus equipment, heavy magnetometers that were formally bolted to the front of trucks, or dragged behind aircraft, radiation detectors from the Civil Defense Program and modified mine detectors from Army surplus stores that collectively required a large truck to haul around, and a fair sized team of mules to load, unload and set it up. There was no such thing as the personal computer, the internet or e-mail, and the world was a much simpler place to live. There were no digital cameras or thermal imaging scanners, and digital recorders were right out of science fiction. The data I collected was sparse, but at times compelling. I was frustrated at the lack of technology specifically designed for paranormal research and embarked on a life time journey of designing and building instrumentation to measure things no one else thought to measure. I have consistently studied the boundaries between the explainable, and the unexplainable.

I talked to anyone who would listen, including medical doctors, optometrists, psychologists, physicists, engineers, and even a few priests. I shared what I knew, encouraged others to duplicate my work and share results, and I also learned from everyone who took the time to offer an opinion. As time rolled by I became more focused, and objective. I learned to debunk and explain scientifically as much of the phenomena that I encountered as possible. In the end, I was left with roughly five percent of data that defied explanation. My life has been dedicated to that five percent.

During this time I have been a soldier, a stereo repair technician, a policeman, an electrical engineer, a technical director of live production, a lighting designer and finally an acoustic and audio engineer. I have brought knowledge from every job I have held into my study of the paranormal. I finally got my Master's Degree in 2007. Currently I am studying Quantum Mechanics. In all of this I have discovered one thing that I believe to the core. Everything that exists is connected.

I have learned the significance of synchronicity, quintessence and the Golden Ratio. I have learned how to find the history of a house. I have learned to value mutual experiences, Deja' Vu', and the connection consciousness plays in it all. Like a filmy spider web, these gossamer strings tie everything together and vibrate at their own special frequencies. This book is a product of that melody. And while the conclusions I reach are my own, they are meant to be a foundation, for others, including you, to build upon and share with each other, as I am about to share with you.

Adelante'

Chapter 1
Photography

"The difficulty lies, not in the new ideas, but in escaping the old ones, which ramify, for those brought up as most of us have been, into every corner of our minds."
- John Maynard Keynes-

My first real 35mm camera was purchased overseas in 1973 while I was in the Air Force. It was a Honeywell Pentax Spotmatic 500, and while it wasn't the best, it was my first ever Single Lens Reflex camera and I cherished it like a new love. It would turn out to be one of my first paranormal tools as well, along with a Yashica J-7 I acquired in 1976. I would eventually add a Nikon F60 to my stable of "analog" cameras and still have the Yashica and Nikon pulling active duty (The Pentax was stolen from me back in the 1980's).

Back in my early days of paranormal investigating, equipment was limited, as was the knowledge of exactly what I was supposed to be looking for. I read everything I could get my hands on, and the primary tools of the trade were a camera and a tape recorder. While I would take the initiative and add to this cadre of technology quickly, my first investigation was performed with three 35mm cameras and a Teak reel to reel tape deck.

Analog film cameras

This term always seems a little funny to me, because film cameras were not considered to be "analog" until the advent of the digital camera. In an "analog" camera, several things control the quality of the photograph. First there is the film itself, which is a plastic based light sensitive medium that has different ISO (**International Organization for Standardization**) / ASA (**American Standards Association**) ratings based on the composition of the film itself.

When you push the button, you trigger the shutter, which opens for a "user determined" interval (shutter speed) and allows the light to hit and saturate the film. The lens then "focuses" the image on the film. The 'focal length' of the lens you use will determine how large the focused image will appear on the film. The Iris or aperture adjusts the amount of light the film is exposed to, and it also affects the focus of the image. Adjusting the aperture process is called the setting the "field of focus". A small aperture opening produces a larger field of focus, allowing object closer and farther away from the actual point of focus to appear sharper. This also reduces the appearance of dust orbs in your image. It is always the best practice to shoot with as deep a field of focus as the lighting will allow. On fixed focus cheapie cameras, the field of focus is near infinity. They automatically apply a flash to enhance the photograph in low light conditions. Of course this limits the usable photographed area to the distance the flash is effective, which is generally less than ten feet. Film cameras will sometimes reveal things that are a product of the film itself, such as impurities in the chemical composition or film medium, or a lack of even chemical embedding for that matter. This is more often than not mistakenly pointed out to be paranormal evidence. It of course isn't.

One thing that film cameras have that digital cameras as of yet do not, is extraordinarily high resolution. Film can excel in revealing highlights and subtle differences in colors and shadow. The beauty of film cameras today are you can purchase a basic point and shoot model that requires little or no skill to operate. Special film media can also be used that is sensitive to specific regions of the light spectrum, such as infrared and ultraviolet. My own research seems to indicate that some paranormal activity may be more visible in these regions of the light spectrum. Film cameras are best utilized in outside areas, where they tend to reveal nuances that digital cameras fail to reveal, due to light reacting with the digital pixelization process. They excel in the environment of a cemetery hunt! In fact, several years ago I was participating in a cemetery hunt in Matawan, NJ at Rose Hill Cemetery. I was working with the New Jersey Ghost Hunters Society and there were several teams of investigators roaming the plots. My team used digital cameras as well as film cameras with IR film. The IR film produced some interesting anomalies. The digital cameras produced a lot of dust orbs.

Unfortunately, film photography can get very expensive, particularly when it comes to processing and doubly so when the camera is in the hands of a novice. It takes some special abilities to use special light film, and it would be a good idea to get someone to train you if you plan to take this path. Just remember, long before we had "Thermal Imaging Cameras and FLIRs, we had 35mm cameras with IR film. As expensive as it may seem, the film camera beats the cost of a FLIR hands down. In a field where it is taboo to charge money for services, either of these paths can quickly put a small investigative group out of business financially, so keep that in mind.

Also consider that unless you have your own darkroom, the quality may not be as good as it could be. Commercial developing resources still available today are set to generic properties using machines that automate the process. While it is possible if you know the employee at the developing center you can persuade them to alter the properties, chances are they are trained to run the machine in a generic fashion. This becomes painfully true when dealing with specialized film media. Also paper photographs must be scanned in to a digital format, which also creates a loss of resolution. A solution to the scanning dilemma is that now most processing houses offer you the option of digital copies provided on a compact disk. Unfortunately, as digital technology improves, film photography may become a thing of the past. It is already getting difficult to find the right film to do the job.

Digital Cameras

There is little question that Digital cameras have revolutionized the photography industry, creating the ability to see your photograph immediately after it is captured, as well as delete it if it isn't to your liking. Digital cameras rely heavily upon digital signal processing; meaning it electronically translates an "analog" image into digital data. The quality of the photograph is based on the amount of the built in processor's resolution capabilities, or the maximum number of "pixels" the camera is capable of producing, commonly expressed in "megapixels". The more pixels the camera produces, the higher the resolution of the captured images. The pixel count is a product of the camera sensor and processor which is typically either a CCD or CMOS chip. Once the picture is captured an analog to digital conversion takes place and the data is assembled and stored on some type of storage medium, such as a diskette, memory card or internal memory chip. Other than that, the digital camera still employs all the basic parts of an analog camera, lens, shutter and aperture or iris. The unique part of a digital camera for paranormal investigative purposes however, is its ability to see into an expanded light spectrum, not just the visual spectrum. Humans can only see in the visible spectrum of light. While we have the ability to glimpse into the other realm of light through our peripheral vision (which may explain seeing things out of the corner of one's eye but not seeing it when looking at it directly), we are limited to perceiving light in the bandwidth rage of roughly 380 to 750 nanometers.

The Spectrum of Electromagnetic Radiation

As demonstrated in Figure 1-1 below, while the visible light segment of the EMF spectrum encompasses a wide range of frequencies, it's over all portion of the EMF spectrum is very small.

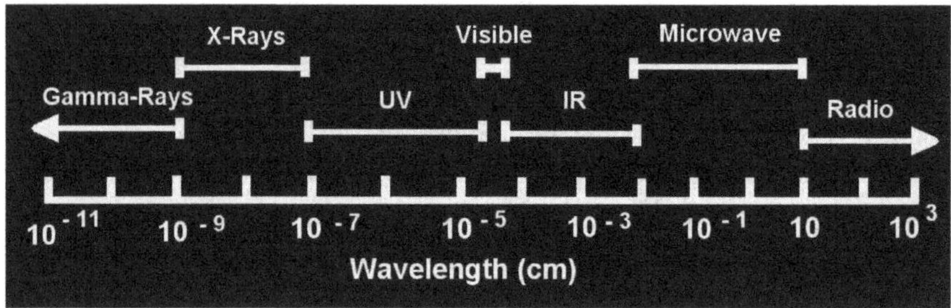

The EMF Spectrum

The light spectrum itself extends from around 200 Gigahertz up to over 3 Petahertz. This is an extraordinary high range of frequencies, and yet the visible spectrum is just a small band of the roughly 400-790 terahertz of the entire light spectrum. As you can see, there is a lot of light that we as humans do not see, no pun intended. Most digital cameras, however, see a good deal more of the light spectrum, which for our purposes will reveal things not ordinarily observed by the human eye.

A common phenomenon captured today is the highly controversial "Orb", or glowing ball that appears in many digital photographs taken by everyone, including paranormal investigators. Photography pundits argue that this is merely a manifestation of dust or other particulate matter captured by the flash and the lens within about four inches from the lens of the camera. For the most part, this is true. But could orbs be real? According to Quantum Mechanics, yes they could!

A flash on a typical camera bombards the environment with an intense emission of photons. These photons are traveling at the speed of light. White light is made up of elements of the entire light spectrum, even though we can't see it. I am sure everyone remembers playing with a prism in elementary school science class. By shining a white light through the prism, you can clearly see a rainbow erupt from the other side. What the prism is doing is breaking the white light down into all of its components, and these elements include small amounts of Infrared and ultraviolet. So suppose these photons bombard a cold plasma-like energy form that is vibrating in the frequency range of ultraviolet light. The plasma would absorb the photons and begin to "glow" brighter in the UV spectrum. Even though our eyes would not be able to tell it, the camera would pick it up and record it. Unfortunately, there would be no way to distinguish a dust orb from a plasma orb, unless you captured the same image of an orb in the same geographical location, by using two different cameras focused on the area from two different angles! Obviously, if you have an orb in one photo, but not the other, it would be dust. But if BOTH photos have the orb depicted in roughly the same place, dust cannot be the source. The trick is to be able to take both photos at approximately the same time. With some practice and working with an associate, you can easily try this on your next investigation.

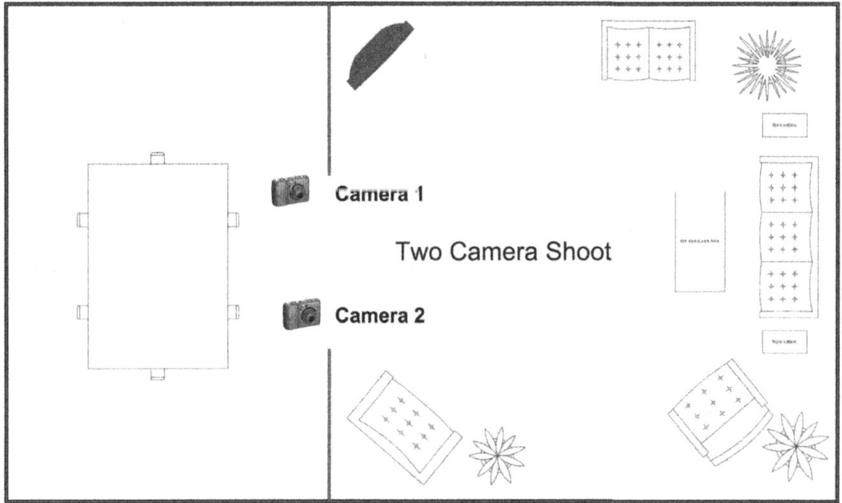

Typical two-camera set up

There are two basic techniques employed using the two camera shoot method; the first and obvious would be to hold two cameras an arm's length apart, and press the shutter triggers simultaneously, catching two photographs of the same area from two different positions and angles. The second and more practical approach would be to use a buddy system technique, in which two team members work together and take the photos from two different positions by synchronizing their photo captures. A simple one, two, three count works well for this method.

Another method is to employ multiple flash units external to the camera. This is possible in Single Lens Reflex 35mm cameras with provisions for an external flash, and SLR digital cameras with the same feature. Multiple flash units give the photograph an illusion of depth lacking from a single flash point, revealing details that may be missed with standard single source flash units.

The use of strobe lights have been advocated for years, with the implication that the light flashing at certain frequencies may "reveal" phenomena that would ordinarily be invisible. Personally I have never captured any phenomena with a strobe set up, but everything should be explored. I can tell you that I have captured questionable orbs using the two camera system from tripods using a synchronous trigger mechanism to take the photos near simultaneously. Does this mean that orbs are ghosts? Certainly not! But it may indicate that some type of phenomena is occurring that is related to paranormal activity.

The advantages of Digital photography are enormous. You can take hundreds of pictures, delete the ones that show no activity, and print them out on your home PC system. The camera itself has extended detection capability allowing it to see into areas that we normally can't perceive. The photographs are digital, so they don't need to be scanned into your PC for analysis, thus losing resolution. Best of all, they are easy to archive, indefinitely. This is a huge bonus and I will relate a personal experience to ratify the point and drive it home. Back in the early 1980's I was dating a woman who went into a rage one night and burned all of my photographic files. This included priceless family photographs that will never be replaced, photographs from my travels overseas while in the Air Force, and hundreds of paranormal evidence related photographs! No, I didn't kill her, but the relationship abruptly ended on that note!

Having said all this, the down side of digital photography is that it is easy to manipulate. There are virtually thousands of instances of faked photos in the field. A photograph in and of itself, regardless of what device is used to capture it, is not acceptable proof of anything because of this. A photograph is, however, a valid piece of the puzzle, that when presented with additional data, builds a case for something unusual occurring. Just like in a crime, it takes a preponderance of evidence to prove a suspect is guilty, or in our case, the possibility that something paranormal is occurring. Photography is not the end all be all, but it is one aspect of the data required to reach that conclusion.

As mentioned previously, and let me reiterate on this, a photograph doesn't really prove anything in and of itself. That being said, the camera is a highly useful tool when used properly in the investigative process. It is particularly useful if you do a preliminary investigation prior to the main event. My team's practice always includes a preliminary investigation during daylight hours to photograph the house for control photos. This will reveal any flaws in the paint, any discoloration, any oddity that is not of a paranormal nature. At the same time we also do the initial interview and take preliminary readings with various instruments around the structure to determine natural hotspots of anomalous readings, and identify any machinery or appliances that may be a source of interference. These preliminary photographs have been a lifesaver when analyzing photographs from the actual investigation, and have allowed us to eliminate false evidence due to mold or mildew.

Additionally, our group gets called upon often to work in historic landmark and museum situations, where because of the nature of the structure content, flash photography is prohibited. This is particularly an issue when dealing with old paintings and artwork. A white flash will fade the paint, causing damage that will require a special and expensive application of a restorative process.

To overcome these limitations as well as open closed doors on investigation opportunities, we employ ultraviolet lighting. UV light does not harm paintings or other artifacts affected by bombardments of regular light. In fact, museums utilize UV light in their examination of artwork and other artifacts that employ artificially applied color. It is also more economical to light up a room with UV light, than by using the more expensive infrared LED lighting systems. Any group can put together an enhanced lighting system relatively cheap. Just go to any chain hardware store and find UV incandescent bulbs on the shelf. These bulbs are often referred to as "Party Lights" or "Black Lights" and can be purchased for 3-5 dollars each. They fit into a standard lamp socket, and a casual stroll through the hardware or electrical section will reveal clip on parabolic lighting fixtures, designed to focus the light in a directional manner. These clip on fixtures range in size from around six inches to 16 inches, with some even larger units available in some stores. The smallest of these "parabolic reflectors" retails for about six dollars. As an added bonus, they will clip on to your tripod legs, and can be used for both still and video applications.

Other lighting tricks involve using night-vision devices with built in illuminators. I have used a Night Owl night vision monocular from our equipment inventory to enhance illumination. In a pinch we can clamp the device on a tripod pointing in the direction covered by the camera, and it will also enhance the available IR light. But no matter how great a tool photography is, you have to utilize it. Case in point:

In 2006 I was investigating a house in Morristown, NJ that was built before the Revolutionary War. While on the second floor, my wife and another investigator heard a little girl's voice, clear as a bell. While we were discussing the possible source for the voice, my wife noticed that one of the bedrooms was filling up with a bluish fog. She called all the investigators up to the second floor as we all watched the room fill, and then the fog slowly dissipate. Twelve investigators watched, all with cameras around their necks, and not s single photograph was taken! Such is the impact of the transitory nature of paranormal phenomena. Don't make the mistake we made!

Photography has other useful purposes in paranormal investigating. It can be used to survey a location for briefing purposes prior to the main investigation. It can be used to record an event on a piece of test equipment, as well as establish a time stamp for the reading. In the end, the key take away to keep in mind is that photography is just one piece of evidence and it takes a preponderance (a lot) of evidence to prove paranormal activity is occurring. In addition to photographs, many different aspects of the environment must be recorded and correlated with that activity in order to reach an accurate conclusion. The camera is simply one of the tools available to the paranormal investigator to perform this task. In my opinion, instead of choosing between analog or digital photography, employ them both, as each system offers different advantages as well as disadvantages in their data producing characteristics.

Remember; take as many photographs as possible. There is no such thing as too much evidence.

Chapter 2
Videography

"Man will occasionally stumble over the truth, but usually manages to pick himself up, walk over or around it, and carry on."
-Winston S. Churchill-

In 1976 when I started out investigating paranormal activity, video was not exactly an affordable proposition. Occasionally I would gain access to a Sony U-matic deck, but that was very rare indeed. As such, the ¾" Sony U-matic was at the time our only option for portable video recording. Due to their high cost we were never able to purchase one, so consequently video from my early years of investigating is virtually non-existent. But the year I started, Sony introduced a new product, the first stand-alone Sony Betamax VCR, the SL-7200, but it was priced at $1295, far more than my budget would allow. I was soon in a partnership with a fellow who worked at a video store, and before long, we were able to purchase one, placing it in service on an investigation in late 1976. We immediately discovered that the one hour format tape created a serious drawback. Betamax, for all its weaknesses was however, the first successful consumer video format ever, opening the door for individuals on a relatively limited budget to film their own video, as well as becoming a much desired tool for paranormal investigators of the day.

In the mid-1970s unlike now, the field had very few amateur organizations involved in paranormal research and there wasn't the "hobby" interest the field shares today. While there was funding available from several universities for different aspects of paranormal research, "Ghost Hunting" was never one of them. The researchers in the field have always been self-financed in their work. The Betamax ½" format made a significant difference to the field due to its price. The U-Matic ¾" decks at the time were priced from $1800 - $2500, making the Betamax a bargain. At one time Sony maintained 100% of the home video market. All of the video machines in use at the time for consumers and all of the pre-recorded movies available to rent were Betamax. Sony lost its monopoly however with the introduction of the VHS format by Japanese Victor Corporation (JVC) in 1976, introducing a tape with two hour storage capability, and the format was shared by all the electronics manufacturers, sounding the death toll for the Betamax format. To carry it a step beyond, the introduction of DVD technology in 1996, would signal the beginning of the end for VHS.

My first use of a video system was somewhat nightmarish. My team which at the time consisted of five gentlemen, and one lady, none of which had any real experience in either ghost hunting or technology, so from the start it was a comedy of errors. We were investigating an old building in St. Augustine and we hooked up a very complicated camera, cables and the recording deck. We placed the camera, turned everything on and were rewarded with absolutely nothing. We would later determine that we had not set up the camera correctly, and there was insufficient light for the camera to pick up anything usable. This would make something painfully clear to me. I would have to learn everything there was about video production in order to properly set up a video system. Unlike today, back then there was no such thing as plug and play. Thank goodness technology has become more user-friendly!

Groups starting out today can take advantage of older technology equipment such as VHS format machines. While they are rare to find new, there are still plenty of good quality VHS video cameras and decks for that matter available at a bargain on E-Bay. VHS has some serious drawbacks though when used in the field of paranormal research. Standard VHS format operates with a limited luminance resolution, based on the luminance carrier frequency of 3 MHz. While this may not mean much to the average investigator, it translates into the cameras needing more light than current digital cameras require. There is also the issue of overall picture quality, as the VHS is limited to 240 lines of resolution, which is relatively low. If you are lucky enough to find the rare super VHS camera, you can get near Hi8 quality due to the increased luminance carrier frequency (5.4 MHz) and the increased lines of resolution (420). However, you must also make sure you get a VCR that is also a SVHS format to get the updated performance from the tape. But it beats having no video at all!

Another issue with VHS cameras is their reliance on visible light to perform well. While some of the more recently manufactured cameras have newer video sensors that can see into the extended range of light the eye can't see, most of the older VHS cameras do not. This can become problematic during an investigation since white light is rarely used during the active part of the investigation. VHS was primarily designed for home entertainment, yet it did expand the market for self produced videos, and became the mainstay format of paranormal investigation for many years. Due to the proliferation of equipment, and its popularity it is still in use by many groups today, and when properly deployed, produce good results.

The key to achieving those results is to provide adequate lighting to insure capitalization of the systems capabilities. You will have to experiment with your cameras and decks to determine the best conditions for video recording with the equipment you have available. The good news is you can use the same tape over and over for testing and it won't cost you anything but time. I would recommend saving all your tape masters from investigations, to preserve any evidence you capture in its original form.

Video 8, Hi 8 and Digital 8

Introduced by Sony in 1985, the Video8 format was introduced as the foundation for the HandyCam series of video cameras. The three formats that exist, (Video8, Hi8 and Digital8) are physically very similar, featuring both the same tape-width and near-identical cassettes. This provides a measure of backward-compatibility in some cases, but not all. The biggest difference between them is in the tape quality. Video8 was the original version of the three formats and was entirely analog in nature. The 8 mm tape format was selected as the smaller replacement of the 12mm Betamax format, using the same technology in a smaller package in order to compete with the compact format VHS-C. Soon, however, recognizing the need for increased resolution, Sony created the Hi8 format. Hi8 was somewhat of a hybrid format, because even though it was still analog in nature, you could purchase professional Hi8 equipment that could store additional digital-stereo PCM sound on a special reserved track on the tape. While this was a neat idea, it did little for the paranormal investigation community as we were still in the camp of recording sound with dedicated audio recording devices.

Digital8 is the most recent incarnation of the 8 mm video format, and the first one I bought into. It retains the same physical cassette design as the earlier versions, and can even record onto Video 8 or Hi8 cassettes, although if you do this, the quality of the video will suffer. All three of these formats are still being used in the paranormal field today. The cameras perform well, are portable, and most have built in IR lighting sources (i.e. night shot, etc). The Digital8 format has the added capability to upload directly to a PC using the USB or Firewire streaming function, saving time in the analog to digital conversion process. Primary applications of the Hi8 is for hand held use to record the team's actions and the environment, as well as using them on tripods to cover areas of a small building. In a typical home investigation, two or three Hi8s can cover a lot of territory. Another advantage is the team member who owns the camera can review it for any evidence, spreading the review/analysis process around the organization.

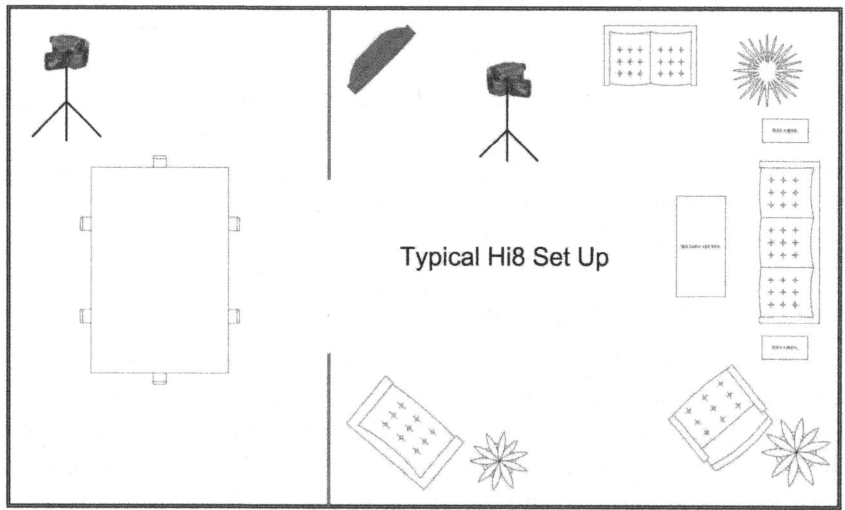

Typical Hi8 set up

For most home investigation applications, personal video cameras are quite adequate for monitoring hot spots. With the advent of newer all digital video cameras, there is no conversion process required for AVI to Mpeg or WMV to Mpeg for archival purposes. The cameras directly record in Mpeg format, with compression. These cameras work just like a Hi8 format camera only they record directly to a digital storage system, either internal flash memory, memory cards, mini DVDs and in some cases direct to hard drive.

In the case of a larger facility, such as an old factory, or a prison for example, this type of video coverage becomes problematic. Most of these cameras have a very limited time in which they can record (usually an hour or so) and changing storage media can become time consuming and cumbersome. For these applications, a digital video management system is the practical approach.

Closed Circuit Television or CCTV uses a set number of video cameras to transmit signal to a media recorder, either analog (VCR) or digital (DVR)

CCTV is often used for surveillance in areas that need monitoring such as banks, casinos, transportation facilities, military installations and convenience stores.

In addition, CCTV systems can operate continuously or be triggered to monitor a particular event based on motion detected by the cameras.

Originally, multiple camera set ups required a multiplexer, in order to record multiple cameras onto the media. This was problematic for resolution, as you were not only reducing the resolution by the number of cameras you were recording, but you also reduced the Fields Per Second refresh rate of the media recorder. Analog VHS tape was capable of around 20-24 FPS at best for one camera. If you were using 8 cameras each camera would record at a rate of 2.5 to 3 FPS, which is far from the established standard of real time recording of 30 FPS per camera for modern digital management systems. Film established a standard at the turn of the twentieth century of 24 frames per second for real time action. Fields per second is roughly a similar concept, but instead of each frame being recorded, the field of the picture refreshes. Below 15 Fields Per Second movement appears very jumpy on review. It is also possible to miss an event if it is too transitory. This is why modern casinos monitor their dealers with cameras that refresh at the rate of 30 FPS. I was introduced to CCTV equipment in the 1990's, when time lapse VHS format VCRs were the mainstream mode of storage, and multiplexers were employed to handle multiple cameras. Because of this, I rejected the idea of using them in this fashion, choosing instead to deploy one camera to one VCR, and capturing full real time video. A typical home investigation would employ five CCTV cameras and five VHS VCRs. This is a winning combination and I continued to use this type of set up until quite recently. I still keep a small inventory of VHS decks around, because in a pinch, you can easily deploy one mated to a CCTV camera quickly and most team members know how to set a simple VCR up.

Modern CCTV equipment can be very expensive; low light sensitive high resolution cameras market from $250 to several thousands of dollars for just one unit. Recording management systems can cost as high as twelve to fifteen thousand dollars per 16 camera feed. The good news is you can get a 4 channel DVR today with 160 GB of storage for around $260.00! Cameras are available on E-Bay with built in IR illuminators for under $50.00, which would allow you to put together a four channel digital video system for under $600.00 dollars, cables included. Other alternatives are available if you have an old PC lying around. Four Channel plug in cards are available to inexpensively convert a PC into a DVR. There are "How To" guides all over the internet.

The important thing to remember when covering a building with video is to try to cover as much as possible, and try to overlap the coverage a bit, so that any unusual phenomena can be "tracked" as it moves from Camera view to camera view. If something happens, you will catch it on film. Even better is to catch it on two cameras from two different angles.

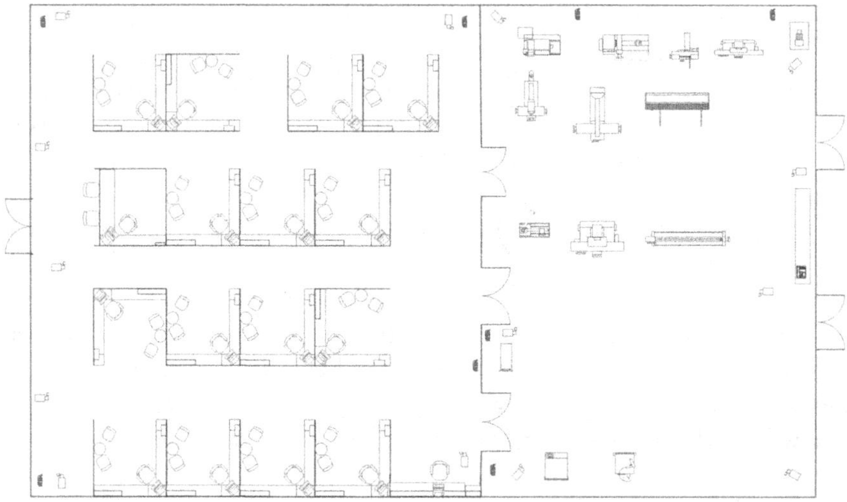

Typical CCTV set up

The main thing to keep in mind is coverage, and more is always better with video. The more area you monitor, the better the chance you have of catching something unusual.

It is also important to use a good mount for your cameras. Camera movement can destroy the validity of any evidence you capture. We use mini-tripods, tripods and fixed bases. We NEVER duct tape a camera to a surface for mounting purposes. That is a disaster waiting to happen.

The most common phenomenon captured on video is a moving orb. The same rules apply in videography as in photography; 95% of the orbs filmed are dust or foreign particulate matter near the lens. Another cause is insects flying near the camera. Other commonly occurring bits of film "evidence" include moving shadows, shadow people and moving lights. Just keep in mind that like I have pointed out in the preceding chapter, something on film by itself proves nothing. You have to assemble a preponderance of evidence. Video is one more piece of the puzzle.

At this point I would be remiss in my duties if I did not mention a phenomenon that is sweeping through the paranormal community like wildfire; the FLIR (Forward Looking Infra Red) Systems Thermal Imaging camera. These devices are tools for thermography. Thermography is the use of an infrared imaging and measurement camera to "see" and "measure" thermal energy emitted from an *object*. Thermal, or infrared energy, is light that is not visible because its wavelength is too long to be detected by the human eye; it's the part of the electromagnetic spectrum that we perceive as heat. Unlike visible light, in the infrared world, everything with a temperature above absolute zero emits heat.

Even very cold objects, like ice cubes, emit infrared. The higher the object's temperature, the greater the IR radiation emitted. Infrared allows us to see what our eyes cannot. Infrared thermography cameras produce images of invisible infrared or "heat" radiation and provide precise non-contact temperature measurement capabilities. But in spite of everything you have been led to believe, it will not measure ambient air temperature, i.e. a "cold spot". I will go into this technology deeper in Chapter 4. If you have plenty of money, then an FLIR system is a good investment. I would however consider how to better use the $8,000.00 required to currently purchase one.

If you are a group leader, it is at about this point that you are most likely starting to realize just how important and valuable a technology savvy person is to a cohesive investigative team. If you have one, treat him or her well. If you don't have one, consider finding one.

Lighting

More so than with photography, lighting is a vital element to gather usable video evidence. General Purpose video cameras work the best with intense white light. Since true white light is rarely available, cameras include a "white balance" adjustment that when performed correctly, helps the camera to record colors accurately. However, most environments for video in paranormal investigations are dark. After all, on TV the investigators always kill the lights before their investigation. But is this really a requirement?

In all of the cases I have investigated, paranormal activity is reported under many varied conditions, including day time as well as total darkness. There is a school of thought that follows if you eliminate the lighting from a scene it makes the environment friendlier to paranormal manifestations. Statistical data does not support this theory. However, a well lit house produces elevated levels of 60 Hertz EMF. This artificially increases the noise floor for audio recordings, as well as EMF measurements. Killing the lights creates a quieter electronic environment. The type of camera you are using will determine what need for lighting you will require. Let's explore some Myths and Facts.

The Myths

MYTH #1: "The new digital cameras don't need as much light." While technically this is true when compared to the lighting needs of older cameras such as VHS and early Video8, lighting still makes all the difference in the world. Just because a camera is rated at 1 lux, don't bank on great quality video. At that light level the picture will look like horrible, grainy surveillance video. While this may do for some, it doesn't let you capture nuances and detail you may need to capture that "special" event. I mean, what good is video evidence if you can't make out what is going on?

MYTH # 2 (a variation on Myth #1): "You don't need lighting with digital camcorders." Wrong! Good video still needs to be lit correctly.

The Facts

FACT #1: The simple truth is cameras can't handle reality. What does THAT mean? Well, even the best broadcast quality video cameras can't handle real life the way our eyes do. Our eyes are incredible instruments that can handle a broad range of brightness. Generally speaking, human beings can easily perceive a contrast range (the range of the darkest area to the brightest area in perception) of about 1000:1. The very best video cameras can deliver a contrast range of only 250:1. Fairly average video cameras (in the $1500.00- $5,000.00 price range) can handle a contrast range of 100:1, or about 1/10th the range our eyes handle. To get the best results with your camera, you'll need to artificially compress the contrast range, by adding ambient (fill) lighting.

FACT #2 Video lighting isn't realistic. The lighting we're used to seeing on TV isn't true to life. In fact, it's extremely unnatural. In nearly every case, it's an enhancement to improve reality for the benefit of the camera. In the case of a typical paranormal investigation, we don't necessarily have to produce broadcast quality video, but we should still strive to produce the best video we can to accurately record a potential piece of evidence.

Ok, so the best case scenario lighting would be to have two light sources, one on each side of your camera position, set at a 45 degree angle in reference to each other aimed at the focus point of the camera. Whether you use monochromatic (white) light as your source, or choose to go the IR or UV route, this is the ultimate lighting angle. To take it a step further, the angle from the height of the lighting instrument should also be mounted at 45 degrees in relationship to the subject being videotaped. This is something one almost is never able to achieve in a typical paranormal environment.

Many cameras today come equipped with built in Near IR light sources (such as Sony's "Night Shot"). This works well for about five feet in front of the camera, but its effectiveness falls off rather dramatically after this distance. Also, by relying solely on the onboard single source lighting, your video will be very flat, lacking depth and will have a limited field of view due to the range of the light. Supplemental lighting on an investigation is almost always required to render the video usable for evidence. IR illuminators are available for this use, but tend to be costly. If you have to shoot in the dark, you can employ other devices with IR illuminators from your inventory, such as night vision viewing devices. As with a digital camera, the new generation of video cameras can also see into the Ultraviolet range of light, so the old Black Light Party Bulb trick will also work to increase the lighting of the investigated area. Combining an incandescent black light bulb with an inexpensive reflector generally gives a decent fill if used in pairs as indicated above with the white light example.

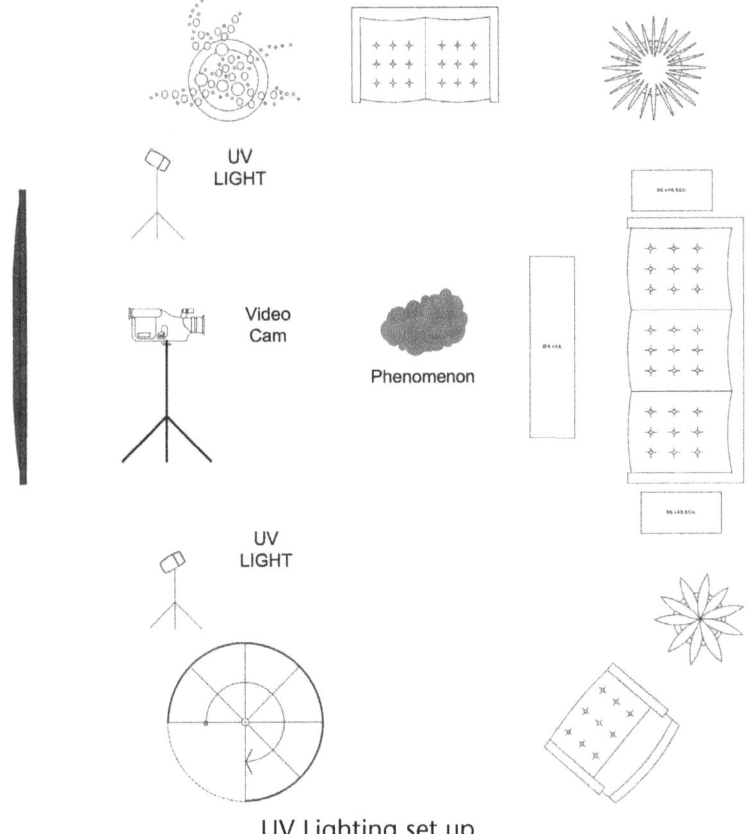

UV Lighting set up

If you expect to capture color images using IR or UV light, you won't. IR and UV lit video is always rendered in Black and White. A good compromise is to shoot the main structure with the normal lighting on, and darken special areas of interest where a concentration of equipment might be arrayed, such as audio recorders and test instrumentation. This allows you to film a darkened room while freely moving around in other areas of the house without dealing with lighting issues and the lack of color in your video. It also creates a "quiet spot" for EVP collection and other EMF/noise effected devices. While video by itself is not very powerful evidence on its own, it can be extremely powerful when coupled with additional corroborating evidence. It is also a valuable tool for documentation, whether you capture any evidence or not.

Something else I have learned over the years is to place test instruments in the camera's field of view. Deploying an EMF meter, a geophone, a Geiger counter or other gear in the field of view of the camera can be very, very useful. Let the camera be your eyes in places you can't constantly watch.

Chapter 3
Audio

"The value the world sets upon motives is often grossly unjust and inaccurate. Consider, for example, two of them: mere insatiable curiosity and the desire to do good. The latter is put high above the former, and yet it is the former that moves one of the most useful men the human race has yet produced: the scientific investigator. What actually urges him on is not some brummagem idea of service, but a boundless, almost pathological thirst to penetrate the unknown, to uncover the secret, to find out what has not been found out before. His prototype is not the liberator releasing slaves, the good Samaritan lifting up the fallen, but a dog sniffing tremendously at an infinite series of rat-holes."
-Henry Louis Mencken-

So far we have talked about the most common tools of the trade for a paranormal investigator; Photography and videography. While these two are prolific and useful tools, they are flawed as evidence collection methods alone due to the ease of tampering with them post recording. By now it should be starting to become clear that if as researchers and investigators we are going to prove the existence of paranormal activity, we will need more tools in our arsenal to provide the preponderance of evidence required. Audio recording, the third most prolific tool for the paranormal investigator, is the next subject we will cover.

I make my living as an Audio Engineer and I design very sophisticated public address systems. I actually manage an audio engineering design department responsible for designing large passenger information systems for transportation facilities as well as the data systems that feed them. Consequently, I could write an entire book just on audio alone. But the goal of this book is to cover all of the technology currently being used to measure and record paranormal activity, so I will try to paint as clear a picture of audio as I can in the confines of one chapter.

What exactly is sound anyway?

The sound that we hear is mechanical in nature. Meaning, sound is a vibration or wave of air molecules caused by the motion of an object. The wave is a compression wave where the density of the molecules is higher than the ambient air. This wave travels through the air (or water for that matter) at a speed dependent on the temperature. A sound wave contains energy, which in turn means it can make things move. However, if the wave strikes something hard and solid, the wave will bounce back in the form of an echo. Depending on the phase relationship of this echo, it may enhance or cancel the source frequencies.

Look at it this way; throw a stone into a still body of water. The rings of waves from the point of entry expand indefinitely in the water until they dissipate. The same is true with sound. Irregular repeating sound waves create noise, while regular repeating waves produce musical notes. When the vibrations are fast, a person hears a high note. When the vibrations are slow, it creates a low note.

Interestingly, sound can travel through all forms of matter: gases, liquids, solids, and plasmas. However, sound cannot propagate through vacuum. The matter that allows sound to propagate is called the medium. As humans, we create sound by inhaling air, breathing out that air through our vocal chords, which in turn causes the chords to vibrate at a series of frequencies. These vibrations physically move the air, changing the pressure levels and we "hear" the vibrations as sound as it vibrates our ear drums.

Hearing is limited to frequencies between about 20 Hz (Hertz or cycles per second) and 20,000 Hz in humans, with the upper limit generally decreasing as we grow older. Animals have a different range of hearing. For example, dogs can perceive vibrations higher than 25 kHz. Additionally, we have developed culture, protocols and technology (such as music, telephony and radio) that allows us to generate, record, transmit, and broadcast sound. These are vital points to remember when doing any kind of Electronic or Aural Voice phenomena research. They can be the source of perceived paranormal activity, due to the ability of that audio to bleed into the environment.

Sound is measured primarily by its frequency and its level, though there are other factors that make up sound as we hear it. Frequency is a measure of the number of occurrences of a repeating event per unit time. The period is the duration of one cycle in a repeating event, so the period is the reciprocal of the frequency.

For cyclical processes, such as sound waves, frequency is defined as a number of cycles, or periods, per unit time. In physics and engineering disciplines, such as optics, acoustics, and radio, frequency is usually denoted by a Latin letter f or by a Greek letter ν (nu).

In the International System of units (SI), the unit of frequency is measured in hertz (Hz), named after the German physicist Heinrich Hertz. For example, 1 Hz means that an event repeats once per second, 2 Hz is twice per second, and so on. This unit was originally called a cycle per second (cps), which is still sometimes used, particularly with technicians and engineers nearing retirement age. When I was taught electrical theory in the early 1970's both terms were commonly used. Now you rarely hear the term "cycles per second". To me, "cycles per second" is a common sense term and I am sorry we moved away from it. It is certainly easier to understand 20 cycles per second when compared to "20 Hertz".

Sound level is measured in one of the most misunderstood terms in audio engineering, the decibel. The decibel, expressed by the letter configuration dB, is a *logarithmic* unit of measurement that expresses the magnitude of a physical quantity (usually power or intensity) relative to a specified or implied reference level. Since it expresses a ratio of two quantities with the same unit, it is a dimensionless unit. A decibel is one tenth of a bel (B). A lot of people refer to this term and have no idea what it means.

The decibel is useful for a wide variety of measurements in science and engineering, primarily acoustics and electronics, but is also found in a few other disciplines. Using the whole concept of the decibel has a number of advantages, such as the ability to conveniently represent very large or small numbers, a logarithmic scaling that roughly corresponds to the human perception of, for example, sound and light, and the ability to carry out multiplication of ratios by simple addition and subtraction. For all of you out there who are allergic to math, this is a boon!

Today's paranormal investigators commonly use audio recording equipment in a paranormal investigation in order to acquire evidence. The motivation for this should be for a variety of reasons, and the most popular of course is to capture an Electronic Voice Phenomena (EVP). There is also a phenomenon known as Aural Voice Phenomena, or AVP, meaning sounds that CAN be heard by the human ear. It is easy to understand how we can record Aural Voice Phenomena, but what few understand is for Aural Voice Phenomena to be created, *matter* is required to move the air and create the sound. In other words there has to be some type of partial manifestation leaving physical evidence in order to generate the sound. Care must be taken though not to jump to a hasty conclusion, as it is also possible for the sound to be a byproduct of Radio Frequency Interference, or RFI which is a perfectly natural and non-paranormal condition. There are situations and conditions that will cause the audio riding on the radio carrier frequency to demodulate. This is essentially how we hear a radio broadcast. The RF carrier frequency passes through a detector in the radio, usually a diode or transistor junction, and the audio is removed from the carrier. This is an overly simplistic explanation, but the important point is to listen to the audio content carefully. If it sounds like an afternoon talk show host, it most likely is.

This becomes a real bone of contention in the way ITC is viewed by the scientific community. Many early experiments by researchers such as Raudive and others employed using a diode instead of a microphone for the input to the recorder. While they believed they had discovered something quite magical, all they did was build a demodulation circuit for any nearby broadcasted radio frequency signals. Every radio ever built has a semi-conductor, diode or tube junction to demodulate the audio from the carrier. This simple misunderstanding, or a better term would be *lack of* understanding of physics and electronics theory is responsible for fueling one of the most misguided segments in EVP research today; ITC, or Inter-dimensional Trans-Communication using radio frequency devices. I will talk about this more in Chapter 19.

EVP however, is something completely different. After thirty years of research I have gathered sufficient evidence to convince me that EVP is an electromagnetic phenomenon. Since the ear can't hear it, it isn't sound. Some have argued that it is infrasound, or subsonic in nature, but evidence does not support this theory. Most recording equipment available to the consumer can only record sound in the human aural spectrum. I will go into how we determined the electromagnetic nature of EVP in a later chapter, but for now, it is important to know how a recording device captures EVP. A microphone is an electromagnetic transducer, and as such, acts as an EMF (Electro-Magnetic Field) sensor, due to the voice coil's response to the field fluctuations. The coil movement induces a current which is recorded by the audio recorder. When we play it back, it sounds like sound, even though it isn't. The principle is used in the law enforcement field to tap phones. An EMF sensor is placed on a telephone line, receiver or punch-down block and reads the EMF onto a tape or digital recorder.

Most teams now are familiar with portable voice recorders. They can range from mini-cassette analog devices to expensive digital recorders with internal memory, including professional grade recording devices designed to record live performances. The most commonly used device now is a pocket digital voice recorder, such as offered by Olympus and Sony. There are inexpensive ones on the market for fewer than thirty dollars, but they require playing them back into your PC to record them digitally for analysis. Spend an extra twenty dollars or so and get a model with a USB connection. You can upload the entire memory of the device in seconds in a digital format. This helps reduce format conversion artifacts from analog recording the files and saving them as an .mp3 or .wav file.

These voice recorders come with a built in electret microphone. The microphone has a fixed charge in an electret material. An electret is a term for a ferroelectric material that has been permanently electrically charged or polarized. Because they are polarized, they respond to electromagnetic fields. However, these microphones are mass produced cheaply and do not have the precision required to produce accurate sound. While it doesn't respond very well to EMF, some interesting EVPs have been captured using the built in "electret" microphone.

The microphone that responds the best to EMF is a standard Dynamic Microphone. I use a model from Radio Shack that costs about ten bucks. I also have expensive Shure, AKG, Audio Technica and other professional grade microphones, but the cheapie works just as well. Dynamic microphones work via electromagnetic induction. There are two basic types: the moving coil microphone and the ribbon microphone. We will concentrate here on the moving coil type. The dynamic microphone works exactly the same as a loudspeaker, only reversed. A small movable induction coil, positioned in the magnetic field of a permanent magnet, is attached to the diaphragm. When sound occurs, the sound wave moves the diaphragm. The diaphragm then vibrates to the frequency of the sound wave, causing the coil to move in the magnetic field at the same frequency. This generates a varying current in the coil through the process known as "electromagnetic induction" and the current is then amplified and stored in the recording device.

These devices are incredibly sensitive to EMF fluctuations, to the point of picking up the 60 Hz frequency that our electric company puts out to feed our homes. Try this and you will see for yourself what I am talking about; hold your microphone plugged into the recorder near an electrical outlet. While there is no sound emanating from the outlet, you will get a loud hum in the recorder from the EMF given off by the outlet. Now remove the microphone and use the built in electret to make a similar recording. The hum is still there, but not as pronounced. THAT is why a dynamic microphone works best for recording EVPs. It is more sensitive to EMF and the fluctuations associated with EVP recording.

There has also been an argument in the last few years concerning the use of analog (Tape) recorders over digital recorders (Memory). Some claim that analog tape recorders work best, while others swear by their digital recorders.

The simple truth is there are pros and cons to each device, and neither one is better than the other. They will both capture EMF and record EVPs. Avoid using internal microphones and always use the same external microphone for all your work, so you have a standard frequency response maintained throughout your research.

There is a lot of disagreement in history as to who actually recorded the first EVP. It unfortunately can't be verified for certain, as we have no surviving evidence in actual recordings, only testimony. It seems that the first reported incidents took place in1949, when Marcello Bacci of Italy began recording voices with an old tube radio and an old magnetophone (The Magnetophone was the pioneering reel-to-reel tape recorder developed by engineers of the German electronics company AEG in the 1930s, based on the magnetic tape invention by Fritz Pfleumer. AEG created the world's first practical tape recorder, the K1, first demonstrated in Germany in 1935). According to reports, local residents would come to Bacci's home in order to talk to their dead relatives. Several years later, two Italian priests named Father Ernetti and Father Gemelli were recording Gregorian chants on their magnetophone, but the machine kept malfunctioning. Father Gemelli became so frustrated, he looked up and asked his father (who had passed on some years previously) for help. Much to his amazement, his dead father's voice answered from the magnetophone, "Of course I shall help you. I'm always with you." And of course there is little other than these gentlemen's "word" to prove their claims. As stated, none of the examples they quote exist today for confirmation.

Perhaps the most well-known EVP researchers of the 20th century was a Swedish opera singer, painter and film producer named Friedrich Jurgenson. In 1959, while recording the sounds of birds singing in his back yard he captured what he believed to be "phantom voices". During tape playback, he heard a female voice say, "Friedrich, you are being watched. Friedel, my little Friedel, can you hear me?" He *believed* it was the voice of his dead mother. However, one must note that it could have just as easily been a neighbor or prankster, as the recording was not performed in a controlled situation. Jurgenson would go on to record many other voices over the next four years, inspiring him to write his two famous literary works, "Voices From the Universe" and "Radio Contact with the Dead." It is unfortunate that Jurgenson didn't have a background in science.

Dr. Konstantin Raudive, a Latvian psychologist, got wind of Jurgenson's experiments several years later. It has been reported that Raudive was initially skeptical of the recordings, but after he used Jurgenson's methodology and recorded many voices, including that of his deceased mother (what is it with mothers?) he became a convert. This is why for many years, EVPs were known as Raudive Voices. When I began my own research in 1976, I had never heard the term EVP.

In the 1960s and 1970s, EVP research became a key area of focus in the paranormal community. While this type of evidence seemed compelling, it was not without controversy. It was during this period that "researchers" began perpetrating fraud in the field that would become known as ITC or so-called Inter-Transdimentional Communications or Instrumental Trans-Communications (both terms have been used). This began in earnest with American researchers George Meek and psychic William O'Neil, who claimed they recorded hundreds of hours of EVPs with radio oscillators. They also claimed to have worked closely with scientist Dr. George Jeffries Mueller. The only catch was that Mueller was deceased. A bigger catch was it is doubtful that he ever existed at all. It seems the primary motivation for the hoax was to secure funding from various corporations to fund building the device and its future modifications. I will cover this in more detail in a later chapter.

Then there is Sarah Estep, one of the most outspoken EVP "researchers" on the planet. Ms Estep founded the American Association of Electronic Voice Phenomenon (AAEVP) in 1982 and has built it into a multi-million dollar 501I nonprofit educational corporation, using tax deductible donations and. She claims to have communicated with thousands of ghosts over the years, as well as with aliens. But for some inexplicable reason, she hasn't won a Nobel Prize yet, or been the subject of earth shattering scientific breakthroughs in proving the existence of ghosts OR UFOs, at least not by the scientific community. Perhaps I lack the required "inner peace" and "spiritual focus" to fully appreciate the "work". A careful read of their site reveals little in the way of any objective evidence. What would be compelling is to monitor these folks in action with sophisticated environmental monitoring equipment to see what is really going on…

My first experience with a Raudive voice took place in December of 1976. I headed a small team of researchers on vigil at an old Victorian home located near Micanopy, Florida. I was using a 9 year old TEAC A4010S reel to reel recorder deck, two Shure M67 four channel mixers (one for each channel of the recorder deck), and eight Shure SM-58 Microphones mounted on Atlas Boom stands. While we considered this to be a portable set up, the weight of this system was incredible. The tape recorder weighed 45 pounds, the mixers weighed 4 pounds 13 ounces each, the microphones weighed 12 ounces each, and the Atlas Boom stands had a per unit weight of 20 pounds, bringing the total system weight to 220 pounds, 10 ounces, and this is just for the audio recorder set up! I drove a Datsun pickup truck back then and this illustrates why.

Getting back to the story, I set up microphones all over the house, but limited the four upstairs microphones to the left channel of the recorder, and the four downstairs microphones to the right channel of the recorder. I managed to capture several EVPs upstairs, but could not identify the exact location, since I had four microphones covering the entire floor. To say this system had drawbacks was something of an understatement! The proper way to record would have been to have the eight microphones each feed a separate channel on the recording deck. That of course would have required an 8 channel recorder, a studio quality device that would have cost ten thousand dollars instead of the four hundred I paid for the Teac. One works with what they can afford. The good news is I captured the EVPs with such clarity because the additive effect of four microphones made for a far more sensitive recording than one microphone could have produced. The take away lesson was that multiple microphones in an environment are accumulative in their effect.

Today, thousands of researchers around the world investigate EVP. Their findings are documented on thousands of web sites, as well as in numerous books on the subject. Of course not everyone believes that the voices EVP researchers hear are otherworldly spirits. Many engineers (including myself) who have studied the phenomenon point out that many EVPs are caused by radio interference. Skeptics will point out that people who claim to hear these voices are either imagining them or are creating meaning out of insignificant sound with their minds, projecting what the person wants to hear on the recording they are listening to. After having many heated debates with proponents and critics of ITC, an interesting pattern emerges; people who expect to speak with the dead do. People who analyze the devices from a purely objective standpoint don't. In my opinion in many cases of EVP as well, the listener is a victim of auditory pareidolia. This auditory pareidolia or apophenia is a key contributor to the EVP phenomenon. The term pareidolia, referenced in 1994 by Steven Goldstein, describes a psychological phenomenon involving a vague and random stimulus, often an image or sound, being perceived as significant. Common examples include images of animals or faces in clouds, the man in the moon, hidden messages on records played in reverse and of course, EVPs. Pareidolia is actually a type of apophenia.

Apophenia is the experience of seeing patterns or connections in random or meaningless data. The term was coined in 1958 by Klaus Conrad, who defined it as the "unmotivated seeing of connections" accompanied by a "specific experience of an abnormal meaningfulness". But, in spite of this, not all EVP (we will address ITC specifically later in the book) is a product of the mind. So how can you tell if you have a legitimate EVP? There is a simple litmus test that will give you this answer; play it privately to five different people. If they all hear the same thing you have an EVP. To date, relating an

EVP to the dead is done solely by the content of the message, or the perceived content of the message. No scientifically acceptable factor has been identified so far to prove any connection to the dead, or aliens for that matter. They are electromagnetic fields from an unknown or unidentifiable source.

In many cases, groups or group members are creating their own EVPs artificially. I am not sure what the motivation would be for this, but it adds nothing to the research and under close analysis, the file can be analyzed and determined to be fake, which in turn can discredit the investigator responsible for its creation.

A case in point, I have a friend who does a lot of voice analysis work for a governmental law enforcement agency and is considered an expert in voice analysis. He has access to sophisticated voice analysis software that can compare two voiceprints and determine how genuine they are to its claimed source. To be qualified as experts in voiceprint analysis, technicians must complete a course of study on spectrographic analysis that generally runs from two to four weeks, complete one hundred voice comparison cases under intense personal supervision by a known expert and be examined by a board of experts in the field. All of the studies that have been done on spectrographic accuracy of voiceprint analysis, including a 1986 FBI survey, show that the people who have been properly trained and who use standard aural and visual procedures get highly accurate results. To make a long story short, it was amazing how many EVPs had a high number of similarities to the voice patterns of those "living" voices on the recordings.

Having said all this, there is a fairly high percentage of EVP recordings that defy explanation. This is because additional evidence confirmed that they were not caused by interference from radio or operator sources. This of course requires additional equipment such as Radio Frequency Spectrum Analyzers and EMF frequency sensors. I will include more about this type of equipment in a later chapter in more detail.

I have a pet peeve in the field today with "rating" systems. In an effort to sound more scientific, people place additional tags to certain phenomena. EVP is unfortunately a prime example of this. The aforementioned AAEVP has endorsed the Raudive rating system for EVP quality that most investigators are familiar with.

Class A: Voices are very clear and easily understandable by everyone. This means that no matter who listens to it, there is agreement on content.
Class B: Voices are fairly loud and clear and are sometimes audible without headphones. This definition is very vague to me. This must be classified as noise induced Pareidolia. Besides, if it is audible, it is Aural Voice Phenomena, not Electronic Voice Phenomena, and the two are very distinct in nature.

Aural Voice phenomena requires mass to move air, indicative of a physical manifestation requirement. Sound is mechanical energy, and as such, requires mass to move the air to create it. EVP is created by EMF in the audio spectrum.

Class C: Voices are very soft and often indecipherable. This too is nothing more than noise stimulated Pareidolia. While it may be interesting, it is in essence, noise, from a scientific standpoint, and can be caused by many natural occurring conditions.

Here is the plain and simple objective truth. If you can't understand it, it is noise. To call it anything else is fantasy from a scientific standpoint. So, the definition of an EVP should be, an inaudible disembodied voice captured electronically that is clearly understood by all who hear it, from a source unknown.

There have been hundreds of articles, books and papers, not to mention blogs claiming to state the proper way to capture an EVP. Some advocate the use of white noise as a means of facilitating the recording. From an evidence standpoint, any signal you intentionally inject into a recording will render the evidence as tampered with and useless, regardless of what you pick up. It will be dismissed outright in scientific circles. A serious researcher works very hard to lift an EVP out of the noise floor that occurs all around us naturally. Increasing that noise floor may obscure a legitimate piece of evidence. Additionally, the injection of noise can cause many things to occur with the recording device, from saturating the input amplifiers to demodulating audio from an RF signal bleeding over into the device. While it may yield interesting results, you have no way of proving what it is because there are too many things it could be. Ideally, capturing EVPs should be accomplished as simply as possible to remove additional opportunities for the evidence to be debunked. To do this, you need two essential pieces of equipment, the recording device and the microphone.

Now back to the pros and cons of recording devices. Analog devices work extremely well, and have done so for years. The issues with them today are most groups are using portable voice recorders that have an internal microphone and use mini-cassettes as a recording medium. The problem is the internal microphone works great when you are talking directly into it, but when it is left in a quiet environment to record, the automatic gain control heads for infinity gain, which allows it to pick up and record the sounds of the motor and tape transport mechanics. To eliminate the problem, an external dynamic microphone should be used. If investigators wire themselves for sound to document the investigation, a lavaliere dynamic microphone pinned on the shirt near the mouth should be used. Unfortunately, at last check, only a few manufacturers such as Shure Brothers still make a dynamic lavaliere microphone (the Shure model SM11), and it is rather costly at $179.00 retail. You can shop around and get them for around $130.00 but this is still costly for the average group. Anchor Audio makes the LM 60, a dynamic lapel microphone that can be found online for around $78.00, and this is about the best deal I have found. But for those on a tight technical budget, I have rigged a small plastic cased dynamic microphone that is available from various online supply houses for less than ten dollars to a simple clip (i.e. duct taping a binder clip to the microphone) and produced excellent results.

If the microphone comes with a standard XLR connector on the end (a special three pin jack used in professional audio application for balanced inputs), a trip to Radio Shack will be required to buy a mini phone plug to either mount on the microphone cable if you know how to use a soldering iron, or simply to purchase an adaptor to allow you to use the mini-phone plug input of the portable voice recorder. A word of warning here, be sure to get the correct plug end. Some digital recorders require a plug with the tip maintaining the same diameter as the sleeve. Some mini-phone plugs use a slightly larger tip to help lock the plug in the jack. If you choose to hack off the XLR plug and replace it with a mini-phone plug search the internet for a wiring diagram. Essentially you tie both signal wires (white and black or red and black) to the center pin (tip) and the shield is soldered to the longer arm of the connector (sleeve). Also be sure to slip the plug sleeve on the wire before you solder the plug tip on.

An additional problem with the analog recorder is that in order to analyze the audio captured, you will need to use software. Since the software is on your computer, you will have to manually record the content onto the PC via the sound card input. This can become a tedious task when you have twelve voice recorders and two hours of audio associated with each one. This also brings into play another set of variables, the quality of your sound card and your ability to properly record the signal from one device to the other. This can add distortion to the recording if done improperly. Additionally, artifacts are created on the recording by the digital conversion process. An "artifact" is essentially noise that is added by the process that alters the wave form. Direct inscription to digital format eliminates those artifacts. One of the key benefits to the digital voice recorder is the availability of a USB interface for instant uploading of the file in seconds. While all digital recorders do not come equipped with this feature, spend the extra money for it. The amount of time this will save you converting files will more than make up for the extra twenty bucks it will add to the purchase price. With the advent of FireWire, even faster modes of transfer (for streaming at any rate) can be achieved, with recorders and computers set up for the format. USB 2.0 also has added a faster download rate option. Most of us are patiently awaiting USB 3.0.

There is one more thing I would emphasize concerning the use of small digital voice recorders. These devices are not of the best quality, and subsequently add a lot of artifacts to the recording that are not related to paranormal activity and yet can be easily misconstrued to be paranormal. Consequently while we use small recorders on people to document the investigator in an investigation, we use a higher quality recording device for actual evidence capture. In our case, the Tascam DR-7 digital recorder, which is capable of producing near studio quality recordings.

Of course there are many other ways to gather EVP evidence besides the portable recorder method. My team also uses several standard home stereo system cassette decks coupled to small microphone mixers for some of our more advanced work. Old VCRs work great for this as well. The point is you can use any recording device you have available as long as you use an external dynamic microphone. We overcome the sound card issues by using a USB interface from SoundBlaster to transfer audio from the cassette deck to the PC or laptop. It converts the material to digital information and uploads it either using optical links or a USB connection.

In my opinion, the biggest problem encountered during the quest for EVP evidence is, as I have hinted at, is ambient noise. Your team members are talking about the investigation, their bad day at work, who they are dating, etc. and this background chatter can obliterate any EVP present. A good rule of thumb is to limit voice communication while on an investigation. Walk and move about quietly to avoid generating unwarranted noise. My team sets up recorders in rooms with suspected activity and leaves them there for the duration of the investigation, coming back on occasion to check on them or change tapes. Some investigators like to attempt communication by asking questions. It is a good idea to decided on a series of questions before the investigation begins instead of coming up with questions on site. You should work up a basic script to follow, and then deviate as required by the circumstances. Questions should include "What is your name?" or "Do you know what year it is?" etc. No matter what path you choose, standardize your protocols and stick to them so your results are consistent.

After you capture an EVP, you will need to analyze it. There are several freeware programs such as Audacity and EXPStudio, which will work wonderfully. There is also a myriad of software available to purchase. My favorites happen to be Sony Sound Forge and Adobe Audigy. Sony's entry-level software, Sound Forge Audio Studio, is only $54.95. We use Sound Forge 9, which retails for around $400.00. Software can be used to filter, clean up and amplify any EVP you capture. Many people claim to be able to tell a real EVP from background voices on the audio. I can tell you they are full of it. Audio signals are audio signals. They will claim an EVP will "ride" on another frequency, which renders it differently than recorded audio. Guess what? Radio broadcasts also have audio "riding on another frequency". While in some cases this is true, very specific audio analysis techniques are required to verify the reality of a recording. Audio analysis is not a foolproof method to determine the reality of an EVP, but it can be used to determine if a recording has been tampered with.

Voice Print Analysis, however can positively identify a voice and associate it with a dead person, if certain conditions are met. The key difference is Voice Print Analysis requires about $12,000.00 worth of software and some laboratory quality equipment as well as an intense training and certification process by the analyzer. It also requires that you have a voice file of the dead person when they were alive for comparison. But can you imagine the impact of making such a positive identification?

There are also many other things to consider when recording EVPs. Is there a high level of RF present? Are there other contributing signals in the background that could potentially be a source for the EVP? Is this just a team member saying something low so that it doesn't sound familiar? Can you discern the content? These are some of the questions that need to be answered to determine the reality of an EVP. We will go into more depth on EVP analysis in a later chapter.

It is my personal belief that EVP evidence is the most compelling single piece of evidence that gives any indication that there may be such a thing as "ghosts". However, it is just another piece of the puzzle that requires many pieces to fit together to make a recognizable picture. As with photography and videography, audio evidence by itself is interesting, but inconclusive. In order to build a preponderance of evidence, we will need to gather far more data, quantify it, and correlate it to a real time event. In order to accomplish this, we will have to add additional information from the environment to put it all in perspective.

Chapter 4
Temperature and Humidity

"The young specialist in English Lit, a correspondent, lectured me severely on the fact that in every century people have thought they understood the Universe at last, and in every century they were proved to be wrong. It follows that the one thing we can say about our modern "knowledge" is that it is wrong. My answer to him was, when people thought the Earth was flat, they were wrong. When people thought the Earth was spherical they were wrong. But if you think that thinking the Earth is spherical is just as wrong as thinking the Earth is flat, then your view is wronger than both of them put together."
-Isaac Asimov-

As we have seen, photography, videography and audio recording can produce some compelling and interesting evidence, but not necessarily credible evidence on its own. In order to strengthen this evidence, it must be quantified by additional changes in the environment correlated with the recorded events, in order to put everything in perspective. In order to do this, we must monitor as much of the environment as possible, and note any transitory changes that occur and their relationship to perceived paranormal activity.

Temperature

Cold spots have long been associated with paranormal phenomena. Probably the next most common piece of equipment found in the hands of today's paranormal investigators is the thermometer. Some thermometers work well in our application while others do not. Some, in fact, won't work at all. The most ridiculous thing I ever witnessed on TV was a team using a laser thermometer to find an ambient cold spot in the air. A non-contact infrared thermometer is useless for this purpose as it can only measure surface temperatures and is *specifically designed* to ignore ambient conditions.

IR infrared thermometers work by capturing the invisible infrared energy naturally emitted from all *objects* warmer than absolute zero (0 degrees Kelvin). Infrared radiation is part of the electromagnetic radiation spectrum that includes, radio waves, microwaves, visible light, ultraviolet, gamma, and X-rays. Every *object* emits IR energy as long as it is warmer than absolute zero. Ambient temperature is area temperature, not object temperature.

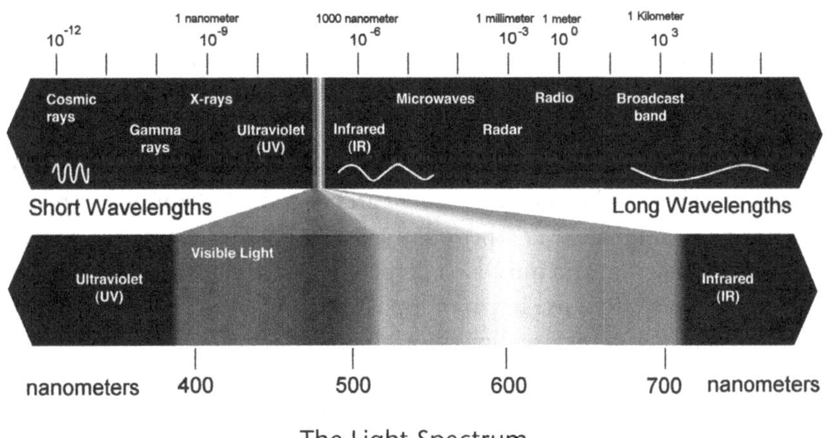

The Light Spectrum

To be extremely specific here, infrared thermometers need a surface to measure. All infrared thermometer sensors are specifically designed so that the air between the sensor and target *does not* affect the accuracy of the surface measurement. Therefore using an IR thermometer to read temperature changes in the air will be unsuccessful. You will be reading the temperature change on the surface the sight beam is hitting. Don't throw your laser thermometer away just yet though. IR thermometers are useful on an investigation to identify sources of drafts, and can be an excellent tool for debunking cold spots caused by "leaks" that are essentially from air conditioning units or cold outside air (they are also useful as pointers for giving presentations on a projection screen).

Due to the popularity of certain television shows the Forward Looking Infra-Red camera has become a popular tool with select paranormal groups for hunting cold spots and "ghosts." I owe this trend to the fact that some people have more money than common sense. If you are going to spend ten thousand dollars on a piece of equipment, it would make sense to take a certification course on how to use it, and how it works. Having taken the course myself, I can tell you that these devices work just like a laser thermometer. IR technology is the same in both devices. The device will measure temperature differentials on *surfaces*, but not ambient temperatures. So unless the cold spot has mass (in which it would be visible) or the ghost has mass (same argument applies) it is useless for finding cold spots in the air. Here in again, it is useful for other things. For example, if someone is hoaxing you, they will show up on the FLIR cam. If they were in an area that had reported activity, they will leave a thermal signature of their presence. It is an outstanding tool for debunking paranormal activity, not proving it.

Basically, FLIR is an imaging device that senses and displays infrared radiation. The term "forward looking" is used to distinguish FLIR systems from sideways tracking infrared systems, also called "push-broom" imagers. Sideways tracking systems were typically used on aircraft and satellites for navigation assistance and data gathering. They were quite primitive, using a 1 dimensional array of pixels which uses the motion of the aircraft or satellite to move the view of the one dimensional array across the ground to create a two dimensional image over a period of time. Such systems cannot be used for real time imaging, and must look perpendicular to the direction of travel. Such a system had little use in paranormal research.

Many FLIR systems use digital image processing to improve the image quality. A byproduct of DIP is that they can display artifacts that are products of this functionality. FLIR sensor arrays often have wildly inconsistent sensitivities from pixel to pixel, due to limitations in the manufacturing process. To remedy this, the response of each pixel is measured at the factory, and a transformer, most often linear, maps the measured input signal to an output level. This creates an averaging effect to smooth out responses of adjacent pixels.

FLIR systems can see through smoke, fog, haze, and other atmospheric obscurants better than a visible light camera can. It is for precisely this reason that it is incapable of reading temperature from the air itself. It is specifically designed to look through the air for a reflective surface.

So if the fancy pistol-like IR thermometers and the thermal imaging cameras are useless for cold spot detection in the air, what is the right thermometer for the job? Temperature changes relating to paranormal activity are very transitory, meaning they come and go without warning. Any thermometer we choose must have the ability to display temperature changes in real time. This means if the temperature suddenly drops ten degrees, the thermometer needs to show that instantly or near instantly. Popular with a lot of groups are small digital indoor/outdoor models such as those offered by Accurite©. While these will work to a certain degree, they have a slow refresh rate. So while you may be able to detect a temperature change, you will not be able to track a blob of cold air across a room with it or map its size and shape, because the display upgrades every ten seconds or so. In order to get an accurate thermometer to test ambient air conditions in real time situations we are going to have to look at the HVAC service industry and the environmental monitoring industry. Most of these professional grade meters not only measure temperature, but humidity as well, offering another good thing to monitor at an investigation. Humidity can affect air pressure and density, and can effect propagation of signals in the air.

I personally use the Extech RH101 Hygro-Thermometer and Infrared Thermometer. Cost is around $160.00 and it will provide ambient and surface (IR) temperature as well as relative humidity in real time. While there are other devices out there, the Extech gives you the most bang for the buck.

Using the thermometer should be part of every initial investigation. An investigator should check and record each room, working in a grid pattern to establish any hot or cold spots in the subject area. The grid pattern is an important tool in any investigation, as it allows you to pinpoint any anomalous condition and physically place a location to it. I will refer to this invaluable process over and over again as we cover the different test equipment used in paranormal investigation. The ambient readings should be recorded, either as notes or on audio recording, along with the time to properly reference the readings. Relative humidity should also be recorded for each room, as well as any unusual readings encountered such as humidity fluctuations. In this manner, you will establish some base readings to work from as the investigation progresses. Also check to see what type of climate control if any is present. Is there heat? Is there Air Conditioning? Where are the vents? All of this should be factored in when doing a temperature survey. Outside air leaks and drafts should also be noted.

After establishing base readings and the investigation continues, what do you do when you encounter a dramatic temperature change? First, try to determine the *area of effect*. You can do this by moving the probe around in the air to determine the size and shape of the cold spot. You can then track its actual movement (if there is any) around the room. Cold spots can be caused by natural sources, such as a Freon leak in the air conditioner, and other Heating, Ventilation and Air Conditioning equipment. These types of cold spots will disperse fairly rapidly and spread out across the room driven by the air currents and eddies in play. If the cold spot maintains its concentration, something else is going on and should be noted as possible evidence.

The common theory concerning cold spots today is that "spirits" rob the air of heat in order to utilize the energy to manifest. While on the surface this may sound logical, there is no evidence to indicate this is the case. There are situations that could cause the temperature change that can also link it to paranormal activity based on certain theories in Quantum Mechanics. For example, in the Multiverse or Many Worlds theory, it has now been mathematically proven that parallel universes must exist. If this is the case, and a parallel universe overlaps or touches our own and a portal is created, matter could possibly transfer from one universe into another, without causing annihilation. This "exotic" matter may affect the temperature as well as other environmental conditions in the room, as the adjacent universe could be venting colder air molecules or other atmosphere into the room via a wormhole type of effect and could move around as frequency instabilities occur. This could also explain other aspects of paranormal phenomena, such as EMF fluctuations, radioactivity, and elevated ion counts. The important thing to remember is to record every fluctuation encountered for future reference.

Other methods of temperature gathering involve the use of constant data monitoring, or data loggers. These devices allow multiple sensors to be attached to an interface, which is then fed to a PC or laptop computer. The data collected from the temperature probes can then be displayed as continuous data based on the temperature each sensor monitors over the course of time. Data logging is quickly becoming a recognized preferred data collection system for paranormal research, but we will address this in greater detail later in the book.

Humidity

The term humidity refers to "relative humidity". Relative humidity is the amount of water vapor in a sample of air compared to the maximum amount of water vapor the air can hold at any specific temperature. This data is reported in a percentage format of 0 to 100%. Relative humidity is an important piece of data used in the forecasting weather. Humidity indicates the likelihood of precipitation, dew, or fog. High humidity makes people feel hotter outside in the summer because it reduces the effectiveness of sweating to cool the body by preventing the evaporation of perspiration from the skin. This effect is calculated in a heat index table. Warm water vapor has more thermal energy than cool water vapor and therefore more of it evaporates into warm air than into cold air. Humidity can also be detected as a mist of fog in a photograph and may lend a false interpretation of paranormal activity.

Humidity is an often-overlooked condition that may also have a correlation to paranormal phenomena. Since the amount of data is so sparse, it is of course impossible to determine at this stage of the game what exactly that relationship may be. However, since temperature can be an effect of paranormal activity, other environmental factors could be as well. Since humidity can affect atmospheric pressure, it may be related to the dip in barometer readings sometimes noted during a paranormal event. Local weather may play a key role as well in the strength and duration of these events. We know humidity affects aspects of evidence gathering. For example, low humidity will increase background static electrical fields, as well as cause an increase in airborne dust particles, that may print as orbs on photographs. Relatively higher humidity will eliminate dust as a factor, due to the moisture in the air weighing down the dust particles to keep them earthbound. However, as previously stated, too much humidity in the air can cause areas of dense moisture that will photograph like fog or even take on an "ectoplasm" type of appearance. Knowing the humidity can assist in the elimination of false evidence or the verification of *possible* evidence.

Humidity changes (dramatic ones) can also be indicative of a parallel universe overlap. It is possible that conditions in the parallel universe leak over into our own, creating a localized effect on the weather or environment. It is important to note that some HVAC systems (Heating, Ventilation, and Air Conditioning) can and do affect humidity. Malfunctions of these systems can cause dramatic level changes in the humidity that can actually be observed, photographed or videotaped. While the exact nature of the effect of humidity on paranormal activity remains elusive, it is important that we as researchers monitor this condition and share any data we collect with each other to establish that possible connection. Otherwise, measuring humidity offers a valuable tool for debunking false evidence. As do the measurement of other environmental factors, as we shall see.

I was involved in an investigation in Key West Florida in 1979 that involved an old house built in the early 1800s. The home had an air conditioning system in it that was rather dated. At one point during the evening it discharges a large mass of water vapor into the air in the living room. The ambient light caught it just right causing it to glow. Everyone on the team observed it and took photographs. We were using 35mm film cameras at the time, so we didn't have the ability to review photographs instantly. However, I noticed moisture forming on my lens as I was near the phenomena and was able to quickly determine that the source of our fog was water vapor from the AC unit. A short time later the system did it again and we witnessed the condition actually occurring. We were able to eliminate the condition as a non-paranormal event and made notes concerning the photograph numbers related to the phenomena. This worked out really well later as upon review of the photos I found we had all caught the perfect image of what looked like a ghost. Had we not performed a detail investigation of the humidity injected into the room we would have mistaken a common system moisture discharge for a possible spirit manfest!

A couple of years ago I was investigating a house in Morristown, New Jersey. While walking around with a temperature sensor, I came upon a rather cold area in the center of a large room that had previously been a living room. I managed to trace around the edges and noted it was a rather large blog of cold, moving at a fairly steady pace. The shape didn't seem to alter much, and it maintained its consistency until it disappeared by an interior wall. I quickly ran around to the next room and found the cold spot continuing to move across that room. The normal ambient temperature at the time in the home was about 52 degrees, and the blob was tipping the scales at 26 degrees F. I tracked the spot across the entire side of the second floor and it passed through walls with ease without losing its relative size or shape. This could not be contributed to draft, faulty HVAC systems, or other rational explanation. To this day I am not certain if it was a ghost, but it sure as heck wasn't the Fuller Brush Man!

Chapter 5
Barometers

"A successful unification of quantum theory and relativity would necessarily be a theory of the universe as a whole. It would tell us, as Aristotle and Newton did before, what space and time are, what the cosmos is, what things are made of, and what kind of laws those things obey. Such a theory will bring about a radical shift - a revolution - in our understanding of what nature is. It must also have wide repercussions, and will likely bring about, or contribute to, a shift in our understanding of ourselves and our relationship to the rest of the universe."
-Lee Smolin-

A barometer is an instrument used to measure atmospheric pressure. It can measure the pressure exerted by the atmosphere by using water, air, or mercury. Pressure tendency is used primarily in meteorology to forecast short-term changes in the weather. Numerous measurements of air pressure are used within a regional geographical area to help find surface troughs, high-pressure systems, and frontal boundaries. Barometers have also been used to predict paranormal activity, as there have been noted instances when barometric pressure dropped just prior to a paranormal event. Hundreds of accounts are posted at such sites as GhostStudy.com, Paranormalsoup.com, and other research oriented paranormal group sites from around the world. In fact, some researchers have speculated that cats and dog may react to paranormal phenomena due to their sensitivity to rapid changes in barometric pressure. My own research has indicated that a drop in barometric pressure is linked to a pending paranormal event. I have documented random drops in pressure that were later correlated to paranormal activity from Florida to Upstate New York. I have performed experiments using helium filled balloons (low pressure will cause a balloon to sink) in areas of reported activity. Watching the balloons helps pass the time on those boring vigils, as well as gives the investigator a wakeup call that pressure is dropping when they sink toward the floor. If a perceived paranormal event occurs, this tends to confirm there is something going on with atmospheric pressure changes and paranormal activity. If you don't have a barometer, take a handful of helium filled balloons with you on your next investigation. You may be in for a pleasant surprise. Additionally, they will demonstrate if there is a draft in the room, as the air currents will move the balloons away from the source of the draft. Helium balloons are a very inexpensive and effective tool for teams on a budget.

Critics of this methodology are quick to point out that the effect may be caused simply by the fact that the investigator enters a room or area of natural low pressure; tunnels, caves and negatively pressurized rooms could account for the drop in pressure. On the other hand, few homes have tunnels, caves or negatively pressurized rooms. Since there are many reports of drops in barometric pressure occurring in perfectly normal spaces prior to a perceived paranormal event, monitoring the air pressure should be a part of any serious researcher's regime. But what could cause the air pressure to drop? An answer may lie in the realm of Quantum Mechanics based on environmental changes caused by a possible worm hole or portal opening up between two worlds. Matter, including air, may be rarefied or sucked in by the opening, only to be replaced with matter of a different mass or concentration of mass, affecting air pressure. But regardless of the theory, it is a condition that needs to be further explored and the cause or source identified so we can confirm or dismiss what we believe it may be based on data, not conjecture.

The key question of course is what type of barometer should a field investigator use? For our purposes as a paranormal investigator, we need a barometer with a relatively quick refresh or response rate or in other words a device that responds to changes very quickly. An aneroid barometer uses a small, flexible metal box called an aneroid cell. This aneroid capsule (cell) is made from an alloy of beryllium and copper. The evacuated capsule (or usually more capsules) is prevented from collapsing by a strong spring. Small changes in external air pressure cause the cell to expand or contract. This expansion and contraction drives mechanical levers such that the tiny movements of the capsule are amplified and displayed on the face of the aneroid barometer. Many models include a manually set needle, which is used to mark the current measurement so a change can be seen. In addition, the mechanism is made deliberately 'stiff' so that tapping the barometer reveals whether the pressure is rising or falling as the pointer moves after the physical tap. These instruments are now available in hand held small sized units resembling a pocket watch and include an altimeter function. While these aren't instant in their response, they will work.

The ultimate barometer for our use, however, is the digital barometer. Now available as hand held units thanks to modern technology, they even come incorporated in wristwatches. They rule the field for speed and ease of use, as well as being simple to calibrate.

To make barometric pressure meaningful during an investigation, the outside air pressure should be monitored to insure any changed noted inside is not a regional condition.

Atmospheric pressure cycles twice a day due to global atmospheric tides. This effect is strongest in tropical zones, with amplitude of a few millibars, and almost zero in polar areas. These variations have two superimposed cycles, a circadian (24 h) cycle and semi-circadian (12 h) cycle. These are important things to keep in mind. The main thing to remember is pressure falls naturally in the evening. Don't let this fool you. Paranormal pressure drops tend to be extremely transient.

As with other indoor weather conditions such as temperature and humidity, barometric pressure can be affected by active HVAC systems. A negative pressure system is used in laboratories and containment buildings to prevent the escape of dangerous bacteria or viruses from lab environments. A positive pressure system is used to pressurize a room or to force material out of it. Both of these conditions will affect barometric pressure, which is why it is important to have a control reading or base reading consisting of the outside air pressure as well as an average of the inside air pressure. As with any measurement, establishing a base reading is tantamount to defining variables encountered during the investigation. To establish a base reading, work the room in a grid pattern and note any deviations. Also work the perimeter of the house outdoors to note any deviation. Any variances noted should be closely investigated for a possible natural source. Bear in mind, in most residential settings, the barometric pressure will cycle up and down with the AC or heating unit turning on or off, especially if it is a forced air system.

The vital role of barometric pressure and its effect on or by the paranormal is still largely unexplored. While conditions have been recorded that seem to indicate a connection, none has been satisfactorily established. There are several specific instruments on the market that will work well for the field investigator in attempting to establish this connection, but just keep in mind that the key option is high refresh rate. Because by nature paranormal activity is so transitory, readings can and will be just as transitory. The faster the device responds to change, the more accurate the data will be. The more data collected, the clearer the picture it paints.

There are several wristwatches now available with built in barometer/altimeters that work well for paranormal investigating. Campmor offers the Altimax Altimeter-Barometer watch for around $150.00, and the Weather

Radio Store online offers brands from around $125.00 to $159.00. If price is an issue, cheer up. Timex offers a barometer watch for under $70.00.

Barometer watches respond quickly and accurately, and are the best solution to portable field measurement as it doesn't require the operator to hold it, only to read it from the wrist. This frees up the hands to hold additional data gathering devices.

Pocket barometers are also very popular, and I will list a few of the common ones here. The BARIGO Pocket Altimeter/Barometer sells for around $103.00 and works well, although you have to hold it in your hand. THOMMEN® makes an excellent barometer, the TX Mechanical Altimeter/ Barometer that ranges from $320.00 to $383.00, while Benmeadows.com offers the "Traceable Precision Dial pocket barometer for $89.90. Amazon. com offers the Mannix analog pocket barometer for $43.14, and E-Bay offers models from $9.00 on up. The mechanical versions will have a slow but steady response time, while digital versions will generally respond faster, but you will pay for the added speed. The altimeter portion of these type of instruments offer a built in calibration protocol. By using popular software applications such as Google Earth, you can stand on a location that you know the exact altitude of, thereby setting the pocket barometer/altimeter to a known value. This procedure will help insure that you are collecting accurate data. Of course, instrument calibration procedures should be routinely followed with all of your measurement instruments as recommended by the manufacturer.

As I have noted previously, the jury is still out concerning the nature of the relationship of barometric pressure to paranormal activity. Many critics point out that there is no reason in the world for ghosts to affect the weather, or vice versa. The critics have a flaw in their perception, however; they are looking at extraordinary events with ordinary points of view. The paranormal by nature requires extraordinary methods to document and understand. If paranormal activity is related to a parallel universe, as I believe it is, then it is conceivable that the pressure changes occur as a result of the differential between the two atmospheres of each respected universe interacting with each other through a portal where the conditions mix. This condition could be measurable on either side of the portal or wormhole. For example, on the other side the pressure may increase as a result of the interaction while it may decrease on our side. So it isn't the "ghost" that affects the environment as much as the possible enabler of the ghostly phenomena. As more correlating data becomes available, a finite hypothesis can be formulated. It is also very possible that we may not only discover the nature of certain aspects of paranormal activity, but we may also discover viable to answers to some of the questions posed by Quantum Mechanics!

Chapter 6
Electromagnetic Fields (EMF)

"In speaking of the Energy of the field, however, I wish to be understood literally. All energy is the same as mechanical energy, whether it exists in the form of motion or in that of elasticity, or in any other form. The energy in electromagnetic phenomena is mechanical energy."
-James Clerk Maxwell-

Perhaps the most abused and least understood condition encountered in paranormal research is an electromagnetic field. How often have you watched an investigator dancing around in glee on some TV program yelling, "I have a spike…I have a spike!" and proudly hailing it as evidence of paranormal activity? If you watch all of the offerings on paranormal investigation on the airwaves, the answer approaches infinity. This always instigates a snicker on my part.

In September of 1976 I acquired a surplus AN/PSS-11 mine detector. This seemingly innocent act would begin my life long quest of modifying equipment designed for one function, into a device that does something else. In those days, there were no hand held EMF meters. Consequently, I wanted to measure EMF and its possible relationship to paranormal activity. I also knew I would want to know the frequency of the EMF and not just the strength of the EMF. I had at my beck and call, a Tektronix 545-B Dual Trace Oscilloscope, which was by no means a very portable device. Built in 1965, it was a masterpiece of over 50 vacuum tubes and analog circuitry that amounted to 78 pounds of nightmare squeezed into a 17" x 12-7/8" x 23-7/8" metal case.

From these humble beginnings I assembled a fairly accurate state of the art (sort of) EMF detection/Analysis device. My very first discovery was that the vast majority of EMF in any dwelling is at the frequency of 60 cycles or Hertz, and is caused by electricity being supplied to the structure. A simple meter would have never revealed that to me, but by looking at the waveform on the scope's screen, I easily identified both the frequency and the relative field strength. This experience drove home to me at the time a very important fact.

The responsibility we have as investigators is to eliminate all of the known causes for EMF as it occurs in a suspected paranormal event and discover and attempt to identify the unknown causes. This is why we identify known EMF field generators, such as appliances, etc. We can only do this by monitoring the EMF frequencies.

The Primary Sources of EMF

The electromagnetic fields produced by electrical appliances are an example of extremely low frequency (ELF) fields. ELF fields generally have frequencies below 300 Hz. Other technologies and electric devices produce intermediate frequency (IF) fields with frequencies from 300 Hz to 100 KHz and radiofrequency (RF) fields with frequencies of 100 KHz to 300 GHz. The effects of electromagnetic fields on the human body depend not only on their field level but on their frequency and energy. Our electricity power supply and all appliances using electricity are the main sources of ELF fields and these are as previously mentioned 60 Hz; computer CRT screens (the old fashion tube type, not the flat screen varieties), anti-theft devices and security systems are the main sources of IF fields; and radio, television, radar and cellular telephone antennas, and microwave ovens are the main sources of RF fields. These fields can induce currents within the human body, which if sufficient can produce a range of effects such as heating and electrical shock, depending on their amplitude and frequency range. (However, to produce such effects, the fields outside the body would have to be very strong, far stronger than present in normal environments.) It is also possible for elevated EMF to affect the mind and perception, at least in some folks.

A little bit about High Frequency EMF

Mobile telephones, television and radio transmitters and radar produce RF (Radio Frequency) fields. These fields are used to transmit information over long distances and form the foundation of modern communications as well as radio and television broadcasting all over the world. Microwaves are RF fields at high frequencies in the GHz range. In microwaves ovens, we use them to quickly heat food. Imagine what it can do to the human body.

At radio frequencies, electric and magnetic fields are closely interrelated and we typically measure their levels as power densities in watts per square meter (W/m^2). Electric and magnetic fields are invisible fields of force created by electric voltage (electric fields) and by electric current (magnetic fields). Wherever there is a flow of electricity, both electric and magnetic fields are present. Electric fields exist when appliances are plugged in. Magnetic fields exist when appliances are turned on.

EMFs are higher in intensity the closer they are measured to their source. In fact, EMF levels are greatest next to an appliance and almost disappear at distances of 3-5 feet. This is one reason why home appliances and house wiring may produce higher levels of EMFs in a house as opposed to a power line that may be nearby or directly overhead.

Common as dirt - 60 Hz EMF

EMF exists everywhere there is power. Here in the U.S. the power standard frequency is 60 Hz. We are exposed to this electromagnetic field by high voltage power "transmission" lines and lower voltage "distribution" lines that provide electricity to our homes, and other buildings. While power lines have been the focus of much controversy concerning health, other and far greater dangers come from the actual internal wiring in buildings, currents in grounding paths such as in plumbing pipes, and electric appliances such as TV monitors, radios, hair dryers and electric blankets (electric blankets are BAD..).

Electrical sources with *high voltage* create strong electric fields, while sources with *strong currents* create strong electromagnetic fields. The strength of both electric and magnetic fields falls off rather dramatically the further you move away from the source. Electromagnetic field strength falls off even more rapidly with distance from device sources like appliances than it does from power line sources. The general rule to remember is that an electromagnetic field is down to "background" level or normal natural levels 3-4 feet from an appliance, while it reaches background level around 60-200 feet from a distribution line and 300-1000 feet from a transmission line. Fields and currents that occur at the same place can interact if they are in phase to strengthen or weaken the total effect. Hence, the strength of the fields depends not only on the distance of the source but also the distance and location of other nearby sources and their phase relationship.

Identification of EMF sources

Sometimes fairly simple measurements can identify the external or internal sources creating elevated electromagnetic fields. For example, turning off the main power switch of the house can rule out sources from use of power indoors. Magnetic field measurements made at different distances from power lines can help pinpoint them as sources of elevated residential EMF. Often, however, it takes some detective work to find the major sources of elevated electromagnetic fields in or near a home. Currents in grounding paths (where low voltage electricity returns to the system in plumbing pipes) and some common wiring errors can lead to situations in which source identification is difficult and requires a trained technician. It is almost always possible to find and correct the sources of elevated magnetic fields when they are due to faulty electrical wiring, grounding problems, or appliances such as lighting fixtures.

As stated, measuring EMF and doing it correctly is most likely the single most important measurement when investigating the paranormal. Rooms should be worked in a grid pattern with hand held devices to identify natural sources of EMF. Any spikes occurring during the course of the investigation should be checked immediately for a source.

As mentioned, there are two main sources of EMF that occur naturally in a paranormal investigative situation. The first represents the biggest problem with interference and actually getting real evidence, and that is 60Hz residential power EMF. This is one of the reasons investigators should extinguish all lights and turn off all electrical appliances possible during an investigation. It reduces the 60Hz background EMF significantly. Nearly all of the current EMF meters on the market today are designed to measure 50 – 60Hz fields for the purpose of measuring EMF levels from power sources for health and safety purposes. This includes all of the current fad meters, such as the Dr. Gauss meter and Gauss Master Meter. There are some notable exceptions, however and they are listed below, along with their specifications. Specifications should be a major consideration when purchasing an EMF meter.

Google the highly popular **Single Axis Digital Gauss/Tesla Meter**, and you will discover that it has an ELF range of 30 - 400 Hz. It provides readout in both mG and microTesla and is calibrated to within 4% ± 3 digits at 50/60 Hz. The **Strong Field AC Gaussmeter** has a 4% ±3 digits accuracy also 50/60 Hz, but can read a range of 30Hz - 300Hz. The **Peak/Hold 2-Range Gaussmeter** has a frequency range of 30 to 400 Hz with accuracy of ±3% + 3 digits at 50/60 Hz. Another meter that is quickly becoming popular is the **XYZ Axis EMF Tester with remote probe**. This meter allows you to check each of the three axis (or dimensions, height, width and depth) separately (the other meters mentioned are single axis only, depending on physical orientation) and while it covers bandwidths from 30 Hz to 300 Hz, it is calibrated at 50-60 Hz and is 4% accurate at best, with a 10% accuracy in the higher ranges. The **Switchable Single Axis and 3-Axis Gaussmeter** can operate in either single or tri-axial mode, and has a range from 0.01 mG to 1999 mG with 3% accuracy from 45 to 5000 Hz but is useful from 13 Hz to 75 kHz. This meter retails for around $280.00 and is a serious laboratory instrument that is capable of detecting possible paranormal EMF but not differentiating it.

I currently use an **FW Bell 4100** series meter that is tri-axial as well as has a frequency response of 30 to 2 kHz with 2% accuracy. It retails for around $325.00. Just remember that you get what you pay for when it comes to lab instruments, and none of these instruments can tell you in what frequency the EMF is propagating.

The Trifield natural meter is another highly accurate potentially useful meter for tracking down possible paranormal EMF even though it is also the most misused instruments available to the general public, so I want to go into significant detail on how to operate this device and its sister devices. It has a frequency response of .5 to 10 KHz and sells for under $200.00. This meter is so sensitive that it can measure changes of as little as 0.5% of the strength of the Earth's magnetic field. In spite of what some people claim, the standard Trifield meter is also an excellent tool to use for EMF measurement. It has been believed by some that the Trifield is designed to operate at 50-60 Hz, which it has been, but it also has a high level of accuracy in lower and higher frequency ranges. Depending on where the knob is set, the meter detects either frequency- weighted magnetic fields (two separate scales), or frequency-weighted electric fields in the ELF and VLF range. So you need to make two measurements, one magnetic and one electric to determine the Electromagnetic field. I have seen NO one do this in the field. Most people have the meter set to the magnetic scales and are measuring the Earth's background magnetic radiation. This meter has significant sensitivity at 100,000 Hz, well past the 17,000 Hz horizontal scan of video displays. The radio/microwave setting can detect up to three billion Hz (3 GHz), which lets you gauge radio-microwave power, CB and cellular phone equipment, and many types of low band radars. The useable frequency response for the electric and magnetic section is 30 – 400 Hz. As previously mentioned, in most homes and offices, a large fraction of the total electromagnetic field is at frequencies around 60 Hz. A TriField meter, when exposed to a 3 milligauss EM field, will read "3" if the frequency of the field is 60 Hz, but it will read "6" if the 3 milligauss field is at 120 Hz. Unfortunately, we don't know what frequency the field is that we are measuring. In contrast, a non-frequency-weighted (the flat response version of the TriField) meter will read "3" in both cases, and a 60 Hz-only meter will read "3" and "0" respectively (even though in the 120 Hz case, the current induced in a conductive body is twice as much.) We use a flat responding Trifield in most cases in conjunction with a frequency-measuring probe on a hand held oscilloscope for frequency identification. In many cases, we have captured EMF with the frequency probe that was not in the set parameters of the Tri-Field meter's range. It made us wonder how much data we had missed due to not knowing what frequencies we were dealing with. The Trifield is also a triaxial meter. Triaxial meters as mentioned previously detect energy along three different planes, all opposing one another, such as up-down, left-right and an angle between both, or think of it as three dimensions, height, width and depth and all points in between where those dimensions intersect. If you have a headache, take two aspirins and hang on. It only gets more complex from here.

Finally, I would be remiss in my reporting of devices if I leave out the infamous **KII meter** "as seen on TV". This has to be the sorriest excuse for an EMF meter I have analyzed to date. It is advertised to operate accurately in both the range of 50 to 1,000 Hz as well as 1,000 to 20,000 Hz which is essentially most of the audio spectrum. Because of its relatively high range (it starts at 50 Hz) it will miss 90% of the frequencies associated with paranormal activity, except for specific EVP work. The other problem with the meter is it is unshielded to the point of where any EMF source creating harmonics within its bandwidth will set it off. Radio transmitters, cell phones, you name it, the KII will respond, not to the fundamental frequency, but to its lower harmonic frequencies. Because of this, it is useless for exact EMF field readings. I use mine as an indicator of the presence of EMF, which gives me a heads up to check a real meter for detected field strength, and a scope/sensor combo for frequency.

Let me reemphasize this. A meter alone cannot and does not give you the full story. As I mentioned over and over, the greatest amount of EMF in the U.S. is from a standard 60Hz and in Europe a 50 Hz residential power source. While you may have a spike in EMF, it may be completely explainable, and in most cases, is. In order to differentiate from a normal EMF and a paranormal one, you must know the frequency and the waveform shape. You must also know what changes have occurred in the electric and magnetic fields. The only way you can know this is to use a sensor and an oscilloscope in conjunction with your EMF meter.

Velleman makes a hand held oscilloscope, the **HPS – 10** that sells for under $200.00. Its high sensitivity (down to 5mV/div) and extended scope functions make this unit ideal for measurements of potential paranormal EMF. Features include a 10MHz sampling rate with up to 2MHz analog bandwidth, full auto set up, 5mV to 20V/div sensitivity in 12 steps, 200ns to 1hour/div time base in 32 steps, Trigger modes of run, normal, once, roll, slope +/-, and X and Y position signal shift. It has digital volt meter readout with x10 option, audio power calculation (rms and peak), dBm, dBV, DC, rms measurements, signal markers for volt and time, frequency readout (through markers), recorder function (roll mode), and most important, signal storage (2 memories)

Couple this excellent and affordable tool with a **Magnetic Sciences MC95 Magnetic Field Sensor (MAGCHECK-95)** which has a 25 Hz to 3 kHz bandwidth in the 3dB range and 5 Hz to 20 kHz in the 15 dB bandwidth and you have a perfect EMF frequency identifier. Each sensor also undergoes a NIST traceable calibration to ensure accuracy of +/- 3% typical calibration tolerance (+/- 5% worst case) from 50 Hz to 1000 Hz. Calibrated to ANSI Standard 644-1987 and the certificate is included. It accurately measures through the eleventh harmonic of the fundamental frequency of the EMF detected with ANSI Standard 644-1987. This set up will tell you not only what frequency the EMF is operating at, but will also display the waveform, allowing an accurate identification of the signal. Only by using a configuration of this nature can you positively eliminate natural EMF from the mix. Additionally, the oscilloscope has other functions in the paranormal investigator's tool box. Remember, specifications translate into ability. Understanding specifications is the subject of an entire book alone, but take it from me; this is a lot of bang for the buck.

Another dead horse I like to beat in case you haven't noticed is using the **Grid Pattern method of data measurement**. This is the best way to document data in an area or room. If your meter is a single axis meter, meaning it reads fields in one direction only, or you are using a directional sensor such as the one I mentioned above, keep that in mind when sweeping the room for EMF. Make note of any high readings and try to locate and identify the source. You will discover that many appliances, air conditioners, aquarium pumps, heaters, TVs etc. put out high levels of EMF. In this fashion you will establish a sort of base level of readings for comparison. Once you have discovered the hot spots and EMF levels make note of their location on a graph paper map of the room or area and leave it in the area or room for each team to use as reference during the active investigation. While retracing your steps through the building, your team or teams can make note of any deviation from the original base readings on this graph floor plan and know right away if they have an unusual condition to explore further. Again, try to narrow down a natural source for the EMF. Use a frequency measuring set up like the one previously mentioned to determine the frequency. If the frequency is below 60 Hz in the US (or 50 Hz in Europe), you may have possible paranormal evidence and you certainly have a situation to investigate further. Try to locate the source. If the frequency is a complex signal, make a note to check your personal voice recorder during the time frame for a potential EVP. The elevated EMF may indicate that an EVP is present.

Once you compile the readings in a time frame, they can be compared to other activity or readings taken by other test gear in order to paint a detailed picture as to what may be happening, and to determine if it is a natural or paranormal source. On my own team, we wire ourselves for sound by using a lavaliere microphone and a portable digital recorder and any reading deviation we observe we state aloud and add the time. This is an invaluable reference for later analysis. We also synchronize all of our time records, from watches to laptops to cameras in order to correlate any evidence captured with a standardized timeline.

Recently, I had a very unusual thing occur while I was in Williamsburg, Va. I was in a house built in 1690. I watched a pewter salt shaker (kind of heavy) slide across a table by itself. I had a very high EMF modulating between 6 Hz and 9 Hz and appeared to be generated from approximately two feet off the floor about two feet ENE of the center of the room, based on triangulation readings from my three field detectors. This mysterious spontaneous EMF broadcasted outward in thin air with no apparent source. All during the phenomenon, I monitored gamma radiation levels of about 350 mRADs, indicating the presence of either high energy radio-isotopes, or particle annihilations.

It is important to note here that EMF that is related to paranormal activity essentially falls into two specific frequency ranges, the brainwave region (1Hz to 18Hz) and the audio spectrum (20 Hz to 20 KHz). Keeping this I mind, here is what this translates into with a little physics:

First, 350 mrad=3.5 milliJoules for N.f=E/h~5.25x10^30 Hz. Fine structure this 'frequency-energy' equivalent into the measured gamma frequencies, say the basis ZPE(Zero Point Energy)-electron/positron frequency of 2.5x10^20 Hz. This means that the observed energy is equal to approximately 20 billion electron-positron annihilations. Since the 'telekinetic' movement has no apparent external energy input as the source then the energy supplied derives from the ZPE as stated. The positional calibrations are varied, as holo-fractal magnification and diminution can apply on many scales and at many levels. However, certain boundary conditions have to be considered.

One very important boundary condition is the Schumann Harmonics.

The perimeter of the earth is roughly 40,000 km as a light path on the surface and has a Schumann basis of 7.5 Hz (300,000,000 km/s/40,000km).

So at or near this frequency, otherwise 'obscured' phenomena can occur.

This frequency also allows the light-matter interaction (characterized in the probability of the electromagnetic alpha fine structure constant as 1 in 137) to maximize.

Another important calibration parameter is the 'size' of the 'merkabah', being the Sqrt (15) as wavelength for a frequency of 77.46 MHz. This 'merkabah' frequency then is in harmonic to the Schumann frequency in 1:10^7. The Schumann frequency also is at its fundamental at 7.5 Hz, but there are in fact many other resonances and harmonics that can come into play. Consequently, so called 'paranormal' phenomena seem to depend on a given region of space-time to become temporarily 'isolated' to partake in the holo-fractal nature of the universe (in other words, become apparent to us human types). The phenomenon of the pewter shaker moving that I observed represents such an isolation, most likely having become 'induced' by either some 'emotional suppressed' energy or possibly from a transmitter at least 2 million kilometers from the center of the earth. Or it is possible that I may have quite simply discovered a "ghost". The Force required for the movement derives as follows:

F=dp/dt=d(mv)/dt=mdv/dt+vdm/dt

Use m=moGamma=(hf/c^2)/Sqrt(1-[v/c]^2)=(hf/c^2)/Sqrt(u)=(hf/c^2).f(u,v,t)

dm/dt=(dm/du)(du/dt) and where u(v)=1-[v/c]^2 for du/dv=-2v/c^2

dm/dt={(hf/c^2)(-1/2)Gamma^3}(-2v/c^2)dv/dt

F={dv/dt}(m+[hfv^2/c^4]Gamma^3) as the relativistic extension of Newton's Law.

The first part applies to a constancy in mass m and the second engages special relativity. However this assumes that the frequency f remains constant as photonic inertia f=mc^2/h.

Then allowing the frequency f to vary:

F= dp/dt=d(hfv/c^2 Gamma)/dt=(h/c^2){f.d[vGamma]/dt + vGamma.df/dt}
F=(h/c^2){f.(v^2/c^2+1-v^2/c^2)Gamma^3.dv/dt + vGamma.df/dt}

F=(h/c^2){fGamma^3.dv/dt + vGamma.df/dt}
F= mGamma^3.dv/dt + (hvgroup/c^2).Gamma.df/dt)

F= Standard Acceleration Force + Quantum Alpha-Force; the latter normally 'occultised' due to the minuteness of the multiplier (h/c^2~10^-50).

The resonance or *wormhole* (that is right...*wormhole*) time differential for frequency is the entropy counter 9x10^60 as the square of the source frequency (of the wormhole). So, to put it in plain English, there is a very good chance I discovered an inter-dimensional or trans-universal wormhole, proving a theoretical aspect of both Quantum and Astrophysics!

I know from personal experience, that the manifestation of a 4th spatial dimension superimposes onto the ordinary Minkowski metric. As I mentioned, the requirement for such a dimensional intersection (3D+Twith4D+T) is the encapsulation of a region of space. This region is quantized in the following manner:

VolumexAngular Acceleration (df/dt)=NxUniversal Constant=NxElectron-Diameterxc^2

V3=2pi^2R^3 as dV4/dR for V4=pi^2R^4/2

Then the normal hyperspace vector is: R/4 related to the Planck-Area quantization of Black Holes (The surface area of a BH is quantized in Planck-Areas/4 as entropy count). You can now calculate the maximum resonance state for maximum entropy df/dt=fmax^2 and which crystallizes the wormhole boundary, i.e. the Black Holes Inner Event Horizon and amenable to both activation as a sourced White Hole or a Sinked Black Hole.

For N=1 then; V=500/9x10^60=5.555x10^-59 cubic meters (or 'quarto' meters in V4)

For V3: R3=1.41x10^-20 meters as Compton-Radius with energy 14.03 TeV (yes this is the maximum energy for the LHC at Geneva, thus designed)

For V4 : R4=1.832x10^-15 meters and a 'reduced' energy of frequency 2.6x10^22 Hz or 0.11 GeV.

Recalling, that the calculations above invoke the maximum resonance state it nevertheless becomes apparent, that the practical utility of wormholes should engage the muon-mass (about 106 MeV), which then becomes coupled to the base-pionic quark-antiquark associations either charged (pion+-~140MeV) or neutral (pion0~135 MeV).

Now this throws open a new physics, because of the manner the quantum geometry (or blueprints) arrange the wave functions of the quarks, coupled to leptonic rings. The muon is a 'heavy' electron, due to the fact, that the up-down coupling is energy-wise insufficient to transverse the nucleon diameter (about 5 fermi as an electron probability distribution and about 3 fermi as the size of a proton). So forming resonance states of the up-quark as a charm quark and a resonance state for the down quark as a strange quark, will increase this energy to the required levels. Detailed analysis then shows you how the unitary SU(3) symmetry of the standard model 'falls into place' as emergence of the quark-lepton family couplings.

But I have a conundrum in regards to the wormhole utility.

Quantum mechanics is precisely applicable and useful at the (3 fermi) scale of the classical electron radius, say in QED. At larger scales, the quantum field theories come into play and with it the 'classical electron' is rendered as a 'point particle' with the associated difficulties of renormalization and finitization of working parameters, such as position and momentum. Now in the calculation above, that the 'muonic electron' requires a frequency of 2.6x10^22 Hz for a 4-Radius vector of 1.8x10^-15 meters (2/3rds of the electron radius). So the requirement becomes a change in the frequency of the 'muonic electron' to accommodate a 'matching' of the frequency upon a quantized holo-fractal background. In the case above, decreasing the muonic electron frequency by a factor of 1.51 would attain this harmonization between the 3-dimensional electron limit and its 4-dimensional extension. Then a frequency of 1.72x10^22 Hz would be able to 'tap' into the matrix-background defined 'classical electron radius' also at that frequency Eigen-state.

Generally, the 4th spatial (Kaluza-Klein) dimension of the hyperspace must become congruent with the 3rd spatial Riemann dimension for the 'phenomena' to manifest. This is essentially wormhole physics at its fundamentals and what I term wormholes opening up and closing is the probable dimensional intersection of the Kaluza-Klein 5D with the Minkowski 4D.

While I am fond of parallel universes as the key motivator, I realize they are not the only possible scientific explanation of paranormal phenomena. After this episode I must also consider the event of hyperspace intersecting the Minkowski space. While multiverses are a physical reality, they remain 'frozen' until the Minkowski metric naturally 'opens' up the 4-radius as described in the above. Once this occurs all of the space-time presently embedded in an 11-dimensional 'Strominger Matrix' of extremal Black Hole Equivalence becomes 5-dimensional, causing the creation, or 'opening of wormholes' as portals and conduits into outer space and 'higher dimensions' as well as to any spatial locale on the space-time landscape. Yes, Virginia, there really is such a thing as traveling in time, or at least being able to glimpse it via peering through the opening. The c-invariance will hold, however due to the 4-Radius and the volumar quantization indicated above, and the 'tyranny of the metric' will become infused by an 'easement of the de Broglie phase-changes' with 'Velocity' as the lightpath/time also becoming a scale factor R(n) multiplied by frequency modulators {V=R(n)F}.

While I am at this point dead certain that I have lost 99% of my reading audience with this tirade, it is a gift non-the-less to that 1% that understands it. But I too am only human, and thinking about these things gives ME an extraordinary headache.

As always I want to reiterate that one piece of evidence is meaningless. Two pieces of evidence is interesting. Three pieces of evidence occurring simultaneously is worth analysis, and four pieces of evidence can be compelling. ***It takes a preponderance of evidence to prove a paranormal event is or has occurred, and that evidence must debunk all natural explanations.*** We will touch on EMF again in the chapter on Spectrum Analysis.

Chapter 7
Magnetic Fields

"Space travel is utter bilge."
-Richard Woolley-
(U.K. Astronomer Royal, in 1956, one year before Sputnik)

Magnetic fields as well as the aforementioned electromagnetic fields are probably the most often monitored but least understood environmental factors studied by paranormal investigators. Part of the problem is the lack of a clear understanding about how earth magnetism is generated. The Earth's magnetism varies widely from place to place and these differences in the magnetic field are generally caused by two things; the differing nature and composition of rocks and strata, and the interaction between charged particles from the sun and the magnetosphere. The Earth's magnetic field is polarized, made up of a static DC (Direct Current) field with north and south poles. The Earth's magnetic field extends approximately 36,000 miles out into space. Note the term "static". ALL magnetic fields are static, meaning of fixed polarity, with current flowing in only one direction. There is NO frequency present, and they are considered to be direct current or DC fields. If it has frequency, or is AC (Alternating Current) it is an Electromagnetic Field.

The magnetic field of the Earth is referred to scientifically as the magnetosphere. The magnetosphere prevents most of the particles from the sun, carried in solar wind, from hitting the Earth, and more important (to me personally and to all life in general), it prevents those particles from killing us. However, some particles from the solar wind do make it through the magnetosphere and these particles excite the Aurora displays (The Northern and Southern Lights) in both hemispheres. Interestingly, the Earth's north and south magnetic poles reverse at irregular intervals of hundreds of thousands of years. Some "Doom and Gloom" prophets think this is an event that is long overdue and on our horizon. It is the number one expectation of the Mayan Calendar believer's theory of the 2012 end of world scenario. We will have to wait and see how that plays out.

As implied by DC current, the force of magnetism flows from the positive side or pole, to the opposite pole. Now I am going to mess with your mind a bit. On Earth, the north (positive) pole of the Earth's magnet field is in fact at its south geographic pole. A compass needle sure enough indicates North, but if you put a compass needle near a bar magnet, it points AWAY from the north (positive) pole of the bar magnet. A compass, by the way, acts as a basic magnetometer. A magnetometer is a device that measures magnetic fields. The amount of needle deflection on a compass can be used to determine the relative strength and polarity of a magnetic field. Magnetometers are used in geophysical surveys to find deposits of iron or other metals because they can measure the magnetic field variations caused by metallic deposits.

Magnetometers are also used to detect archaeological sites or even shipwrecks and other buried or submerged objects, as they too create anomalies in the local magnetic field. Magnetic anomaly detectors, which are a form of magnetometer, detect submarines for military purposes. Geostationary Operational Environmental Satellites (GOES) employ magnetometers in order to measure the magnitude and direction of the earth's magnetic field. Magnetometers are used in directional drilling applications for oil or gas in order to detect the azimuth of the drilling tools and are most often paired up with accelerometers in the drilling tools so that both the inclination and azimuth of the drill bit can be found. But magnetometers, like all other equipment used by the paranormal investigator, were not designed to be specifically used to find "ghosts". Consequently, while the magnetometer is a popular tool in paranormal research it is also highly misused and its readings misunderstood, primarily because most people have a limited knowledge base as to how to properly use the equipment and what the measurements mean.

Magnetometers can be divided into two basic types, the scalar magnetometer, which measures the total strength of the magnetic field it is exposed to, and the vector magnetometer which has the capability to measure the component of the magnetic field in a particular direction or axis. For example, the use of three orthogonal vector magnetometers allows the magnetic field strength, inclination and declination to be accurately recorded. Examples of vector magnetometers are the common fluxgate magnetometer so often written about, and the not so common superconducting quantum interference devices, or SQUIDs. While some research has been conducted using Fluxgate Magnetometers, their cost generally prohibits them from widespread use in the paranormal investigative community, so most of us have to take these individual's findings at face value without independent correlation by several thousand other researchers.

The most common magnetic sensing device currently used on a paranormal investigation is the compass and it will serve quite well in determining the presence of magnetic fields. Any deviation of the needle from magnetic North should be noted, not as a paranormal event, but as an anomaly whose source should be identified. The world and most homes are full of magnetic deviations, and 99% of these deviations will have a natural, non-paranormal source. I will go into these natural causes of deviation a little further in the chapter, so bear with me for a bit.

Another common device in widespread use is the Pocket Magnetometer, and many models are available on the market. I use an old Annis model originally designed for the government geological survey teams, but any of the current magnetometers can be useful, as long as they have a -20 to +20 Gauss range maximum. Any more than that is not sensitive enough to be of much use.

The most common hand held magnetic sensing meters on the market today employ solid-state Hall Effect sensors. These sensors produce a voltage proportional to the applied magnetic field and also sense polarity. There are many of these devices on the market, and you can pay from $200.00 to $600 dollars for a decent example.

A fluxgate magnetometer on the other hand consists of a small, magnetically susceptible core wrapped by two coils of wire. An alternating electrical "Bias" current is passed through one coil, driving the core through an alternating cycle of magnetic saturation (i.e. magnetized, un-magnetized, inversely magnetized, un-magnetized, and magnetized). This constantly changing field induces an electrical current in the second coil, and this output current is measured by a detector. In a magnetically neutral background, the input and output currents will match each other. However, when the core is exposed to a background field, it will be more easily saturated in alignment or in phase with that field and less easily saturated in opposition to it. Hence the alternating magnetic field, and the induced output current, will be out of phase with the input current. The extent to which this is the case will depend on the strength of the background magnetic field. Often, the current in the output coil is integrated, yielding an output analog voltage, proportional to the magnetic field. Fluxgate magnetometers, paired in a gradiometer configuration, are commonly used for archaeological prospection. There are also numerous locations on the web that has plans for building your own magnetometer. My favorite one is at the website http://www.magnetometer.org/ and I recommend checking it out.

So what can a magnetometer really tell us concerning paranormal activity? Understanding the Earth's magnetic field and knowing what it should be gives us a piece of the environmental puzzle concerning the conditions present during a paranormal event. Since one way magnetic fields are produced is by the movement of the molten iron core of the earth and because they vary in strength by geographical location, knowing the base or control levels locally is important if fluctuations are to have any significant meaning. Additionally, the local magnetic field can be affected by seismic activity, and thunderstorms. But they can also be greatly affected by solar activity and to a lesser degree by stellar radiation from the cosmos. This is the primary reason why space weather is important to the paranormal investigator. If the magnetic survey of a site should be 4.7 gauss, and it is 5.9 gauss, one may assume something was going on of a paranormal nature, when the reality is a geomagnetic storm is peaking. Reported data seems to indicate that magnetic fields peak during a paranormal event and our own research certainly reinforces that there is a relationship between magnetic anomalies and perceived paranormal activity. Before we examine the possible ramifications of this, let's go over some rules for making magnetic measurements in relation to a paranormal investigation.

Before you make a single measurement, there are things you need to know. First, you must know what the current space weather is, and know if you have sunspot activity, high solar wind, geomagnetic storms, etc. Next, you must know what the geomagnetic field of the area should be. If you live in North America, this information is easy to get. Real time information is available at:
http://geomag.usgs.gov/.

If you don't know what your readings should be, then what you read is meaningless. A lot of work is required to establish a magnetic control reading for a specific area. Fortunately, USGS offers maps of all areas in the USA. Once you have your control data, you can refine it even further by inspecting the area around the data point or area of measurement to insure there are no obvious man made causes for a static magnetic field (a stack of railroad rails, old radio tower parts, abandoned farm equipment, etc.). Note any local deviations from the published magnetic field data. Taking the time to assemble this background information upfront guarantees that you will reduce the risk of mistaking normal deviation readings and believing you have an anomaly related to paranormal activity. In paranormal investigating, you must remain objective in your measurements, regardless of the parameters you are measuring, and don't get excited when you get a spike in the magnetic field (or any of your readings, for that matter). Just like Electromagnetic fields, a spike alone doesn't mean much. While it appears that magnetic fields may be related in some way to paranormal phenomena, it doesn't mean that any deviation from the norm is indicative of activity. It is all too common of a mistake to jump to this conclusion without being armed with control figures from a reliable, unbiased source. Remember that natural sources of magnetic fields exist everywhere, including the haunted house up the street you plan to investigate. Your magnetic anomaly may be due to someone simply flushing a toilet.

ALWAYS begin your investigation by taking baseline readings of the target site to determine specific background magnetic fields as well as identify areas of increase field strength. As stressed above, compare these readings to the published data available from the USGS. Also compare your readings with known null areas, or areas that no activity has been reported. This will give you a good overall survey of the site to work from. Magnetic fields in general do not appear to increase and decrease like EMF does, since EMF is more than likely the result of power consumption by manmade equipment or appliances. Magnetic fields tend to alter more subtly, unless of course our sun goes nova, in which case your investigation becomes a non-issue.

ALWAYS record your data in some form or fashion. Include a time check with your readings at regular intervals. Again, for the sake of speed, a personal voice recorder is an ideal log for noting measurements. You can begin with a time and end with a time, and you can figure out any activity in between after the fact by using the timeline on your audio editing software when viewing the recorded wave file and using simple math. This will give you accurate data points to compare with other readings made at the same time by others when you correlate all the data after the investigation concludes. It is a little more work, but it yields far more information concerning relationships with data and phenomena.

While most investigators use the "spot check" method of collecting data, a much more valuable method is to record "continuous data" to compare with other recorded activity and data from the investigation. There are several ways to do this, with the simplest being to rig up a small video camera on the measuring device and leave it running. More sophisticated methods include data loggers and special sensors designed for automated data collection and storage. It is always best to monitor the data at several places on site, so a data logger with 6 magnetic sensors is a great way to gather magnetic fluctuation data over a wide area.

We were investigating a home in Flemington, NJ not too long ago that had been the subject of a previous investigation in which we had collected some highly controversial evidence concerning a rocking chair. As is our policy, anytime we capture something that is impossible to explain, we go back and concentrate on the specific area with a battery of equipment. In this case, we placed a Trifield Meter on the rocking chair, and then used low light IR illuminated video cameras to document the results. While we were not able to duplicate the previous capture, we did discover a highly fluctuating magnetic field was present in and around the chair, with no specifically identifiable source!

Many paranormal investigators confuse electromagnetic fields with magnetic fields. They are completely different, with unrelated natural sources. An electromagnetic field as previously mentioned is dynamic or alternating in frequency, meaning the field is propagating at a specific frequency or medley of frequencies, and those frequencies or frequency will swing positive and negative from a center reference point at a measurable rate. Magnetic fields are static or direct current flow in nature, meaning the energy always flows in one direction, from negative to positive or from South Pole to North Pole. Electromagnetic fields are non-polar, constantly changing their polarity based on the frequency they are propagating in. Magnetic fields are polar in nature, meaning they always have a North and South Pole. Electromagnetic fields are for the most part the product of manmade devices, such as house current, radios, cell phones, appliances, computers, monitors, etc. Light is also an electromagnetic field, as are gamma rays and other cosmic radiation. The main sources of magnetic fields, on the other hand, are rock strata at a local level, the sun and the core of the earth. It remains to be seen if magnetic fields actually have a viable relationship with paranormal activity. The current level of data is non-conclusive.

Having a map to make reference notes on is invaluable. ALWAYS graph out the floor plan of the building, room or location. The best arguments for performing a preliminary investigation prior to investigating a site is to scout it, document, and map it for your team's use, as well as conduct interviews in a neutral environment. But let's get back to the actual investigation. Log readings you believe to be anomalous in the area on the floor plan where they occur. After the investigation, thoroughly search those areas to try and locate a natural source for the field strength recorded. We have investigated crawl spaces, inspected the ceiling in basements to trace out wiring, and documented water pipe currents to locate potential sources. But natural contributors must be eliminated as well. For example, land with rich iron ore deposits underground can have a high level of residual magnetic fields. Remember also that elevated magnetic fields have been reported to affect human consciousness just as elevated levels of EMF effects consciousness and behavior. While eye witness accounts are considered anecdotal evidence, if you find a correlating magnetic hot spot where activity has been reported, you have to keep in mind the observer or witness may have suffered from sensitivity to the elevated magnetic field that could be causing hallucinations or altered perceptions and there may actually be nothing paranormal present at the site at all. For your data to have any strength at all, you must debunk evidence or propose its possible paranormal nature with equal veracity.

So, back to the question on what does measuring a magnetic field do for our insight? Well the Earth's magnetic field is actually not one field, but a composite of several magnetic fields generated by a variety of sources. These fields are superimposed on each other and through inductive processes interact with each other sometimes adding, sometimes subtracting, and thereby creating a varying measurable magnetic field across the Earth's surface. The most important of these geomagnetic sources for our purposes are the Earth's fluid outer core, magnetized rocks in Earth's crust and fields generated outside Earth by electric currents flowing in the ionosphere and magnetosphere. One of the reasons we monitor space weather is to eliminate cosmic radiation, geomagnetic storms as well as sunspots and other celestial activity from being a possible source of "paranormal activity" or to establish any correlation between elevated natural sources of magnetic activity to suspected paranormal activity.

Elevated geomagnetic fields may also contribute to a quantum singularity that could open a gateway or wormhole between two parallel universes, or another dimension. Some theorize that a phenomena known as a vortex may be just such a wormhole. Elevated levels could indicate a "tunnel" or gateway has opened between two dimensions or two universes of one level of magnetic field strength, to another of higher or lower value. This could mean that paranormal activity is normal, or a process based on natural and yet unexplainable phenomena, and not a "ghost" at all. On the other hand, it could indicate that "ghosts" are simply transferred consciousness from one universe or dimension to another. The whole point of research is to find the answers, and to find the answers we need to do controlled research. I have heard many people say that we will never find the answers, because we can never find controls. If this were the case, there would be no atomic bomb or space travel! Monitoring magnetic field strength may add understanding to this picture, by correlating the changes with other data changes occurring simultaneously. Just remember, one of the "controls" that exist in paranormal research is correlation. Therefore we need to correlate, correlate, and correlate!

In 1977 I was in St. Augustine doing an investigation in a home that was built in the late 1600's. I was using a compass to map out any magnetic anomalies in the home by working each room in a grid pattern and then making notations on a hand drawn map of the room. I had just completed the survey of the master bedroom when suddenly the compass began spinning wildly in a clockwise direction. Simultaneously the hair on my neck and body stood out from the skin as if under the influence of a static field. The temperature around me dropped rather suddenly from 85 degrees F to 42 degrees! We could never find a viable source for that event. Did we have a brush with a parallel universe or did the spirit of a long dead Spaniard interface with our reality? We have no way of knowing for certain because we did not have enough evidence correlated to make a judgment call. My opinion however for what it is worth, is that both were probably the case.

Chapter 8
Ions

"Nothing tends so much to the advancement of knowledge as the application of a new instrument. The native intellectual powers of men in different times are not so much the causes of the different success of their labors, as the peculiar nature of the means and artificial resources in their possession."
-Sir Humphrey Davy-

Recently there has been a lot of controversy concerning the measurement of ions during a paranormal investigation. This is due to a drastic misunderstanding of what ions are and why we want to measure them in the first place. Ions are atoms that have either "acquired" or "shed" an electrical charge. They are created naturally as air molecules that break apart due to a variety of reasons including sunlight, radiation, moving air or water. Depending on who you read or listen to, ions are very important or have no connection to paranormal activity. This translates into "no one really knows one way or the other". Concrete evidence of ion importance simply hasn't been established, making the study of ions and their possible relationship to paranormal activity, paramount. I have personally explored the ion question for many years, and my evidence indicates that artificially increasing ion levels does not "cause" paranormal activity. The data leads me to believe that noted increases in ion counts during a paranormal event may be the effect, not cause of the event. This opens up tantalizing possibilities. The essential question remains, "what causes the atom to acquire or shed a charge? Is it normal, or "paranormal"? To get a handle on the questions, let me relate the story of our research into the matter.

We know from a huge volume of independent research that ions affect us and every other living thing. The simple fact is one in three human beings are sensitive to the effects of negative and positive ion bombardment (an interesting study would be are these are also the same 1 in 3 that are sensitive to EMF). This research on ions and their effects on humans indicate that negative ions make us feel good, and positive ions make us feel bad. If you feel sleepy when you are around an air-conditioner, but feel immediately refreshed and invigorated when you step outside or roll down the car window, then you are definitely sensitive to ionic effects. It is well known that air conditioning depletes the atmosphere of negative ions. The question my team of researchers has tried to answer is, since we believe that ion count is connected to paranormal activity, what could we do to determine if it was a contributing source of the activity, or caused by the activity. Our solution was to monitor the controlled injection of ions into the air at a reported active location. The idea being if we as living beings respond to ion concentrations, then it stands to reason that it may be possible that we as dead people (assuming paranormal activity is caused by dead people) also react to ion bombardment. Also, is it possible that elevation in ion concentrations may be related to an interaction between two parallel universes, or the interaction of other dimensions on our own four dimensional existence? My poker chips are placed on the high probability these two suppositions being the case.

The first question we approached is whether positive or negative ions or both would affect paranormal activity. The second question is if ion counts do not affect paranormal activity, what is causing elevated ion counts during reported paranormal activity? This led to theoretical discussions such as, is the ion count a precursor to the manifestation of paranormal activity, or is it a product of it? What is the source of these ions, and how does the ratio of positive and negative change and affect the phenomena? This led me to design an experiment to attempt to find out, and I have included this experiment in Chapter 22. It is called the Ion Bombardment Experiment, and I invite everyone to copy the experiment and let me know your findings.

We have run the ion experiment at many locations to date. So far, we have not recorded any noticeable effect on paranormal activity by increasing positive or negative ion counts. We have noticed increased amounts of positive and negative ions present from no identifiable source just prior to and during a paranormal event. This would indicate to me, that whatever is happening in a paranormal event, something creates an increase in ionized air at the actual event horizon. This is of course a preliminary finding that bears multiple repetitions. And what do I mean by "event horizon"? I mean we may actually be witnessing the opening of a small Lorenzian Wormhole!

As mentioned earlier, many self proclaimed professional skeptics out there dismiss ion level monitoring as a waste of time, citing the inaccuracy of the meters (some meters can have as much as a 20% error rate). While this is certainly true, it doesn't disqualify ion measurement from paranormal investigation, and here's why; we are looking for comparisons, not accurate counts. In other words, if there is a 70% increase in ion levels, the increase tells us something, even if the exact count is inaccurate. And on a separate but relevant note, there are metering devices available to the general public with much greater accuracies available if an exact count is desired. They just cost more money!

An interesting foot note is that indoors, ions "live" an average of 30 seconds before touching a surface and shorting to ground. Outdoor ions usually "live" several minutes more than indoor ions. Any concentration lasting longer durations are most likely being generated by a source. Locating the source will explain what is really going on, and if the relationship to paranormal activity is coincidental. In our case, the source appeared to be a spot in the middle of the room a few feet above shoulder height, with no apparent source. Spontaneous ion generation from thin air! This takes us back to the potential wormhole discovery from Chapter 6, adding additional evidence for my conclusion. The question it poses is, does the wormhole interconnect with a parallel universe, or is it a dimensional connection? Time will tell.

Normal fair-weather ion concentrations are 200 to 800 negative and 250 to 1500 positive ions per cubic centimeter. Indoor levels as a rule are generally lower. Several hours before a storm, positive ion concentration will increase dramatically, sometimes exceeding 5000 ions per cubic centimeter (cm3). During a storm, negative ions increase to several thousand while positive ions decrease, often to levels below 500. Is this related to increased paranormal activity during thunderstorms? Possibly!

Ion Distribution is, however, not an exact science (nor is the measurement of ion concentrations). Typically, a high concentration (1000 cm^3 or more) of both may be found in one area outdoors while low concentration (300 or less) may be measured a few feet away. A cloud of pure positive ions (no negative ions) with a concentration of 1000 ions/cm^3 is highly unstable and would fall apart if the cloud diameter expanded beyond a hundred feet or so. Because of this effect, high concentrations of exclusively positive or negative ions tend to be compact, and don't extend beyond 60 to 100 feet in area.

The one noted exception is during thunderstorms, when strong atmospheric electric fields can maintain a high concentration of one ion polarity. While testing indoors, you may find high negative ion counts in one area of a room and high positive in another, particularly if the rooms are large in size. Is there a correlation between this phenomena and paranormal activity? Possibly!

Humidity also affects the total ion count as well. The higher the humidity, the lower the ion count will be. High humidity also reduces dust in the air as the moisture weighs it down, reducing dust orb photos but possibly increasing moisture orbs in photos, none of which are paranormal in nature.

Another key factor to bear in mind when measuring ions is that your breath contains about 20,000 to 50,000 - ions/cm3 from the evaporating water, but you must be grounded to exhale a concentration this high. If you are insulated from ground, you will become more positively charged with each exhalation (by about five volts DC due to static electricity accumulation) since your breath is removing negative charge. This is a very important factor to keep in mind if you are holding the sampling device.

Another tidbit of knowledge that is helpful to your client is that indoors, near ground level or in the basement, most positive ions come from radon. The total number of ions is directly proportional to radon concentration multiplied by average ion lifetime. Also remember, strong electric fields indoors will act to reduce the ion lifetime. Since it is unlikely that a high level of 1000 positive ions/cm^3 can result from anything else other than flame, smoke, or a hot electric heating element, it is probable that 1000 positive ions/cm^3 in a basement signifies the presence of at least 4 pCi/L (picocuries per liter) of radon (2000 ions/cm^3 = 8 pCi/L, etc.) 4 pCi/L is the maximum allowable amount / limit in the U.S. and this information SHOULD always be reported to the client for further testing for health purposes. My own team has uncovered numerous radon contaminations that were unknown to the client. Additionally, if radon is the source of the elevated ion level, the concentration of ions will be approximately equal throughout the basement, unlike any naturally occurring ions which would be cluster in an uneven distribution.

However, the entire basement should be tested to insure this is the case. For instance, if you measure 1000 positive ions near the hot water heater but only measure 100 positive ions/cm^3 in other areas of the basement, the probability is that radon isn't the source. Furthermore, a slightly higher concentration of positive ions near cracks in the concrete foundation or near corners could indicate the radon is entering into the basement. If the average positive ion count is low (less than 100), then there is essentially no radon present. It is not possible to "hide" the ions that radon produces. "No ions" means "no radon".

How to measure ions

Prior to an investigation, when the site is inactive, the area to be investigated should have a complete ion sweep performed using a "grid" pattern making a note of the ion concentrations found in the dwelling. I want to add that while measuring data with portable hand held devices is not the ideal methodology for research with active paranormal occurrences due to their lack of data logging capability, it is an excellent methodology to use to establish control readings prior to the investigation starting. Since they are used to establish a normal level, they are a reference point only. If you begin logging data and the readings fall within the established measurements, then YOU know nothing is going on yet. Since the focus will be on variations from the norm, it is the variations that are the more questioned data you will collect, and this is what the sensors or their software management should log on a chart or as data figures.

After these measurements are completed and the notes have been made, prior to starting the investigation, it is a good idea to run several negative air ionization units (air purifiers) at full power in different parts of the house. Negative ionization of the air removes most of the particulate matter that floats in suspension. Under normal conditions, dust and other particles are suspended in the air by the normal convective air currents present in the room. By running the ionizers and keeping the windows closed, you will effectively remove much of this "dust" from the air. This will help reduce the photographing of dust orbs. This also dramatically increases the negative ion count in the room, and alters the ratio of negative and positive ions present. This should be standard operating procedure before any investigation that you plan to employ photographic evidence collection as part of the protocol.

Once the room has been swept of dust by the negative ion generators, air sampling should be taken again. Some of you are wondering how long does it take to ionize the air in a room, and that will be determined by the output of the air purifier you are using. Refer to the individual owner's manual for this information, and plan your investigation activities accordingly.

Note the ion counts, both positive and negative. A constant monitoring of the ion count should proceed from this point forward until the investigation ends. Make note of any changes in ion counts and note the time for future reference. Also, make sure your ion counter is grounded for best results. Continuous consistent data will tell you far more than sporadic spot checks of a room from time to time. Find the area with the most reported activity, and let the ion counter run there. If you can't be there to monitor it, place a camera on it and video the meter with a time reference. We use an ALPHALAB, INC. ion counter, but it is recommended to follow the procedure outlined by the manufacturer of the meter you use. With most forced air meters, there are a few tricks you should be aware of.

If you are measuring ions while walking, hold the Ion Counter vertical and at arm's length. This will cause the moving air to flow perpendicular to the forced air flow through the Ion Counter caused by the internal fan. In windy conditions, hold it (or set it down) so it is vertical or at least perpendicular to the wind direction. If changing conditions require that it is sometimes parallel to the wind direction, have the air flow into the top (as opposed to into the bottom or fan side). This procedure will assure the most accurate readings. When air is rapidly flowing into the top, the Ion Counter will read slightly high, but if air is rapidly flowing into the fan side, it may read very low.

Also remember that you are building up a static charge if you are exposed to the output of an air ionizer (air cleaner or filter) or simply walking on a carpet. This may attract or repel ions, (depending on the polarity of the static charge) and it can even create positive ions due to our natural highly negative charge. When walking on a carpet, do not wear plastic-soled shoes as this can build up a static charge and affect accuracy. While measuring, touch a grounded object frequently to avoid too much static buildup. Another method that helps reduce static interference is to set the Ion Counter on a glass tray or on a sheet of glass (plastic will not work because it acquires a charge). Hold the glass instead of the actual Ion Counter while measuring and touch the Counter to ground before starting measurements. Most ion counters come with a ground clamp and this also works quite well, as long as the other end of the cable is connected to a grounded object. I try to use the center screw on an electrical outlet or switch when in a home, but a cold water pipe works well also.

Another interesting piece of information is that holding a counter near any radiation particle source will produce very high positive ion readings. It can therefore be used as a Geiger counter. While this isn't as accurate as a radiation meter, it will work, and is something to keep in mind when purchasing equipment.

There are many theories concerning ion counts and paranormal activity, and to date, none have been proven or disproven scientifically. I believe this is due mostly to the lack of serious, scientific methodology when deploying ion counters on investigations, and misinterpreting what a high ion count means. I also believe that most people have no idea how to properly use an ion counter in the field. A good example of scientific methodology in using ion counters in paranormal investigations can be found by reading "Hauntings and Poltergeists: Multidisciplinary Perspectives" by James Houran and Rense Lange. Their research points out that many paranormal incidents may be caused by the effect of positive ion concentrations on the brain. Since high ion counts have been associated with haunting activity, this certainly justifies more research and underlines the one thing we all need to do; accept nothing as fact until you prove it to yourself. Once you prove it to yourself, you are obligated to share your findings so others may prove it too.

Several years ago my team and I were investigating a historical building in

Perth Amboy, NJ. During the investigation, there was an increase in negative ions that was rather dramatic, on the second floor of the building. The increase was measured throughout the entire floor. Shortly after the increase, a column of flame like mist was photographed in one area of the floor, while a shadow person was captured in the hallway. Did the increase in ionic content signal a precursor to the appearance of these phenomena? The evidence suggests that it does. We have encountered this increase prior to paranormal activity on nearly every active investigation we have participated in. In some cases, for example a recent case in Pennsylvania, we encountered an ion reading so high we were unable to measure it! The air literally caused our skin to tingle. In the same location, we measured a negative RF transmission. While this was obviously a meter malfunction, we could not reproduce the readings after we left the area. Regardless of what the critics say, ion count levels are a critical part of the puzzle and should not be ignored for what they may indicate, which is in my opinion, the presence of an open portal.

Chapter 9
Radiation

"There are many examples of old, incorrect theories that stubbornly persisted, sustained only by the prestige of foolish but well-connected scientists. Many of these theories have been killed off only when some decisive experiment exposed their incorrectness. Thus the yeoman work in any science, and especially physics, is done by the experimentalist, who must keep the theoreticians honest."
-Michio Kaku-

Radiation is energy that comes from a source, travels through space and may be able to penetrate various materials. Light, radio, and microwaves are types of radiation that are called non-ionizing and we will talk about them later in the book. The kind of radiation discussed in this chapter is called ionizing radiation. Ionizing radiation is different because it can produce charged particles (ions) in matter.

In the preceding chapter on ions we explored how ionizing radiation is produced by unstable atoms. Unstable atoms differ from stable atoms because unstable atoms have an excess of energy or mass or both. High-voltage manmade devices such as x-ray machines can also produce radiation.

These unstable atoms are referred to as being "radioactive". In order to reach stability, these atoms give off, or emit, the excess energy or mass as "radiation". There are several types of radiation including electromagnetic (like light, radio transmissions, etc.) and particle based (i.e., mass given off with the energy of motion). Gamma rays and X-rays are examples of electromagnetic radiation. Gamma radiation originates in the nucleus while x-rays come from the electronic construct of the atom. Alpha and beta radiation are examples of particulate radiation. Alpha and beta radiation can be commonly found in private residences. Gamma radiation in any concentration generally speaking, is not normally encountered.

Interestingly, there is a "background" of natural radiation everywhere in our environment. It comes from outer space in the form of cosmic rays and from naturally occurring radioactive materials contained in the earth and in living things.

The radiation one typically encounters is one of four types: alpha radiation, beta radiation, gamma radiation, and x radiation. Neutron radiation is also encountered in nuclear power plants and high-altitude flight and is emitted from some industrial radioactive sources. So what is the relationship between radiation and paranormal activity?

I tested a reportedly active paranormal site for radiation for the first time in 1977. I did so in an effort to identify the forces at work during a perceived paranormal event. I used an old Civil Defense Geiger Counter. CD meters were produced by a number of different firms in the 1960s under government contract. Victoreen, Lionel, Electro Neutronics, Nuclear Measurements, Chatham Electronics, International Pump and Machine Works, Universal Atomics, Anton Electronic Laboratories; Landers, Frary, & Clark; El Tronics, Jordan, and Nuclear Chicago to name a few. Mine was a Victoreen Model CDV 700. The CDV-700 is an actual Geiger counter with a Geiger tube and detects beta radiation and gamma radiation with the detecting wand's beta shield open, or gammas only when the shield is closed. I chose this model back then because unlike many CD meters, the 700 could detect low levels of radiation, but had to be used in conjunction with a survey meter in high-radiation areas.

The CDV-700, was a true Geiger Counter, not a radiological survey meter that was only capable of measuring the high levels of radiation normally associated with a nuclear event. It was capable of measuring ambient environmental radiation levels. This was important, as ambient radiation levels would have to be monitored in order to detect the slightest of changes corresponding to an event.

Today, technology has made quite a few leaps and bounds, specifically in miniaturization and accuracy. My team employs a Radiation Alert® Monitor 4 hand held meter for monitoring low levels of radiation, but additionally I still use old CD meters. We have 3 CDV-715s which are by far the most popular meter on the used equipment market today and the most widely used in paranormal investigating because of low cost. Here is something to keep in mind though. Unlike the CDV-700, the CDV-715 is a simple radiological survey meter, specifically designed for high-radiation fields for which Geiger counters will give incorrect readings. Survey meters do not read alpha or beta radiation, only Gamma radiation. They work by radiation penetrating the case of the unit and the enclosed ionization chamber to produce a visible reading between .1R/hr and 500R/hr. If you can get this unit (or any other like it) to react to any source of radiation for a prolonged period, you need to evacuate the area immediately!

However, a simple modification will allow the device to read beta radiation. Simply provide vent holes in the case and remove the shielding from the ionization chamber. You can determine whether the readings are from Beta or gamma radiation by covering the vent holes with aluminum foil. If you still get a reading, it is gamma radiation.

We also employ 1 CDV 717, which is similar to the CDV-715, and also reads from .1R/hr to 500R/hr. It too is a survey meter with an ionization chamber; however this unit's chamber is detachable, designed originally for hanging outside a fallout shelter or basement. When used, the ionization chamber would be inserted into a yellow anti-contamination bag, tied off, and hung outside a bomb shelter to measure radioactivity levels from a safe distance. An extension coaxial cord, typically stored inside the unit, is then run from the outdoor chamber to the indoor meter. The coaxial spool is used to prop the meter up for reading. This would allow those hiding to wait until outside radiation levels have fallen to a "safe" level before emerging. When using the extension cord, a slight delay in measurement readings occurs, but this is not really an issue as outdoor radiation levels are unlikely to change quickly. We employ these modified meters in general areas to measure any large spikes in radiation. The fact is, however, that most of the radiation meters in use in the paranormal field are unmodified survey meters; this would explain why few researchers talk about radiation being a factor during paranormal activity.

But there is a great deal of evidence that it IS related. I have miles of recorded audio bytes and tape from investigations where the audible beep from the Monitor 4 detector is sporadically going off at irregular intervals, indicating a small recurring spike in radiation. Since radiation has a steady, slow decay rate, sporadic radiation is not a natural occurrence. The areas also seem to move about, indicating no fixed source. While it may be possible that the spikes are being caused by something natural in the environment, to date no source has been identified. The Monitor 4 is capable of monitoring Alpha, Beta and Gamma radiation. In order to determine the type of radiation present, you have to employ shielding. A piece of paper will stop Alpha radiation, so if you still get spikes after covering the sensor with a piece of paper, you know it is not Alpha radiation. Next, to further refine the identity of the radiation levels, a piece of aluminum foil is placed over the sensor. Aluminum foil stops Beta radiation. If you still have a spike, it is Gamma radiation. I have noted all three present at active locations. If you are going to test for radiation spikes as part of your paranormal research, there are a few things to keep in mind.

Alpha Radiation

There are natural sources of radiation that can be encountered in a home or commercial building. We have already mentioned Radon. Radon is a colorless, odorless gas, and a byproduct of radium. It is a part of the natural radioactive decay series starting with uranium-238. It is radioactive with a half-life of 3.8 days, decaying by the emission of alpha particles causing it to degrade to polonium, bismuth, and finally lead in successive steps. Hence, Radon is a good example of Alpha radiation encountered in the home, as mentioned above. Alpha particles are emitted by radioactive nuclei such as is found in the minerals uranium, thorium, actinium, and radium. The process of this emission is called alpha decay. Alpha decay often leaves the nucleus in an excited state, resulting in the emission of a gamma ray to shed the excess energy. Unlike beta decay, alpha decay is affected by the strong nuclear force. According to classical physics, alpha particles do not have the energy to escape the nucleus. However, something called the quantum tunneling effect or wave-mechanical tunneling allows them to escape. The quantum tunneling is due to the behavior of particles illustrated by Schrödinger's wave-equation. All wave equations exhibit fleeting or dispersing wave coupling effects under the right conditions. Wave coupling effects mathematically equivalent to those called "tunneling" in quantum mechanics sometimes occur in Maxwell's wave-equation and with the common non-dispersive wave-equation often applied to waves generated by plucking strings or other acoustic conditions. These are fairly complex concepts and I won't go into them here, but you can certainly research them on the web. The bottom line is alpha particles escape. This has a lot to do with particle-wave duality, another headache creating concept of quantum mechanics.

When an alpha particle is emitted, the atomic mass of an element decreases due to the loss of two neutrons and two protons. The atomic number of the atom also goes down by two, as a result of the loss of two protons and the atom morphs into a new element. This is evident by the morphing of uranium into thorium, or radium into radon gas. Both are products of alpha decay.

The energy of an alpha particle can vary widely, with higher energy alpha particles ejected from large nuclei and less energy from smaller nuclei. Generally speaking, however, in a home environment most alpha particles range between 3.0 and 7.0 MeV or "million electron-volts". Don't let this relatively low number fool you though. This is a substantial amount of energy for a single particle. However their high mass translates into a lower particle speed than any other radiation type. Due to their charge and relatively large mass, alpha particles are easily stopped by a simple piece of tissue paper, and their travel is limited to only a few inches in air. Additionally they can be absorbed by the outer layers of human skin and are not generally dangerous to life unless the ingested or inhaled such as with the gas Radon.

Most smoke detectors contain a small amount of the alpha emitter americium-241. This isotope is extremely dangerous if inhaled or ingested, but the danger is minimal if the source is kept sealed. Many municipalities have established programs to collect and dispose of old smoke detectors, to keep them out of the general waste stream. This is another example of radiation commonly found in a home or business. Be sure you aren't close to a smoke detector when your radiation meter goes off!

Another thing to consider is that while alpha particles occur naturally, they can have energy high enough to participate in a nuclear reaction. This offers an interesting group of probabilities and possibilities to the paranormal mix. In fact, the study of alpha radiation contributed much of the early knowledge of nuclear physics. Physicist Ernest Rutherford used alpha particles emitted by Radium bromide to infer that J. J. Thomson's Plum pudding model of the atom was fundamentally flawed. In Rutherford's gold foil experiment conducted by his students Hans Geiger and Ernest Marsden, a narrow beam of alpha particles was established, passing through very thin (a few hundred atoms thick) gold foil. The alpha particles were detected by a zinc sulfide screen, which emits a flash of light upon an alpha particle collision. Rutherford hypothesized that, assuming the "plum pudding" model of the atom was correct, the positively charged alpha particles would be only slightly deflected, if at all, by the dispersed positive charge predicted. It was found that some of the alpha particles were deflected at much larger angles than expected, and some bounced back. Although most of the alpha particles went straight through as expected, Rutherford commented that the few particles that were deflected was akin to shooting a fifteen inch shell at tissue paper only to have it bounce off, again assuming the "plum pudding" theory was correct. It was determined that the atom's positive charge was concentrated in a small area in its center, making the positive charge dense enough to deflect any positively charged alpha particles that came close to what was later termed the nucleus. While this may seem like basic high school physics, you have to remember that at the time it was not known that alpha particles were themselves nuclei nor was the existence of protons or neutrons known. Rutherford's experiment led to the Bohr model (named for Niels Bohr) and later the modern wave-mechanical model of the atom.

Beta Radiation

Henri Becquerel is credited with the discovery of beta particles. In 1900, he showed that beta particles were identical to electrons, which had recently been discovered by Joseph John Thompson.

Beta radiation is actually an ejected electron. Beta radiation may travel several feet in air and can be moderately penetrating. It has been known to penetrate human skin to the depth of where skin cells are produced. Needless to say if high levels of beta radiation particles are allowed to remain on the skin for an extended period, they can certainly cause skin injury. Like alpha energy, beta-radiation is harmful when ingested. Bottom line here is to avoid eating or breathing the radiation.

Beta radiation for the most part can be easily detected with a survey type meter and a thin-window G-M probe. However, some beta materials produce very low-energy that may be very difficult or impossible to detect. These materials would include hydrogen-3 (tritium), some carbon-14, and sulfur-35. Additionally, unlike alpha radiation, clothing can provide some protection against beta radiation. Strong beta radiation materials are strontium-90, carbon-14, tritium, and sulfur-35. If you are investigating an industrial setting, keep in mind that abandoned radiation sources may have been left behind. If you discover such a radioactive source, leave the area immediately and report it to the authorities!

Gamma and X Radiation

Gamma radiation and x-rays are high energy electromagnetic radiation that is extraordinarily penetrating and requires special materials to shield them. They can travel a long way in air and clean through the human body. It takes very dense materials like lead to shield a person from the effects of this type of radiation. While clothing won't shield the effects of gamma radiation and x-rays, it will help prevent contamination of the skin by gamma-emitting materials. Gamma radiation is easily detected by survey meters with a gamma detector probe as well as standard radiation detectors. Gamma radiation and X-rays are frequently associated with the emission of alpha and beta radiation during radioactive decay. Some examples of Gamma emitters include cesium-137, cobalt-60, iodine-131, radium-226, and technetium-99. Gamma radiation and X-rays should not be present in any quantity in a house or business. If it is encountered, leave the building immediately and notify the owners and authorities.

Measuring radiation for paranormal research purposes

Here in the United States, "radiation absorbed dose", "dose equivalent", and "exposure" are most commonly measured units called RAD, REM, or roentgen (R), respectively. In regards to gamma and x-ray radiation, these units of measure for exposure or dose are assumed equal. For our research purposes, we don't normally deal with high levels of radiation, and usually it is in the form of a burst, or spike, rather than a typical radioactive decay cycle. Consequently, we need to measure small amounts of radiation that are transitory in nature. Smaller fractions of these measured quantities often have a prefix, such as milli (m), which means 1/1,000. For example, 1 rad = 1,000 mrad. Micro (µ) means 1/1,000,000. So, 1,000,000 µrad = 1 rad, or 10 µR = 0.000010 R. The International System of Units (SI) should anyone be curious, is now the official system of measurement for radiation in scientific circles and uses the "gray" (Gy) and "sievert" (Sv) identifiers for absorbed dose and equivalent dose respectively. The conversions are as follows:

1 Gy = 100 rad
1 mGy = 100 mrad
1 Sv = 100 rem
1 mSv = 100 mrem

There exists today a large variety of handheld instruments for detecting and measuring radiation. The most common handheld or portable instruments are Geiger Counters, with common measurement units being roentgens per hour (R/hr), milliroentgens per hour (mR/hr), rem per hour (rem/hr), millirem per hour (mrem/hr), and or counts per minute (cpm).

Another type of device that is used in paranormal investigating is the MicroR Meter, which uses a Sodium Iodide Detector. An SID is a solid crystal of sodium iodide that generates a pulse of light when radiation hits it. This pulse of light is converted into an electrical impulse by a photomultiplier tube (PMT), which then can drive a meter movement or LED readout. The pulse of light is proportional to the amount of radiation hitting the crystal. A common accessory on these meters is a speaker, and the pulses can be used to trigger an audible click or "beep", a useful feature when looking for an unknown source (such as a ghost, portal or wormhole opening up). Common readout units are in these units are microroentgens per hour (µR/hr) and counts per minute (cpm). Some of these units employ a special plastic or other inert crystal "scintillator" in place of the sodium iodide crystal. This reduces the cost significantly and performance isn't affected.

The Portable Multichannel Analyzer is starting to be explored, but so far its use has been limited due to cost. I am sure as surplus units begin to appear on E-Bay it will only be a matter of time before they make a wider appearance. This device consists of a sodium iodide crystal and PMT as described above, coupled with a small multichannel analyzer (MCA) electronics package. When gamma-ray data libraries and automatic gamma-ray energy identification procedures are employed, these handheld instruments can automatically identify and display the type of radioactive materials present. When dealing with unknown sources of radiation, this is an incredibly useful feature. Particularly if you are at a site and get a spike that says "source unidentifiable". For the most part, these devices are employed to measure Gamma radiation.

Just keep in mind that there are few "cheap" solutions for accurately detecting radiation. The old fashioned civil defense meters are perhaps the least expensive and easiest to acquire, but the best device is a small hand held Radiation detection meter, and be prepared to spend at least $300.00 to get one.

To use a radiation detector on an investigation requires using the same grid search pattern that I have preached about continuously throughout this book. As with the other instruments we have discussed up to this point, any event should be recorded and noted for time and location. But there is an additional methodology that is now available for the Monitor 4 Geiger counter, and this new methodology is called Data Logging. I will go into Data Logging later in the book. But there is a meter out there that can be used and log data by itself with a software application available that allows analysis with a laptop computer or desktop PC.

Specifically, the Monitor 4 Handheld Radiation Detector is made by SE International, who now offer a software package called "Observer". The current price of the modified monitor 4 is about $289.00, with the software costing an additional $79.00. The procedure is to set the monitor 4 up and running, and connected to a laptop computer via the USB cable. The device is turned on, and using the software, a constant data file is created as a permanent record of every radiation event. This is the recommended procedure to use for any measurements taken by any equipment, as it creates a time based record that can be correlated to other real time data collected by other instrumentation. However, it is not a universally offered option with all of the aspects of the environment that we currently monitor. Hopefully this will change in the future. But what this type of set up allows the researcher to do is to match up events and the effects on the environment in a record format that can be used for detailed analysis to correlate effects. Using this type of configuration allows for the easy discovery of a very real relationship between paranormal activity and radiation. Even better there is the probability that soon you will be able to purchase a radiation sensor that will allow you to use it with a standard multi-channel data logger so it can be easily kept in context with multiple environmental sensors such as temperature, EMF, humidity, barometric pressure, etc. (what a concept). Beware of naturally occurring radiation in the building you are investigating. These natural sources are listed below.

SMOKE DETECTORS: Some smoke detectors contain americium-241, a radioactive isotope used in the smoke sensing mechanism. This can create a dangerous situation if the isotope seal is breached.

CAMPING LANTERN MANTLES: In the past, some lantern mantles were made with radioactive Thorium. Since we don't as a rule use lanterns on investigations, this really doesn't apply to modern conditions. However, if you investigate an old mine and light an old lantern on the wall (a lot of ifs I admit), take care not to inhale or ingest the ash residue created by the burning mantle.

CLOCKS, WATCHES, AND TIMERS: Older timepieces may have dials painted with radium to make them glow in the dark. Now days Tritium is commonly used to do the same thing. Tritium is radioactive but the emissions are so low that they cannot penetrate the lens of the timepiece; therefore they only present a hazard to jewelers.

JEWELRY: Also in the past gold was used to encapsulate radium and radon in the field of medicine. During the gold crunch many years back, this gold was improperly reprocessed became "radioactive jewelry". Today, electron beams and accelerators are used to irradiate gems to enhance their color. These are not generally put on the market until they become inert.

ROCK COLLECTIONS: Some rocks contain radioactive materials. If you encounter a "rock hound" in the course of your investigations be sure to adequately vent the rooms in which these items are on display and be careful to avoid inhaling any residue from these minerals. Your radiation meter will certainly be able to identify any questionable rocks. Be sure to make the client aware of the situation.

POTTERY: Uranium oxide was used for many years to glaze certain types of pottery. To the best of my knowledge, this process has been discontinued, although some of these pieces are still in circulation. Again, scan any older looking pottery with your radiation meter to determine if it is active.

Gamma radiation is a vital piece of the paranormal puzzle. It is starting to look like paranormal events may trigger bursts of gamma radiation. Since there are only a few things that could cause this to occur, the possibilities are fascinating. For example, after the experience I had in Williamsburg, Virginia that I recounted in Chapter 6, I have employed additional equipment together to try to lock down the real explanation of what I encountered. Consequently, I recently performed an investigation in which we captured a series of EVPs that seemed to be coming from a spot in the center of the room. The following conditions were noted:

1. Barometric pressure fell from 30.31 to 29.23
2. Positive ions began increasing from 105 cm^3 to 1080 cm^3
3. Negative ions began increasing from 96 cm^3 to 3678 cm^3
4. Air conductivity increases 200%
5. Relative Humidity drops from 78% to 61%
6. Temperature dropped from 72° to 65°
7. Magnetic field increased from 21 mG to 310 mG
8. Static electricity increased from – 225 volts to – 510 volts
9. There were no measurable Radio Frequencies active
10. A burst of Ultraviolet light was recorded
11. Low Frequency EMF is suddenly present, spontaneously appearing and traceable via triangulation to the center of the room at about a five foot height.
12. EVPs were captured. The waveforms of the EVPs matched the low frequency EMF.
13. No substantial radio frequencies were present.
14. Geomagnetic field increased from 28 mG to 104 mG.
15. Intermittent bursts of Gamma Radiation were measured, ranging from 365 mRAD/hr to 590 mRAD/hr.
16. Time shifts were noted using the time shift detector. This is a temperature controlled device that beats two oscillators together to form an audible tone. When the audible tone changes, time has shifted. (More on this device later).
17. A slight decrease in gravity was noted for the duration of the event. (Gravity was measured by using a combination of several applications on an Apple iTouch utilizing the built in accelerometer perfected by the author, more on this later).
18. Cold plasma formation in the form of an orb was present, captured and measured in excess of 600 volts and 500 ma.

Again, I am left with little to explain this phenomenon other than a possible wormhole or type of portal opening up. This preponderance of evidence is quite compelling based on the gamma ray emissions, which seem to indicate some type of annihilation is occurring at a very small scale, caused by not necessarily anti-mater/matter collisions, but phase differential matter/matter collisions. This would indicate that the two parallel universes are near compatible. This may indicate that the afterlife is all around us; it is just vibrating at a different resonant frequency in a different universe occupying the same spatial region as our own.

Chapter 10
Static Electricity

"Even if there is only one possible unified theory, it is just a set of rules and equations. What is it that breathes fire into the equations and makes a universe for them to describe? The usual approach of science of constructing a mathematical model cannot answer the questions of why there should be a universe for the model to describe. Why does the universe go to all the bother of existing?"
-Stephen W. Hawking-

Static electricity is a condition caused by the accumulation of an electric charge, either positive or negative. The word static implies Direct Current, or DC voltage, hence you will either have a positive or negative accumulated charge. The effects of static electricity are familiar to most of us, particularly those of us who live in a cold climate that requires the seasonal use of heat, as we have painfully discovered what happened when you walk across the carpet and touch the metal door knob. If we have forgotten over the summer, the initial zap is an educational reminder of how well we actually conduct electricity to ground.

Causes of static electricity

Everything around us is made up of atoms and molecules that are electrically neutral, meaning they have an equal number of positive charges or protons, in the nucleus of the atom, and negative charges or electrons, in the shell surrounding the nucleus. This harmony crumbles when the phenomenon of static electricity rears its ugly head. Static electricity requires a sustained separation of positive and negative charges. But how does that happen? One way is called a contact induced charge separation, or what scientists call a

Triboelectric effect. What actually happens in a Triboelectric effect is electrons get exchanged when two separate materials touch one another. A material made up of weakly bound electrons will shed them on contact when touching a material that has a thinly populated shell. The end result of course is that two materials without a charge end up being two materials with opposite charges, one positive and one negative. This is the most common cause of static electricity that we encounter in our normal daily life.

Another type of Static charge can be caused by a pressure induced charge separation, or a Piezoelectric effect. This has to do with certain types of crystals and ceramics creating a separation of charge in response to applied mechanical stress. For example, in certain Native American cultures, shaman or medicine men will go to a spring or river and slam a large quartz crystal hard against a rock. If the crystal survives, the year will be plentiful. If the crystal shatters, it is a bad sign, particularly for the shaman who was holding the crystal, as he will absorb about 25,000 volts of static discharge, often resulting in his doom. This type of discharge is rarely encountered in our everyday life.

There are materials that can generate a separation of charge in response to heating. A Heat induced charge separation is called the Pyroelectric effect. Interestingly all pyroelectric materials are coincidentally piezoelectric as well, which results in a double wammy. This is almost never encountered in normal everyday life either.

The type of phenomena we as paranormal investigators are most interested in though, is a charge induced charge separation or what is commonly referred to as an Electrostatic induction. This occurs when a charged object or particle (such as an ion or cloud of ions) is located adjacent to an electrically neutral object or particle. This causes a separation of charge within the conductor material as charges of the like polarity repel and charges of the opposite polarity attract. This interaction is subject to something called a "proximity effect", meaning that the force created by the interaction decreases in intensity rapidly with increasing distance, so consequently the effect of the closer attracting polarity charged particles is greater and the two particles come even closer together. This can create a collision of particles and depending on how great the velocity, annihilation can occur.

This also leads to an Electrostatic discharge, or the infamous spark that arcs across the air gap from that door knob and knocks the manure out of you in the winter time. In general, significant charge accumulations only occur in an area of low electrical conductivity. In essence, neutral atoms and molecules in the air are violently torn apart to form separate positive and negative charges which then propagate through the air in opposite directions as an electric current, effectively neutralizing the accumulation of charge. Air typically breaks down in at approximately 30,000 volts-per-centimeter depending on the relative humidity. The discharge superheats the surrounding air causing the bright flash, and produces a shockwave causing the clicking sound, and of course rattles your teeth and in my case, causes the emission of a stream of explicatives. The resulting "shock" is the product of nerve stimulation as the neutralizing current flows through you. Fortunately, one almost never encounters a dangerous currant, merely an annoying one.

To a paranormal researcher, there are essentially two kinds of static electricity; that which is a natural product of the environment, and that which is not. Naturally occurring static electricity may facilitate paranormal intensity by adding energy to the environment. Paranormal static electricity may be a byproduct of whatever causes the entrance of paranormal phenomena into our environment. Then, there is lightening.

Lightning is a rather dramatic natural static discharge. We don't yet fully understand how exactly the charge separation of lightning works but it is believed to be linked with ice particles in the storm clouds. Whatever the mechanics involved, the end result is an upscale version of dragging your feet across that carpet in the winter. The flash occurs because on a grand scale the air in the discharge path is super heated until it glows incandescent. The thunder is caused by a shockwave created as the superheated air literally explodes.

Static electricity build up in the air is indicative of the ability of air to conduct electricity. Static electricity increases as the conductance increases. Static electricity in the air is also indicative of increased ion counts present. If you are in an area of low humidity, increase of static electricity potentials are not unusual, as the low humidity prevents natural grounding of the energy. However, if the air is relatively high in humidity and static electricity increases, something very unusual is going on. Static electricity meters are used in conjunction with ion counters to determine the actual conductibility of the air. We have gone as far as to build a free air conductance device that also measures the ability of the air to conduct electricity. We will talk about this device in a later chapter, but it is used in conjunction with the static electricity meter and the ion counter. Increases in Air Conductance are a noted precursor to paranormal activity.

In the field, I use a Kapital SM-1 Static Meter, with scales of 0-3000 volts and 0-30,000 v. It is not uncommon to watch the static field increase over a period of time with a corresponding increase in paranormal activity occurring alongside the increase. Think of it this way; static electricity builds when electrons leap between two objects or surfaces that have opposing electrical charges. A common example of this is when a handshake occurs between one person that has a negative charge, and another person who doesn't. Both get a jolt because of the differences of potential.

Now when dealing with air, atoms are mostly neutral in potential, with the same number of protons and electrons. When an atom's proton and electron numbers are altered to become uneven, the electron dance begins. So what we are witnessing is two different materials next to each other, air, and rarified air. When the rarified air associated with a paranormal event touches normal air, electrons will start jumping from the rarified air to the normal air. This transference is determined by the ability of the air to either conduct electricity, or insulate from electricity. Conductive materials such as metals and carbon hold onto their electrons tightly, and are normally not affected by this proton and electron alteration. On the other hand, insulating materials, such as plastic, can be charged by friction because they easily gain or lose electrons. In the case of air, depending on the conductive properties of the air in question, it can either conduct or insulate, depending on a series of conditions present. By using a static electricity meter, we can determine whether the air is conducting or insulating. If it is conducting, it is time to pay attention to the orchestra!

So, if you encounter an elevated ion count (positive, negative or both) an increase in capacitance and an increase in static electricity, keep your eyes peeled for activity. Chances are you are about to witness something abnormal. The BIG question is what causes these conditions to change? To answer this question, we have a series of smaller questions to resolve. What has the power to affect the air in such as fashion to make it rarified when compared to normal air? And what exactly do I mean when I say rarefied air?

Simply put, rarefied air is any air rendered potentially different by an unknown source. Based on our reading, we have to acknowledge that some type of "different" air mass is colliding with normal air in a paranormal event horizon. A paranormal event horizon is the area affected by paranormal activity. It is an extremely local area of effect. But where does it come from? What is its source? The short answer is we don't know, yet. But we do have some ideas, and we will explore them later in the book. For now it is important to understand that ion count, humidity, conductance and static electricity are all related to each other directly, so when one is affected, all are affected. They are in essence, "entangled". This is another very important piece of the paranormal puzzle.

To take static electricity readings, the same basic methodology applies as with taking any other hand held device readings. Work the area in a grid pattern and note any area of high potential. Cross reference other readings at any high potential area. And keep your eyes open, recorders running and camera ready!

And don't touch the door knob...

Chapter 11
LIGHT

"What I am going to tell you about is what we teach our physics students in the third or fourth year of graduate school... It is my task to convince you not to turn away because you don't understand it. You see my physics students don't understand it... That is because I don't understand it. Nobody does."
-Richard P. Feynman-

Here is a heads up. This chapter is important and will get a bit more technical than previous chapters because I will introduce quantum mechanics into the mix. I will try to keep it as understandable as possible, but I may lose some of you. Quantum Mechanics is an area of science that holds the most promise for finding answers to paranormal questions, so if you are a serious researcher, read on. Yes, this means you!

Light is a magical phenomena. After thousands of years of studying it, we are still not really certain what it is. Light is intimately tied to photography, Videography, as well as our eye-sight, and without it, all of these tools are rendered null and void. For our purposes as paranormal researchers, there are some things about light that we need to be familiar with and understand. The first of these things is to understand that there are two types of light, generally speaking. We are most familiar with *visible light,* which is electromagnetic radiation of a wavelength that is visible to the human eye, generally ranging between 400–700 nanometers. But then we have what is called *Invisible light,* which is the electromagnetic radiation that occurs below and above the visible bandwidths, composed of infrared at the lower end of the bandwidth to ultraviolet at the upper end of the bandwidth. We as humans see only a small percentage of the total light waves radiated. Most animals, however, can see well into the invisible light spectrum. This may explain why pets react to paranormal activity more than we do.

To break light down further, there are three primary properties of light. If we are to measure light as a function of our investigation, we need to understand these measures.

1. Intensity

There are several measures of light commonly used for intensity:

First there is what is called *Radiant intensity,* which is a radiometric quantity, measured in watts per steradian (W/sr). In radiometry, radiant intensity is a measure of the intensity of electromagnetic radiation. It is defined as "power per unit solid angle". The SI unit of radiant intensity is "watts per steradian" and is noted scientifically as ***"W·sr-1"***. It is different from intensity defined by irradiance or radiant existence which measures the radiation involving a surface area.

A brief notation is now required. The International System of Units is abbreviated SI from the French Le Système International d'Unités, and it is the modern form of the metric system based on the number ten. It is the world's most widely used system of measurement, both in everyday commerce and in science. Because the SI is not static, units are created and definitions are modified through international agreement among many nations as the technology of measurement progresses, and as the precision of measurements improve. We will refer to SI units all through this book, so get use to seeing them. It is a form of standardization that we must employ at every opportunity.

Now back to business. Radiant Intensity is measured with a device called a *Spectroradiometer*, which is a laboratory grade instrument that costs between $4500.00 and $10,000. Unfortunately its high cost puts it out of reach for most paranormal research groups. Consequently, for most groups, this avenue is not an option. Let me add that it is, however a better investment than say...a thermal imaging camera

A more common method is *Luminous intensity,* which is a photometric quantity, measured in lumens per steradian (lm/sr), or candela (cd). In photometry, luminous intensity is a measure of the wavelength weighted power emitted by a light source in a particular direction per unit solid angle, based on the luminosity function, a standardized model of the sensitivity of the human eye. The SI unit of luminous intensity is the candela (cd), an SI base unit.

Keep in mind though that Photometry deals only with the measurement of visible light *as perceived by human eyes.* The human eye can only see light in the visible spectrum and has different sensitivities to light of different wavelengths within that spectrum. When adapted for bright conditions, the human eye is highly sensitive to greenish-yellow light at approximately 555 nanometers. Light with the same radiant intensity at other wavelengths has a lower luminous intensity. The curve which measures the response of the human eye to light is a defined standard, known as the *luminosity function.* This curve is based on an average of widely differing experimental data from scientists using different measurement techniques. It isn't important to us how it was defined, but if you are interested, feel free to read up on the subject.

Luminous intensity should not be confused with another photometric unit, luminous flux, which is the total perceived power emitted in *all* directions, or what we may refer to as "Ambient Light". Luminous intensity is the *perceived power per unit solid angle.* Luminous intensity is not to be confused with radiant intensity, the corresponding objective physical quantity used in the measurement science of radiometry. Luminous intensity is measured with a LUX or Foot Candle meter, or a light meter, like the ones photographers and movie maker's use. These can be purchased relatively cheap, from around $50.00 to hundreds of dollars for units with computer interface capability. These meters can be sensitive to both the visible or invisible light spectrum, but be sure to check the specification to insure the unit's effective bandwidth. This is the most common tool for the paranormal investigator to employ in light measurements. It can be used to insure you have proper lighting for your cameras, as well as detecting stray light.

Irradiance is another radiometric quantity, measured in watts per meter squared and expressed scientifically as ***W/m2***. The equivalent quantity in other branches of physics is *intensity.*

Radiance is commonly referred to as "intensity" in astronomy and astrophysics. *Irradiance, radiant emittance, and radiant exitance* are radiometry terms for the power of electromagnetic radiation at a surface, per unit area. "Irradiance" is used when the electromagnetic radiation is incident or bouncing off the surface. "Radiant exitance" or "radiant emittance" is used when the radiation is being transmitted or given off from the surface. The SI units for all of these quantities are watts per square meter and is noted thusly, ***W•m-2***.

All of these quantities characterize the total amount of electromagnetic radiation present, at all frequencies of light. It is also common to consider each frequency in the spectrum separately. At the risk of getting even more confusing, I will stop right here.

But the take away is this; if a light bulb radiates light uniformly in all directions and there is no material to absorb it, then the irradiance decreases in proportion to the distance from the light bulb squared, as the total power is constant and is spread over an area that increases with the square of the distance from the light bulb. This is a big help to keep in mind when searching for a paranormal light bulb, or an unknown source of light radiation.

2. Frequency or wavelength

Light waves also come in many frequencies within a set range associated with light in the electromagnetic spectrum. The frequency is defined as the number of waves that pass a point in space during any time interval, and the common interval we use is one second. Frequency is measured in units of cycles (waves) per second, or Hertz (Hz). The frequency of visible light is referred to as color, and ranges from 430 trillion Hz, perceived by the human eye as red, to 750 trillion Hz, and perceived as violet. Again, the full range of frequencies extends beyond the visible spectrum, from less than one billion Hz, as in radio waves, to greater than 3 billion, billion Hz, as in gamma rays. Staggering figures, but the EMF spectrum is manifested all around us by many natural sources!

As noted above, light waves are waves of energy. The amount of energy in a light wave is proportionally related to its frequency. In other words, high frequency light has high energy; low frequency light has low energy. Thus gamma rays have the most energy, and radio waves have the least. Of visible light, violet has the most energy and red the least.

Light not only vibrates at different frequencies, it also travels at different speeds, depending on the medium of travel. WAIT A MINUTE DAVE! Didn't Einstein say the speed of light was constant?

No, not exactly, he said the speed of light was constant in a *vacuum*. Light waves move through a vacuum at their maximum possible speed, 300,000 kilometers per second or 186,000 miles per second, which makes light the fastest known phenomenon in the universe. Light waves slow down when they travel inside substances, such as air, water, glass or a diamond. The way different substances affect the speed at which light travels is vital to understanding the bending of light, or refraction, which we will discuss later.

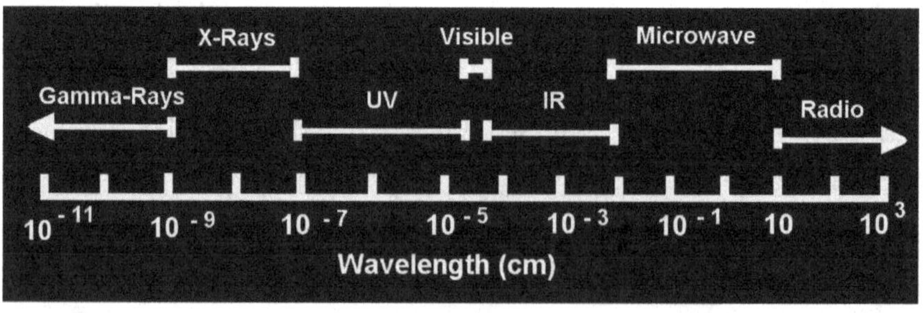

The bottom line is light waves come in a continuous variety of sizes, frequencies and energies. We refer to this realm as the electromagnetic spectrum (Figure 1-1). Figure 1-1 is not drawn to scale, as in reality visible light occupies only one-thousandth of one percent of the spectrum.

3. Polarization

Polarization is a property of waves that describes the orientation of their oscillations or frequency. For transverse waves, it defines the orientation of the frequencies in the plane perpendicular to the wave's direction of travel. Longitudinal waves such as sound waves in liquids and gases do not exhibit polarization, because for these waves the direction of oscillation is by definition along the direction of travel. Some media can carry waves with both transverse and longitudinal oscillations. Such waves do have polarization. Let me give you an example of polarization you can grasp. This requires you to perform a little experiment.

Get a pair of polarized sunglasses. If you have a flat screen LCD or plasma TV great, if not, find a friend with one. Now look at the TV normally. The picture is clear, although a bit darker due to the sunglasses filtering properties. Now turn your head sideways and look at the TV. What you are now seeing is caused by the effect of your polarized sunglasses cancelling out the polarization of the TV, and you can no longer see the picture!

Polarization is used in areas of science and technology that deal specifically with wave propagation. Examples that come to mind are optics, seismology, and telecommunications. For light, the polarization is defined by specifying the direction of the wave's electric field. According to the Maxwell equations, "the direction of the magnetic field is uniquely determined for a specific electric field distribution and polarization". For transverse sound waves in a solid, the polarization is associated with the direction of the shear stress in the plane perpendicular to the propagation direction. I could write an entire book on polarization alone, so again let me stop right here. Polarization is measured by using Ellipsometers and Polarimeters, very expensive laboratory level equipment, placing it out of reach for most paranormal research groups.

Light can exhibit properties of both waves and particles, i.e. photons. This property is referred to as wave/particle duality. The study of light, known as optics, is an important research area in modern physics. So is it a Wave or a Particle? It depends on where and when you measure it!

Speed of light

The speed of light in a vacuum is presently defined to be exactly 299,792,458 meters per second or about 186,282.397 miles per second to be precise. Additionally, as we discussed, the speed of light is affected by the nature of the medium in which it is traveling. Its speed is lower in a transparent substance than in a vacuum. Theoretically, it may be slower or faster in a parallel universe. Additionally, each potential universe may have its own laws independent of our own. We need to keep this thought in the back of our mind.

Different physicists have attempted to measure the speed of light throughout history. Galileo attempted to measure the speed of light in the seventeenth century. An early experiment to measure the speed of light was conducted by Ole Rømer, a Danish physicist, in 1676. Using a telescope, Ole observed the motions of Jupiter and one of its moons, Io. Noting discrepancies in the apparent period of Io's orbit, Rømer calculated that light takes about 22 minutes to traverse the diameter of Earth's orbit. Unfortunately, this was not a value that was known at that time. If Ole had known the diameter of the Earth's orbit, he would have calculated a speed of 227,000,000 meters per second. Close enough for government work maybe, but light years off in astronomy. He would have significantly missed the mark.

Another, more accurate, measurement of the speed of light was performed in Europe by Hippolyte Fizeau in 1849. Fizeau directed a beam of light at a mirror several miles away. A rotating cog wheel was placed in the path of the light beam as it traveled from the source, to the mirror and then returned to its origin. Fizeau found that at a certain rate of rotation, the beam would pass through one gap in the wheel on the way out and the next gap on the way back. Knowing the distance to the mirror, the number of teeth on the wheel, and the rate of rotation, Fizeau was able to calculate the speed of light as 313,000,000 meters per second. Close again, but no cigar.

Léon Foucault used an experiment which used rotating mirrors to obtain a value of 298,000,000 meters per second in 1862, which was remarkably close to the real Havana. Albert A. Michelson conducted experiments on the speed of light from 1877 until his death in 1931. He refined Foucault's methods in 1926 using improved rotating mirrors to measure the time it took light to make a round trip from Mt. Wilson to Mt. San Antonio in California. The precise measurements yielded a speed of 299,796,000 meters per second, or pretty close to the real Cuban Cigar! (Sorry, I love Cuban Cigars).

Two independent teams of physicists were able to bring light to a complete standstill by passing it through a Bose-Einstein Condensate of the element rubidium, one led by Dr. Lene Vestergaard Hau of Harvard University and the Rowland Institute for Science in Cambridge, Mass., and the other by Dr. Ronald L. Walsworth and Dr. Mikhail D. Lukin of the Harvard-Smithsonian Center for Astrophysics, also in Cambridge. Now THAT is pretty awesome!

Refraction

Refraction occurs when light crosses a medium and alters speed causing it to alter its direction. This is a quality normally encountered with lenses and filters. Lenses are frequently used to manipulate light in order to change the size of images. Magnifying glasses, spectacles, contact lenses, microscopes and refracting telescopes are all examples of this manipulation. Filters are used to diffuse or refract light for effects or to alter the perceived lighting in photographs or in Theatrical productions. I am keenly familiar with this as I use to be a lighting designer in my younger days, and designed lighting and effects for plays, operas, dance and live musical performances. Light can be a special effect. There are also reports of light phenomena encountered during paranormal events. Is refraction occurring due to matter transference between two co-existing universes vibrating slightly out of phase from one another? Maybe you will be the one who finds this answer. This is one of the reasons we measure light. In relationships with Quantum Mechanics, the study of light is a vital element.

Electromagnetic theory

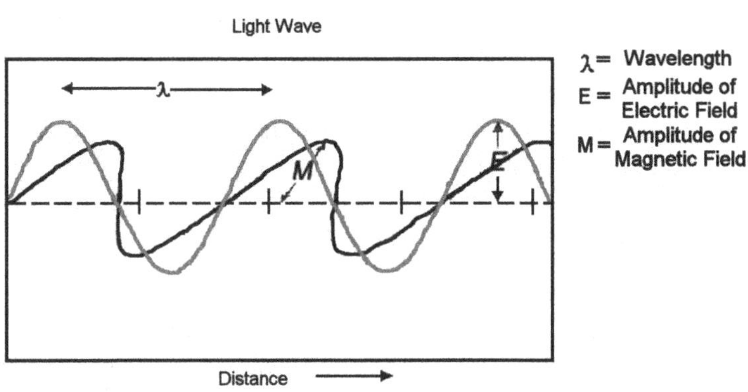

Electromagnetic Theory

A linearly-polarized light wave frozen in time and showing the two oscillating components of light; an electric field and a magnetic field perpendicular to each other and to the direction of motion (a transverse wave).

It was Michael Faraday who discovered that the angle of polarization of a beam of light passing through polarizing material could be altered by a magnetic field back in 1845. This effect is now called "Faraday rotation" and was the initial clue to science that light had a relationship with electromagnetism. Faraday actually went so far as to proposed that light was a high-frequency electromagnetic vibration in1847. He correctly postulated that it would propagate in a vacuum.

James Clerk Maxwell studied electromagnetic radiation and light. Maxwell discovered that electromagnetic waves were not only self-propagating but that they could travel through space at a constant speed as well, and he discovered that the speed in which they traveled was the velocity of light. This was a huge discovery! This is what led Maxwell to correctly identify light as electromagnetic radiation. Maxwell's theory was later confirmed by the work of Heinrich Hertz who experimented with transmitting and receiving radio waves and showing that these waves acted like visible light, identifying properties of reflection, refraction, diffraction, and interference. These experiments by both gentlemen fathered the development of radio, radar, television, electromagnetic imaging, and wireless communications. So, we measure aspects of the environment like barometric pressure, temperature, humidity, ions, etc. and we observe and record changes to quantify what we observe. Audio, magnetic fields, electromagnetic fields, radiation, radio frequency field strength, and light are also a dynamic part of the environment, and few investigators are properly monitoring these parameters in their research. We in effect have to measure the entire EMF spectrum to observe what changes that occur during a paranormal event in order to get the complete picture of what is being altered during a paranormal event. Amazingly, all of these parameters are related to each other.

The special theory of relativity

In the nineteenth century all optical and electromagnetic phenomena was explained by wave theory. But by the end of the century some troublesome anomalies remained that could not be explained by wave theory. In fact, some of these anomalies were at odds with Wave function. One of these anomalies involved the speed of light. Maxwell's equations predicted the constant speed of light and confirmed by the Michelson-Morley experiment. Unfortunately this contradicted the mechanical laws of motion that had been around since Galileo. "All speeds are relative to the speed of the observer". Albert Einstein solved this perplexing riddle in 1905 by revising Galileo's concept of space and time. Called the special theory of relativity, it was a splash of cold water in the face of physicists at the time, and turned physics on its head. Einstein of course is most well remembered as the discoverer of the special relationship between energy and mass with his famous equation

$$E=mc^2$$

E is energy, *m* is mass at rest, and *c* is of course the speed of light in a vacuum. There, I had to squeeze Einstein's equation in this book somewhere; it may as well have been here...

Enter the Dragon: Particle Theory

Another anomaly that defied the wave definition was the photoelectric effect. When light hits a metal surface it causes electrons to be ejected from the surface, which in turn causes an electric current to flow across an applied voltage. Research indicated that the energy of these electrons was related to the *frequency*, and not the *intensity*, of the light. Additionally, at specific lower frequencies, no current would flow no matter what the level of intensity. This spelled real trouble for the now embattled wave theory, and for years physicists remained stumped by this. Einstein resolved this with the "particle theory of light" which offered an explanation for the phenomenon. Because of the preponderance of evidence in favor of the wave theory, however, Einstein's ideas were met initially by great skepticism among established physicists. In time Einstein's theory of the photoelectric effect would prevail, and it formed the foundation for wave/particle duality and much of quantum mechanics. Which leads us to the science that holds the most promise of providing us with answers,

"Quantum Theory"

A third anomaly reared its ugly head in the late 19th century. This one involved thermal radiators, or so-called black bodies and the discrepancies between the wave theory and the EMF measurements. This would come to be known as the "ultraviolet catastrophe", and it would give physicists a fit for several years. Max Planck developed a new theory in 1900 that addressed the whole black-body radiation and the observed spectrum. The crux of Planck's theory assumed that black bodies emit light as well as other electromagnetic radiation as discrete bundles of energy. These bundles are called quanta, and the proposed particle of light is the photon. A photon has energy, *E*, proportional to its frequency, *f*, by

$$E = hf = hc/\lambda$$

here h is Planck's constant, λ is the wavelength and c is the speed of light. Also the momentum p of a photon is directly proportional to its frequency and inversely proportional to its wavelength:

$$p = E/c = hf/c = h/\lambda$$

While this theory did not explain the wave/particle duality of light, Planck would eventually expound theories that addressed these issues. As a founding father of Quantum Theory, Planck received the Nobel Prize in Physics in 1918. We are grateful for his spasms of lucidity.

Wave–particle duality

Today we are firmly entrenched in the notion of wave–particle duality, as described by Einstein in the early 1900s, and Confirmed by Planck. The notion that the energy of a photon is proportional to its frequency was also a brain fart of Einstein's and his theory states that all matter has both a particle nature and a wave nature, and that various experiments can be performed to demonstrate these natures. What we have discovered is that the particle nature of matter is easier to manifest if an object has a large mass. But it was not until 1924 that the scientific community realized that electrons also exhibited wave/particle duality. This was due in large part to the work of Louis de Broglie. In 1927 the wave nature of electrons was further demonstrated by the work of Davisson and Germer. In 1921 of course Einstein would receive the Nobel Prize for his work with the wave/particle duality on photons and de Broglie won it in 1929 extending the theory to encompass other particles. I know that some of you have developed a deep migraine from reading all of this but I am about to make the point so stick in there.

Quantum Electrodynamics

These theories continued to refine and evolve through the 1920s and 1930's, and hit their crescendo during the 1940s with the development of the theory of quantum electrodynamics, or QED. This quantum field theory is possibly the most comprehensive and experimentally successful theory ever formulated to explain natural phenomena. QED was the brainchild of physicists Richard Feynman, Freeman Dyson, Julian Schwinger, and Shin-Ichiro Tomonaga. And, guess what? In 1965 Feynman, Schwinger, and Tomonaga shared the Nobel Prize in Physics for their work. In fact, Quantum

Mechanics has had its share of Nobel Prize winners over the years, and will continue to cultivate both headaches and Laureates for many years to come.

Light Radiation Pressure

And now for the point I have been faithfully approaching and driving some of you crazy with the foundation I have tried to lay. We now know that Light pushes on objects in its way, just as the wind pushes leaves and other debris before it. This pressure is explained in particle theory as photons hitting and transferring their momentum to the mass impacted. Light pressure is capable of making asteroids spin faster, pushing on their irregular shapes like the sails of an ancient ship. The concept of making solar sails to accelerate vessels in space is currently being explored by NASA and other space agencies. Is it possible that light may also affect physical conditions during a paranormal event? Absolutely! In fact, it may be that light has a lot to do with specific aspects of reported paranormal activity, such as shadow people, apparitions and even orbs. For further entertainment, I recommend reading John Walker, founder of Autodesk, Inc. and co-author of AutoCAD, who wrote an interesting piece on paranormal theory: http://www.fourmilab.ch/documents/gtpp/

Everything in the universe is dynamic. Everything dynamic has a frequency. From the Schuman Resonance to Cosmic Radiation, everything we deal with has frequency. It is therefore important to correlate any changes that occur during a paranormal event, from the lowest frequencies of subsonics and brainwaves to the highest that we know of, Gamma Rays. Light is a part of that study.

I use an AEC CA811 Ambient Light Meter with Foot Candle/Lumens scales. I have captured spontaneous bursts of light during a paranormal event. Since I could find no source or explanation for the phenomena, it is quite possible that it may originate in a parallel universe and becomes visible momentarily when a vortex or wormhole occurs. And throughout this book, we will build that case.

Chapter 12
RF Measurement/Analysis

"Every known fact in natural science was divined by the presentiment of somebody, before it was actually verified."
-Ralph Waldo Emerson-

It is a very distinct possibility that paranormal activity may be influenced by radio frequency energy, either from known or unknown sources. It is very probable that some EVPs (Electronic Voice Phenomena) may be the direct result of interference between two very real frequencies, and the resulting differential frequency being a "voice" in the audio frequency spectrum, being recorded as audio by the recording equipment. It is also a very real possibility that demodulated audio may be present if there is a radio transmitter in close proximity to the site being investigated. For this reason, measuring radio frequencies cannot be overlooked by a thorough researcher.

First, before we attempt to measure RF, we should understand what it is and what is out there. Radio frequency (RF) is a frequency or rate of oscillation within the range of about 3 KHz to 300 GHz in the Electromagnetic Spectrum. But wait! Isn't 3 KHz (3000 Hz) firmly planted in the audio spectrum? Yes, Virginia, it certainly is. However, there is little use of radio transmissions in the audio spectrum for lots of practical reasons, such as the length of the antenna required, and most of all, FCC regulations. Realistically, radio frequency use in the U.S. begins at about 9 KHz for radio navigation. Frequencies below that are not allotted by the FCC. But this raises a point everyone needs to be aware of. There is Radio Frequency activity in the audio spectrum, and sometimes this can be an issue! An excellent chart of RF assignment in the U.S is available from http://www.ntia.doc.gov/osmhome/

allochrt.pdf and I would recommend every team in the U.S. to print this out for reference.

Electrical currents that oscillate at RF (radio frequencies) have special properties not shared by direct current or static electricity in the air. One such property is the ease with which it can *ionize molecules and atoms* to create a conductive path through air. Another special property is an *electromagnetic* force that allows RF current to travel along the surface of conductors, commonly called the skin effect. Another property is the ability to flow through paths that contain insulating material, such as the dielectric insulator of a capacitor. The intensity of these effects is dependant largely on the frequency of the signals.

Of vital importance to realize here is RF can ionize the air, thus increasing ion counts. It is also important to remember that it is a form of EMF. This is why it is so very important to identify the frequency of ALL EMF present at a paranormal event. Unidentified radio waves can cause false readings on many of the instruments we use for measuring the environment. In other words, that symmetrical EMF wave you are monitoring at 9.1 KHz may not be paranormal at all, but may instead be a navigation beacon. Spectrum analysis will tell the story. More on this later.

To repeat this: Radio waves are *electromagnetic* waves occurring in the radio frequency portion of the *electromagnetic* spectrum. A common use that most of us are aware of is to transport information through the atmosphere or outer space without wires via propagation. Radio waves are distinguished from other kinds of electromagnetic waves by their frequency and wavelength. In the grand scheme of the EMF spectrum, Radio waves exhibit a relatively long wavelength as compared to light, cosmic and gamma radiation, as well as X-Rays.

Propagation is a term that describes the travel of electromagnetic waves. As such, there are three main modes of propagation. The first and most common is a straight line travel as demonstrated by radio waves traveling through deep space and ignoring gravity deviations under proposed in the theory of relativity. A second way, and a method used by amateur radio operators and others, is called "skip". Skip involves RF waves bouncing between the surface of the earth and the ionosphere. The frequency range of 3 MHz to about 30 MHz is the most reliable band for this kind of propagation. The third way is to hug the surface of the earth, following the curve of the planet. Radio waves of very low frequency most often travel this way, which is why low frequency RF is used for navigational purposes. Locating and identifying the source of low frequency radio waves is a vital task to perform at the beginning of any paranormal event, and once identified, they should be monitored, as these low frequencies correspond to certain frequencies also present during a paranormal event.

Measuring RF

There are several instruments you can employ to measuring RF energy. Beginning with the lowest priced, is the RF scanner. While a scanner will not give you signal strength, it will tell you if signals are present, and what frequencies are active in the area. We use a Radio Shack PRO-82 portable scanner that monitors Public Service bands, weather, aviation and amateur radio as these are the most common interfering frequencies besides broadcast radio (AM and FM). This type of device ranges from $99.00 to $600.00. A scanner can tell you what frequencies are active, and you can generally figure out the source if you listen to it long enough.

RF Signal Tracers are another device for not only determining relative field strength, but can also be used to locate the source of the transmissions. Radio frequency tracers are useful in locating stuck transmitters or bugging devices in a room or automobile. RF-Tracers are not typical receivers like radio-scanners. Transmitters must be very closed to the Tracers, like within 1-3 meters for low power devices, or they can be further away if the transmitter is very high powered. By using a scanner in conjunction with a tracer, you can identify some RF sources found on a site such as wireless internet or other WiFi transmitters, as well as cordless telephones. We use an ACECO FC6002 MK 2 unit for this application. Signal tracers can be purchased from about $100 on up.

RF field density meters detect the electric field of radio and microwaves (RF) as a rule from .5 MHz to 3 GHz, and express the field strength as power density (.001 to 2000 microwatts/cm2). These meters are extremely sensitive and can accurately measure RF background even in remote rural areas far from any known transmitters. The meter reads true power density directly on the display.

RF field density meters are generally directional and they detect only the component of the electric field which has the same polarization as the long axis of the meter. That is, if only a vertically-polarized RF wave is present, but you turn the meter in the horizontal direction, it will essentially read zero. If you subsequently rotate the meter to vertical, it will then read the full power density of the RF wave. Most RF radiation has only vertical electric field, so the full strength can be read by holding the meter vertically. Keep this in mind when making field measurements in a home. We use the Trifield RF Field Strength Meter that sells for about $320.00 at the time of this writing. There are meters that cost less, and meters that cost much more. Look for high sensitivity as a factor when purchasing. The field strength meter will tell you how strong the RF field is in the home, but it will not identify the frequency present.

A spectrum analyzer is a device used to examine the composition of electrical, acoustic, or optical waveforms, based on its frequency response. There are analog and digital spectrum analyzers. An analog spectrum analyzer uses either a variable band-pass filter whose mid-frequency is automatically tuned through the range of being measured or it can take the form of a super-heterodyne receiver sweeping its local oscillator through a range of frequencies. A digital spectrum analyzer calculates the discrete Fourier transform (DFT), a mathematical process that transforms a waveform into the components of its frequency spectrum.

Some spectrum analyzers (such as Tektronix's family of "real-time spectrum analyzers") use a hybrid technique where the incoming signal is first down-converted to a lower frequency using super-heterodyne techniques and then analyzed using fast Fourier transformation (FFT) techniques. But no matter what type of spectrum analyzer you can acquire, it is a very useful tool. The important thing to keep in mind is a spectrum analyzer WILL tell you what frequencies are present and how strong they are. For use with very weak signals, a pre-amplifier can be used, although harmonic and inter-modulation distortion may lead to the creation of new frequency components that were not present in the original signal. If you need to use a preamp, get a low noise, low distortion, high gain RF wide band preamplifier.

Unfortunately the down side is RF spectrum analyzers are incredibly expensive, and no device exists that will measure the entire RF band due to bandwidth and electronics limitations. However, a wise choice would be something that goes up at least to 2.4 GHz, in order to identify any common wireless operations that may be a contributing factor to the investigation site. We use a Thurlby Thandar Instruments Limited PSA2701T that utilizes a Palm Pilot as the processing platform, and it sells for around $2300.00. And that is CHEAP. Most RF Spectrum Analyzers range from $8,000 – $25,000, placing them out of reach for most groups. However, you can sometimes get a good deal on E-Bay if you know what you are looking for. You might also recruit a radio technician to work with your group. Most radio techs, Ham operators and other radio folk have a spectrum analyzer and know how to use one. Knowing what signals you have at a location may reveal insights as to what is actually going on in the environment.

Spectrum analyzers, like oscilloscopes are a basic tool used for observing RF signals. The key difference is oscilloscopes display signals in the time domain, while spectrum analyzers display signals in the frequency domain. Hence the spectrum analyzer displays the field strength of signals on the vertical scale, and the frequency of the signals on the horizontal scale.

To set the frequency of a spectrum analyzer, you must first select the center frequency. This will determine the frequency centering point on the scale of the analyzer, as displayed. Some analyzers have a scan mode in which they will automatically search for different frequencies. I begin by checking all of the scales on the spectrum analyzer just to see what is out there. We will also need to set the span or the size of the region on either side of the center frequency that is to be measured. Think of the span as the bandwidth of your search, or the spread of frequencies that you can monitor.

There are other adjustments that will need to be performed. We will have to properly adjust the gain or attenuation of sections to achieve a proper signal level. If the internal amplifiers are overloaded, then distortion will cause the generating signals within the unit that will read like an external frequency, but will in fact be an internally generated form of interference. This will produce false readings and may send you on a wild goose chase. To avoid this unfavorable condition it is necessary to ensure that the input stages are not overdriven and attenuation is applied to reduce the signal level. Be careful not to use too much attenuation as this will require additional gain to be applied (IF gain) in the gain chain which in turn will increase the background noise level which could mask or hide lower level signals. Much like the fable of Goldilocks, you have to get it "Just right." Fortunately, most modern day digital analyzers do this automatically when used in "auto mode".

The spectrum analyzer scans the frequency span from the low to the high end of the selected spectrum or bandwidth. Due to the transitory nature of paranormal phenomena, it is essential to maintain a high scan rate to guarantee that measurements are made as quickly as possible. In older, manually selectable analyzers the filter scan rate and bandwidths are linked to make sure the optimum combination is selected. Again, most modern Spectrum Analyzers perform this function in "auto mode".

Last but not least, we need to adjust the filter bandwidths within the instrument. Adjusting the IF filter determines the frequency resolution. Selecting a narrow bandwidth enables us to view adjacent frequencies that lie in close proximity to each other. This can be a double edged sword, however, due to the relationship between scan rate and bandwidth. Narrow band filters do not respond to changes as quickly as wider band filters do, requiring a slower scan rate to be selected when employing them. Again, for the novice, "auto mode" is a beautiful thing.

Other filter adjustments are the video filters, which allow an "averaging" effect to be applied to the signal. This will reduce the variations caused by noise and reveal signals that may not otherwise be measured. As with all whistles and bells, using video filtering limits the speed at which the spectrum analyzer can scan. The trick is to arrive at a happy medium that allows you to get the best data possible. Spectrum analyzers are not for the beginner. Again, let me repeat my earlier advice; find a good Ham or radio tech and draft him or her into your group. They make a great contribution to your team's ability to gather data, and most of the time, have their own equipment to add to the mix.

Below is a simplistic chart of radio frequency allocations:

Frequencies

Name	Symbol	Frequency	Wavelength	Applications
Extremely low frequency	ELF	a 3–30 Hz	k 10,000–100,000 kilometers	Directly audible when converted to sound, communication with submarines
Super low frequency	SLF	b 30–300 Hz	j 1,000–10,000 kilometers	Directly audible when converted to sound, AC power grids (50–60 Hz)
Ultra low frequency	ULF	c 300–3000 Hz	i 100–1,000 kilometers	Directly audible when converted to sound, communication with mines
Very low frequency	VLF	d 3–30 kHz	h 10–100 kilometers	Directly audible when converted to sound (below ca. 20 kHz; or *ultrasound* otherwise)
Low frequency	LF	e 30–300 kHz	g 1–10 kilometers	AM broadcasting, navigational beacons, low FER
Medium frequency	MF	f 300–3000 kHz	f 100–1 kilometers	Navigational beacons, AM broadcasting, maritime and aviation communication
High frequency	HF	g 3–30 MHz	e 10–100 meters	Shortwave, amateur radio, citizens' band radio
Very high frequency	VHF	h 30–300 MHz	d 1–10 meters	FM broadcasting, amateur radio, broadcast television, aviation, GPR
Ultra high frequency	UHF	i 300–3000 MHz	c 10–100 centimeters	Broadcast television, amateur radio, mobile telephones, cordless telephones, wireless networking, remote keyless entry for automobiles, microwave ovens, GPR
Super high frequency	SHF	j 3–30 GHz	b 1–10 centimeters	Wireless networking, satellite links, microwave links, satellite television, door openers
Extremely high frequency	EHF	k 30–300 GHz	a 1–10 milimeters	Microwave data links, radio astronomy, remote sensing, advanced weapons systems, advanced security scanning

Again, there is a complete radio frequency allocation chart maintained by the U.S Government and available for free here: http://www.ntia.doc.gov/osmhome/allochrt.pdf

Chapter 13
Other Environmental Testing And Debunking

"Science knows no country, because knowledge belongs to humanity, and is the torch which illuminates the world. Science is the highest personification of the nation because that nation will remain the first which carries the furthest the works of thought and intelligence."
-Louis Pasteur-

There are other parameters that have nothing to do with the paranormal that should be investigated by a thorough researcher. Not only should we seek paranormal phenomena and try to explain it, but we should also seek normal conditions that may contribute to the environment, conditions that may explain what the client is experiencing or believes to be experiencing. For example, exposure to carbon monoxide is most commonly accompanied by the following symptoms: Headache, dizziness, nausea, flu-like symptoms, fatigue, shortness of breath on exertion, impaired judgment, chest pain, confusion, depression, hallucinations, agitation, vomiting, abdominal pain, drowsiness, visual changes, fainting, seizure memory and walking problems

Therefore it stands to reason that since some of these symptoms are reported by victims of reported paranormal phenomena, we should test for carbon monoxide levels. This can be accomplished by using a Carbon Monoxide detector such as the ones sold for home monitoring and available with the smoke detectors at any hardware store. They range in price from around $29.99. We also use an Extech CO-10 Carbon Monoxide Meter, which retails for about $230.00. Either one will do the job, with the Extech being more sensitive, of lab quality, with a more accurate readout and quicker response time. I can't tell you how many times we have discovered dangerous levels of CO in a home or business that both was life threatening, and was a direct cause of the "haunted" experiences.

Carbon Dioxide can be another contaminant present in sufficient qualities to cause issues. A Carbon Dioxide detector can be pricey, ranging from $300.00 on up. It may be something you recommend to the client to have an air quality test performed by their Heating/AC serviceman. Carbon Dioxide poisoning symptoms include delirium, headaches, and shortness of breath and reduced alertness. If dampness is a factor, in say the basement, there may be a toxic mold problem in the home. Symptoms include memory loss, anxiety, personality disorders, nosebleeds, and shortness of breath, abdominal pain, hair loss, skin rashes, fatigue, and numbness in extremities, headaches, mood swings, and pain in the extremities, cough, sore throat, rectal bleeding, tremors, and fibromyalgia.

Other symptoms of toxic mold include: destruction of brain tissue, open skin sores, fungal infections, lung diseases such as Aspergilliosis, and chronic sinus problems. It certainly sounds like a demonic possession, doesn't it? Again, if you suspect a mold problem, recommend to the client that they test their home for mold. In fact, always recommend that a client follow up on any dangerous condition you encounter.

Other conditions to check for or recommend to the client to check are toxic fumes from chemicals or paints and other flammable material, Radon levels, and elevated levels of electromagnetic radiation. Some people suffer from sensitivity to EMF and can have adverse reactions. Commonly reported symptoms of EMF poisoning include sleep disorders, headaches, vision and perception problems, sensitive skin, dizziness, chest pain and nausea. As the level of radiation increases, the severity of the symptoms increases.

High EMF near the electrical panel may indicate an unbalanced system and could pose a fire hazard. Any of these adverse conditions should be reported to the client upon discovery, with a recommendation that a qualified service person check it out and correct any problem.

Additional things to test for are hidden vibrations. Vibration may cause things to move by themselves, may alter a person's perception based on the frequency of the vibration and can even cause hallucinations. A study conducted by Cornell University discovered that vibration has a significant effect on the human body. Some of their key findings were: When an object is vibrated at its resonance frequency, the maximum amplitude of its vibration will be greater than the original amplitude (I.e. the vibration is amplified). Wind blowing on a building can cause vibrations!

Vibrations in the frequency range of 0.5 Hz to 80 Hz have significant effects on the human body. Individual body components, cavities and organs have their own resonant frequencies and can vibrate separately. This can cause amplification or attenuation of input vibrations by certain parts of the body due to their own unique resonant frequencies. The most effective resonant frequencies for vertical vibration happen to fall between 4 and 8 Hz. Vibrations between 2.5 and 5 Hz generate a strong resonance in the vertebra of the neck and lumbar region with a potential amplification of up to 240%. Vibrations between 4 and 6 Hz set up resonances in the trunk with amplification of up to 200%. Vibrations between 20 and 30 Hz set up the strongest resonance between the head and shoulders with amplification of up to 350%. Whole body vibration may create chronic stresses and sometimes even permanent damage to the affected organs or body parts. In fact, it is possible for vibrations affecting the spinal cord to cause graphic hallucinations.

Suspected health effects of whole body vibration include: Blurred vision, Decrease in manual coordination, Drowsiness (even with proper rest), low back pain/injury, insomnia and headaches or even upset stomach.

To take this a step further, the vibration effect on the eyes can cause us to see things that simply are not there. For example, if a vibration occurred that approached the resonant frequency of the person's eye, he could see visions of things that were not there, based on the effect the vibration has on the liquid in the human eye. Also, it is possible that vibrations can stimulate the optic nerve to produce visions that are not there.

A simple test for vibration is the liberal use of a mechanic's stethoscope. This is an extraordinary inexpensive way to locate, and identify the source of low frequency building vibrations. Vibrations present could be a cause of perceived paranormal phenomena. Another useful tool is a geophone, a device used to monitor seismic activity, and of course an industrial vibration meter.

According to experts, positive ions rob us of our good senses and dispositions as well as cause headaches and other health problems. Negative ions enhance our mood, stimulate senses, improve appetite, and provide relief from allergies. Consequently, an unusually elevated level of positive ions in the environment should be investigated as a possible cause for alleged paranormal perception. The environment must under no circumstances be overlooked in a paranormal investigation. Period!

By exploring these conditions we not only are able to debunk some paranormal activity, we also do a service to the client.

Chapter 14
The Computer

"I think there's a world market for about five computers."
-Thomas Watson- (Founder of IBM)

Some of the technology we have today did not exist at a consumer level when I began my journey researching paranormal activity and the computer is at the top of the list. The computer has become a workhorse in the analysis of evidence for the paranormal investigator. It has allowed the detailed dissection of audio files, video files, photographic files, data files, you name it. The market is flooded with software options that can do anything you want to do with information. While the computer is an indispensable tool to the scientific researcher no matter the discipline, it has brought a few negative aspects as well. Certain types of data can easily be faked under the influence of a skilled operator and the right computer and software. Digital photos are no longer accepted as standalone evidence. Today, in order for any evidence to have weight, there needs to be a lot of it, and it needs to be correlated. Thankfully, the computer can also handle this task. But what makes a lot of data harder to fake than a little data? Few people in the field have any idea how to fake lots of different data to paint an accurate picture of the relationships of different aspects measured. Additionally, if they somehow did know those relationships, the software simply doesn't exist to manipulate all the data. And if it did, none of us could afford it. For example, a full suite of Photoshop goes for $1000.00 now, but you can get a consumer level copy of the program for around $140.00. An alternative is Corel's paint Shop pro which sells for around $100.00. For audio, Sony Sound Forge is popular software, a tool used by audio professionals. It ranges from $300.00 for the pro Suite to $55.00 for a consumer grade application. But there is plenty of freeware out there to choose from that will do the job. For a list of applications, go to download.com and search for freeware audio programs, video editor programs, test equipment software and whatever else you can think of.

Some of the freeware for audio applications that I have tested and used are:

Audacity, WavePad, Expstudio Audio Editor, Audioblast, Wavosaur, Kangas Sound Editor, SoundPad, Acoustica SE, QuickAudio and SoundEngine. For photographic analysis there is DriveHQ Batch Photo Editor, PhotoScape, Pos Free Photo Editor, PC Image Editor, Photo Editor, Zoner Media Explorer Classic Image Analyzer, Aoao Photo Editor and Free Image Editor. Free video analysis includes ZS4 Video Editor, Video Edit Master and Avidemux.

While the PC has been a revolutionary tool for paranormal research analysis, the laptop has been a quantum leap forward in field research and data gathering. Now it is possible to run multiple channels of data logging in the field, design elaborate audio recording, video recording, and environmental measuring device management on a fairly grand scale. Laptops can manage data acquisition devices. A data logger is a device that allows multiple sensors to be monitored in real time, on a moving graph, that shows everything happening in real time and in relation to each other. The laptop also revolutionized this portable application of data gathering and made real time data display possible. Real time continuous data will tell you way more information than using a few hand held devices. It will not only reveal oddness as it occurs, it shows what relationship that oddness has to many different aspects of the environment, depending on what sensors you employ.

Additionally, Apple laptops have some handy devices built in that can be used with commercially available applications, such as SeisMac, which is a free Mac OS X application that runs on a MacBook or MacBook Pro and turns the built-in accelerometers into a three-component seismograph. These Mac laptops are installed with a sudden-motion sensor designed to lock up the hard drive if the laptop falls to the ground. There are other commercially available software applications to create a gravimeter, accelerometer, and other tools useful in paranormal research.

The laptop allows for onsite analysis, real time data viewing, record direct to digital, DVR management, radiation monitoring, and more. Just about everything you can think of to measure, a laptop can measure with the right combination of sensors and software. Another advantage is that if you have an air card you can get up to the minute space weather and weather reports on site as your investigation progresses. You can also video-tape your investigation and stream it up on the net for others to watch, as it is happening.

Test equipment software is also available. Some of the freeware associated with test equipment emulation I have tested and used includes oscilloscope software such as Wavetools and ScopePar, as well as spectrum analyzer applications like Voice Balancing System, AudioAnalyser and RightMark Audio Analyzer. All are invaluable tools to have available during an investigation. New software is introduced daily that has potential for our use, and every serious researcher should do a search once a week to keep up on new developments in software.

If you have a laptop, think about what it can do for you and your group in the field. If you don't have a laptop, get one. My organization has entire data collection platforms based around a laptop. In fact we operate 6 laptops in the field at the date of this writing, and are preparing to deploy several more. With the advent of E-Bay, used laptops can be acquired for very reasonable prices. In most applications, older laptops work well for performing specific tasks. A good rule of thumb is to have a processor speed of at least 1 GHz, and a RAM of at least 512 Mb. Hard Drives should be 40 Gb or more. I have picked up used Dell Latitude machines from $100.00 to $300.00 that needed various refurbishment or component upgrades such as bigger hard drives, or more RAM. Considering new laptops can run from $600.00 to $4000.00 E-Bay is a great, affordable alternative. Something else to consider is to add a computer geek to your team line up, or become one yourself. Who knows you may even develop and sell a specific application to assist other ghost hunting researchers, and supplement your operating expenses!

We will further discuss using laptops in more detail in the exotic equipment chapter later on.

Chapter 15
Cell Phones, iPods and PDAs

"Genius is one percent inspiration and ninety-nine percent perspiration."
-Thomas Alva Edison-

While the development of the personal computer and laptop may be the crowning achievement in personal technology, at least by the end of the twentieth century, second place most certainly belongs firmly with the hand held family of devices known as cell phones, iPods and PDAs. Until the deployment of the Quantum computer, these devices will become the new king of personal technology in the twenty-first century. Let's start off with the cell phone.

A cell phone is a relatively short range device used for voice and/or data communication over a grid of base stations called cell sites. Besides being a phone, many current devices support a variety of additional services and applications, such as text messaging, email, internet access, gaming, Bluetooth applications, infrared photography and control, camera functions, video recorder, MP3 player, radio and GPS to name a few of the most common. There are several categories of mobile phones to choose from, starting with basic phones to specialty devices such as music phones, camera phones, smart phones, and more. Several phone series have been introduced to target a specific market sector, such as the BlackBerry for the enterprise/corporate customer email needs and net surfing capabilities or the Sony Ericsson Walkman series of music phones for the audiophile and Cybershot series of camera phones for the photo enthusiast; the Nokia N-Series of multimedia phones offer a lot of bang for the buck, and of course application rich Apple iPhone, which comes with everything but the kitchen sink, and even THAT is an available application!

Well, not really, but you get my point.

Paranormal Applications

Because the Cell phone is a radio type of device, it broadcasts a signal at a specific frequency. Currently these frequencies are 850 MHz, 1900 MHz, with 700 MHz being the targeted future operating band. Because this is a transceiver, and because it uses cell stations to communicate, the cell phone generates high levels of EMF. This is a vital piece of information to remember.

A few years ago a famous television show offered software downloads if you subscribed to their site that claimed to "find Ghosts". The technology was supposedly based on the ability of the phone to detect EMF.

Hailed as the single greatest mobile application of all time, the sponsoring channel offered downloads of "the ghost detection program for compatible cell phones" for free, as long as you signed up for a subscription to its featured TV show website. Sounds too wonderful to be true doesn't it? Sign me up so I can find ghosts with my cell phone!

Well, the truth of the matter is somewhat clouded by the sponsors, but it turns out the phone really will detect EMF, but only in the high frequency RF band, i.e. 800 MHz. In other words, the phone detected background high frequency EMF variations, primarily from normal sources, i.e. its cell sites! Most paranormally related frequencies are far lower, ranging below 500 Hz. Incredibly, it was also advertized that any EMF encountered would be instantly uploaded to the shows nationwide database to "map EMF Ghost Activity". This was a short lived fad when people discovered they were reading the transmissions of their cell phone and not a ghost. It is of course no longer being offered, as it was a gimmick to get subscribers to pay for site membership.

More recently, another popular TV show has offered a free IPhone application that claims to be a "ghost detector". Unfortunately, it isn't what it is claimed to be. Here is the description from a popular iPhone app website, with emphasis added:

"The (name of show) iPhone application turns your device into a *simulated* EMF meter… switch to manual mode and fool your friends by sliding your finger along the green line to control the action of the needle."

Note the carefully used word "simulated". The program is nothing more than a useless toy. Interestingly, Apple currently offers no applications that either detects EMF or Ghosts. In fact, in order to measure EMF, you would need a coil to detect it. This coil would be far larger than the cell phone to detect low frequencies. It could use the antenna to detect EMF in the RF spectrum, but that is EMF from a non paranormal source. Additionally, anything offered by a third party without Apple's endorsement would be subject to scrutiny. In fact, nearly all the fancy scientific applications are simulations, or emulators, such as X-Ray – Convert your IPhone into a personal X-Ray Machine". Can you imagine how much your iPhone would weigh with the lead shielding required if that were real? Keeping all this in mind, is there anything a cell phone or iPhone can do to enhance an investigation? Yes indeed!

It is a good idea to have a phone on you while investigating for the obvious reasons: Texting your team members for communications purposes as well as push to talk or phone conversations, or IM or E-mail. Just remember when you use the phone to transmit you are adding EMF to the environment and your meters will register EMF increases. Applications such as GPS are handy, as well as Google Earth and other mapping software. The ability to surf the net to glean insight to the location is also a handy application as well as being able to reference things such as background geomagnetic fields from geomagnetic surveys of the area. There are weather applications, space weather applications and other applications relevant to the investigation available. My favorite application is Space weather:

http://www.apple.com/webapps/weather/
spaceweathersolarandgeophysicalactivity.html

Perhaps the most useful built in tool and application of the cell phone is its ability to take photographs and movies. Originally, camera phones employed very low resolution, under a megapixel. Today's offerings have considerably higher offerings. My Blackberry Curve has a 2.0 Megapixel camera with video capture built in, which is the same as the iPhone. While it isn't as good as current digital camera technology, it is a useful tool none the less. Additionally, most camera phones see into the IR and UV light spectrums. There are a lot of claims on the web concerning the ability of phone cameras to capture "ghosts" better than normal digital cameras. The fact that the internet is loaded with examples of ghost photographs made with camera phones is offered up as evidence of this.

Unfortunately, most of these photographs can be easily duplicated using simple photo editing techniques. To demonstrate how easily a faked photo or video can be created, I made a ghost image using a felt marker on a piece of clear plastic used to seal ID cards to protect them. This was cut into a small strip so I could manipulate it with my fingers in front of the lens on the front of the camera away from the prying eyes of those standing next to me. In video capture mode, I held up the camera before my friends and told them how easy it was to capture a ghost on film. While explaining this, I moved the clear strip with the shadow figure drawn on it across the lens before their eyes and they went crazy! I let them rant and rave for a few minutes until I finally revealed to them what I had done. The point I was trying to make is not to trust a photograph as evidence of anything by itself or a movie either for that matter, as they can be easily manipulated, in some cases, before witness's eyes! Of course if I ever do capture a ghost on film, no one will ever believe me after that stunt!

While smart phones offer promising technology for future application, they aren't really that useful yet as test instruments using existing applications, unless you have an iPhone, or an iTouch. They are however, extremely useful communication tools and can be used as an audio, video or photographic recorder that fits in your pocket. I have specifically mentioned the iPhone and iTouch because some recently developed applications have created a quantum leap in technology that is a fantastic set of tools for the paranormal investigator.

iPods

Generally speaking, the iPod is not thought of to be much in the way of a test instrument. However, with the advent of some new applications, this has dramatically changed, and it spurred me to rush out and by an iTouch. The first of these applications is a suite of audio tools called "AudioTools". AudioTools Includes sound pressure level measurement protocols, acoustic analysis tools, line input calibration applications, speaker testing applications and various utilities including microphone calibration, and a signal generator! AudioTools when coupled with a microphone pod such as the Blue Mikey becomes a complete audio/acoustical analysis suite.

Also, the iTouch as well as some of the newer generation iPods have the built in accelerometer. This allows you to use applications like Acceleron, AccelGraph, ContextLogger, Gravitometer, iSeismograph and signal scope.

Acceleron is software that displays the record of the accelerometer built in to the iPhone (or, iPod touch). The data display method that Acceleron employs is raw data, accelerometer value on X, Y, Z axis, and timestamp. Each accelerometer value has a High-pass & Low-pass filter. The user can take out recorded data from a device by an E-mail. An accelerometer can be used as a three axis gravimeter that measures absolute gravity.

AccelGraph displays the acceleration applied to the iPhone or iPod Touch by utilizing it's built in motion sensor graphically. The features include

High-Pass filtering, Separate X,Y and Z-Axis graphs, 3 different sampling frequencies, Pause/Resume acceleration measuring, Turn On/Off acceleration measurement on each axis individually, Record acceleration on all axes, Four different recording frequencies, Acceleration measurement automatically saved, Email acceleration measurement, G-Force-Meters menu, G-Force meters for all axes, and four different backgrounds to chose from

ContextLogger is an application that records and interprets the built in accelerometer data. Each event can be logged to reference it to an actual paranormal event. You can create up to six different labels for each recording, and the application allows you to live view data on a graph, and upload the data to any computer on the same network.

Gravitometer measures G-Force and centrifugal force on 3 axes, and all 3 axes can be combined. This application can measure absolute gravity.

iSeismograph samples acceleration in X,Y, and Z direction in g-force and measures seismic activity along three axes. SignalScope turns the iTouch into a powerful real time spectrum analyzer and oscilloscope. Frequency response is in the audio spectrum only, but this is a great tool in the palm of your hand.

The gravitometer app is a huge discovery for me. In doing my own research, I have required the need to monitor absolute gravity during a paranormal event, and I will go into the why later on. Suffice to say, an inexpensive application gives me the same information that would require a $15,000 piece of test equipment, and it is faster and easier to use! I am still roaming the iTunes store looking for useful applications, but so far these are the best for our needs.

PDAs

Personal Digital Assistants or PDAs as they are called have also become invaluable tools. There are many devices and test beds built on the PDA framework that saves you a ton of money. For example, an RF spectrum analyzer can cost between $12,000 and $200,000, yet a software based modification to a Palm pilot can deliver you the same performance for a little under $3,000. The processor built in to the Palm Pilot makes this possible. Other useful applications include GeoMagneticInfo, an application for the Palm OS that computes the magnetic declination, inclination, and magnitude for any location on Earth. Its main use is to give the current magnetic declination to correct a magnetic compass. For our use, it detects geomagnetic anomalies. RecorderX is a powerful recorder for the Treo smartphone. It can be used to record phone conversation, make voice memo, make conference notes, or capture any sound. When coupled with a dynamic microphone it will capture EVPs. There is even a science freeware site for Palm devices. You can go there and find all sorts of free applications that are not only fun and easy to use, but incredibly useful.

http://www.freeware-palm.com/tag-science.html

Handheld communication technology of the 21st century has added an inexpensive hi-tech option to data collection. And, we can make phone calls to our team to find out where they are and why they are late!

Chapter 16
Data Logging and Data Acquisition

"Nothing seems of more importance, towards erecting a firm system of sound and real knowledge, which may be proof against the assaults of skepticism, than to lay the beginning in a distinct explication of what is meant by thing, reality, existence: for in vain shall we dispute concerning the real existence of things, or pretend to any knowledge thereof, so long as we have not fixed the meaning of those words."
-George Berkeley-

I have been championing the array concept and the use of data logging in documenting paranormal activity for the past few years now, ever since my online association with Timothy Hart of the MESA project began. Tim is THE pioneer in this field, having assembled an apparatus to monitor twelve different data points and employ the technology at various investigations around the Midwest for some time now. It was my initial exposure to Tim's work that made me push the development envelope for my own organization to develop a DAQ system deployable in our research activities. Simply put, MESA, the Multi-frequency Energy Sensor Array, is a portable data acquisition and analysis system that simultaneously measures a variety of energies commonly associated with haunt phenomena, and has been used at over 150 survey sites. At present, the system collects data on incident infrared, visible, and ultraviolet light intensities; natural and artificially generated electromagnetic fields, gamma ray radiation, galvanic skin response of a human subject, infrasound, and vibration. MESA researchers also deploy digital still and video cameras, a unique two-camera system connected to a magnetometer, as well as audio recording - all to document haunt phenomena.

I wanted to build upon Tim's concept and extend it a bit further; while understanding the energies is a vital part of the equation, understanding changes in the environment are just as important. In order to determine source, we need to understand infrastructure. In the case of paranormal phenomena, the environment IS the infrastructure. Understanding the energies, and what the environment does prior to, during, and after the spontaneous propagation of these energies it key to understanding "cause", as well as "effect".

Admittedly, my first attempts to document data was very crude, as I had to work with what I had, which was a battery of hand held instruments that couldn't be interfaced to any sort of data logging system. Consequently we concentrated these devices in a compact area, and then monitored the instruments and the operator with video cameras. While this was a less than ideal solution, it was revealing none-the-less. On our first foray into the field, (an old vaudeville theatre) we confirmed several of our suspicions concerning the relationship of EVP, EMF, ion levels, radiation, barometric pressure, temperature, air conductance, static electricity, magnetic fields, infrasound and seismic activity to a paranormal event. The problem was the film archive was not revealing enough to be used as viable evidence, as it was impossible to show all aspects of the room, the instruments and the operator in high enough definition. But we knew we were on the right track.

About this time, I was admitted into a new professional engineering organization, the International Frequency Sensor Association (IFSA). As such, I hope to contribute to sensor design, which will open new realms of data acquisition as it applies to this field. Make no mistake about it; the future of paranormal research will be in data logging and data acquisition.

Data Loggers are devices that allow you to graph multiple sensors in real time on a laptop computer. With a time base on events, you will be able to correlate everything as it happens. Sensors can be run some distance from the logger, allowing the remote placement of the devices without a human being relatively close to the array. Data Acquisition on the other hand, is the gathering of information about a system or process. It is a vital element in analysis of a system or process. Parameter information such as temperature, pressure, radiation, light etc. is gathered by sensors that convert the information into electrical signals. The signals from the sensors are transferred by wire, optical fiber or wireless link to an instrument which conditions, amplifies, measures, scales, processes, displays and stores the sensor signals. This is the Data Acquisition instrument.

Data Acquisition equipment began as largely mechanical apparatus, using smoked drums or motorized chart recorders. As technology advanced, electrically powered chart recorders and magnetic tape recorders were used. Today, powerful microprocessors and computers employing digital technology can perform Data Acquisition faster, more accurately, more flexibly, with more sensors, more complex data processing, and elaborate presentation of the final information. And we ALL know, more IS better.

Data loggers and DAQ (Data Acquisition) devices have been around for some time in various scientific disciplines as well as with maintenance functions such as in association with HVAC (Heating, Ventilation and Air Conditioning) systems, but they have only recently been employed in the paranormal research field, and then by a limited number of researchers. These devices allow the use of multiple sensors, real time data recording via software, and add the ability to observe conditions changing in relationship to an event and each other. While DAQ systems and their software can be very expensive, there are affordable options.

For our purposes, the low cost DAQ (Data Acquisition) module is the best choice for capturing the extremely transient changes associated with paranormal phenomena. My choice is the Measurement Computing model USB-1208FS, which is a USB-based DAQ module with 8 analog input channels, 12-bit resolution, two D/A outputs and 16 DIO bits. I use a pair of these in conjunction with a laptop giving me 16 channels of analog sensor inputs. I manage the devices with TRACER DAQ Pro software, also available from Measurement Computing. The units retail for about $200.00 each and the software is another $200.00. Sensors can be challenging, as you have to tinker with the various offerings available to find the right mix. I have found that there are major differences in operation from sensor to sensor, so make sure you purchase a sensor that will operate correctly with your DAQ or know how to modify it to do so accurately. An issue I discovered early on was that the on board power for the sensors is limited to the 5 volt power supplied to the DAQ via the USB port. While this works in some cases, it is problematic for some sensors since the current available via USB is limited, and the voltage is low. Some sensors give better accuracy with higher voltages, such as 12 or 24 volts. Because of this, I decided to incorporate a 450 watt PC power supply as part of my set up to give me more power options. This way, I have a power station that includes 3.3 volts (which I use for low wattage lighting) 5 volts, + 12 volts and – 12 volts as well as a super 24 volts. With these options, the sensor horizon opens up to infinite possibilities.

We currently are measuring temperature and barometric pressure and are working on adding magnetic fields, electromagnetic fields, IR light, UV light, radiation, audio, infrasound, and vibration to the mix. Additionally, my team is constantly working on identifying other parameters to measure with each new investigation we perform. Analyzing all of these parameters during a paranormal event is very revealing. By gathering data, analyzing and reassessing the environmental issues encountered, we often get inspiration into measuring other factors we never initially thought of. This is what inspired the development of measuring the conductance of air in the room while looking for EVP.

A word of caution here; do not attempt to tackle data acquisition unless you are either an experienced electronics technician, or have an experienced electronic technician in your group or access to such a person. There is no real how to guide out there to modify sensors to work with various DAQ systems and you will have to know the parameters of the DAQ and the sensor, and understand how to interface them. But if you pull it off, you will be standing on a new threshold of discovery. Perhaps this should be the subject of a future book.

Traditionally, "ghost hunting" teams have used a variety of hand held instruments to monitor different aspects of the environment. While this is a good method to use for detection, it is a lousy way to record data, since most devices do not have the ability to save the data they measure. As such, there is no permanent record of the data associated with a paranormal event other than the operator's written report, which does not carry much weight in research circles. There have been some exceptions to the rule, as mentioned previously, such as the use of video cameras to record meter responses, but due to the nature of video cameras, the resolution is less than desirable when put into context with the room, and useless if the shot doesn't show enough of the room to establish that no one is artificially affecting the readings.

On the other hand, if you use a DAQ system, all that is changed. Not only can you monitor the events and their effects on various parts of the environment, you can save it as a proprietary record and can share it as a screen shot or as the actual data program file for archiving and analysis by other researchers. It effectively eliminates the "fudge" factor when reporting data, and reduces fraud to requiring a software hacker and data specialist hours and hours of work, making it hardly worth the effort. DAQ data is difficult to fake, and the software is nearly impossible to hack in order to alter it. Hence, DAQ data is reliable, and gives a fairly complete picture of what all the sensors are doing in relationship to each other. While any system can be "beaten if you throw enough time and money into it, I don't know of any researchers who are serious enough to use this equipment that would do such a thing. Again I can't stress the importance of this.

Pairing real time data with audio and video can reveal some very compelling evidence that can be analyzed by various disciplines of science for a realistic assessment of what may really be going on, making it much easier to either find a real solution in real science, or to eliminate a possible non-paranormal cause for the phenomena encountered. It may also prove to reveal what is actually the probable cause of paranormal activity. The real beauty of this is it is a format accepted by empirical science!

Another great advantage of the DAQ system is the ability of a central monitoring observer to monitor remote areas of the building being investigated, and by using DAQ in conjunction with CCTV, and dispatch personnel to an area of suspected activity quickly to provide human interface as well as instrumentation. By combining video, audio and data, you can sync them all to form a very complete picture of what is going on in the environment and respond to it proactively to gain additional experiences and insight.

As researchers, we are constantly seeking to record data, and to make as complete an assessment of that data as humanly possible. We are also constantly trying to tie in the data we collect to highly transient events that so far have defied all rational explanation. The copious use of DAQ technology threatens to turn the scientific world on its head concerning the "reality" of paranormal phenomena. While this isn't the panacea of the field, it is certainly a giant step in the right direction.

Chapter 17
Exotic Equipment

"Every honest researcher I know admits he's just a professional amateur. He's doing whatever he's doing for the first time. That makes him an amateur. He has sense enough to know that he's going to have a lot of trouble, so that makes him a professional."
-Charles Franklin Kettering-

NOTE: Greater detail on these devices and plans and procedures for assembling them can be found at my website, www.spinvestigations.org

So far I have discussed commercially available equipment that has basically been designed to do specific jobs unrelated to paranormal phenomena and the effective use of those devices. The fact that we as researchers have discovered them, adapted their use to our own needs, and deployed them speaks highly of the field's malleability with technology. But if we are to discover the hidden meaning of the paranormal world it will not be the result of using this approach alone. Researchers on the cutting edge in the field will have to push the technology envelope. We will have to design, adapt and configure new devices and apparatus to look deeper into the mysteries we discover upon finding the few answers the current technology provides. While there are some individuals out there marketing dubious devices that turn data into voice and other such useless toys, there are others who strive to build real equipment that will give you real information, not randomly trigger a dictionary of specially selected words. In that spirit, I have included in this chapter devices, setups and apparatus that has developed as a result of my own research.

One of the first experiments in gathering continuous real time data was based on what I previously expounded on, the "Sensor Array". The reality of the situation would more accurately be described as the "Equipment Array" as all we did was centrally locate all of our test and measurement devices and ran them with an operator, under the scrutiny of a multiple camera set up for recording. I touched on this when I brought up the MESA project championed by Timothy Hart. MESA researchers also deploy digital still and video cameras, a unique two-camera system connected to a magnetometer, as well as audio recording, all in an effort to document haunt phenomena. But in the previous chapter, I did not go into the process that created MESA.

The idea that became MESA was first conceived of by Tim Harte in 1981. Over a delicious Godfather's pizza shared with technically-minded high school pal David Black, Tim presented an idea to "wire up" a room with a variety of energy sensors, record their output in a computer and analyze the results. In 1994 Tim asked Dave to design and build it. MESA was first realized using a compact laptop computer with custom A/D hardware, sensors and software. Soon afterwards Mike Hollinshead joined the group, contributing a unique vibration sensor, community web site (Paranormal House), and much more. Since MESA's inception many improvements have been made, primarily through the generosity of others in donations of equipment, new ideas and encouragement.

Tim is a visionary in the field paranormal research of a caliber that you rarely come across. I owe a lot of the current direction of my own research to Tim's research and input. MESA now has its own website, http://mesaproject.com/ and I encourage you to go there and read. Now on to some of my Frankensteinian inventions...

Radio Frequency Logging Console

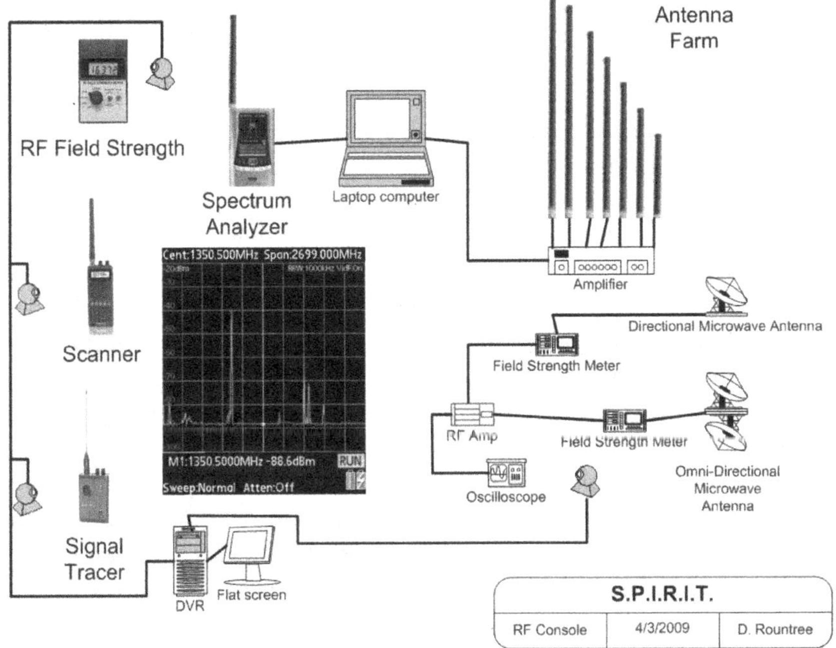

RF Data Console

By far the most troublesome phenomenon we encounter in the field isn't paranormal at all, but is often misread as such. Radio Frequency Interference or RFI is often the cause of EVPs, and can in some circumstances be the cause of EMF spikes in the higher frequency spectrum.

Radio waves are everywhere. We are constantly being bombarded with Microwave from satellites in space and Communication towers, Ultra UHF from Cell phone towers and the phones themselves, Public Service Radio systems (Police, Fire, etc.) Wi-Fi networks for wireless internet, cordless phones, walkie talkies, you name it. RF is everywhere. So with all this noise out there, how can one separate the wheat from the chafe?

Electromagnetic interference (or EMI, in addition to a similar phenomenon, radio frequency interference or RFI) is an undesirable disturbance that affects an electrical circuit due to electromagnetic radiation emitted from an external source. The disturbance may interrupt, obstruct, or otherwise degrade or affect operation. The source may be any object, artificial or natural, that carries rapidly changing electrical currents, such as an electrical circuit, the Sun or the Northern Lights.

EMI can be induced intentionally for radio jamming, as in some forms of electronic warfare, or unintentionally, as a result of spurious emissions and responses, inter-modulation distortion, and other mysterious but explainable propagations. It frequently affects the reception of AM radio in urban areas. It can also affect cell phone reception by creating null points (areas with signal cancellation), as well as FM radio and television reception, although to a lesser degree. *It can also affect complex test instruments or instruments with insufficient shielding used in paranormal research.* EMI or RFI may be broadly categorized into two types; narrowband and broadband.

Narrowband interference usually arises from intentional transmissions such as radio and TV stations, pager transmitters, cell phones, etc. Broadband interference usually comes from incidental radio frequency emitters. These include electric power transmission lines, electric motors, thermostats, bug zappers, etc. Anywhere electrical power is being turned off and on rapidly is a potential source. The spectra of these sources generally resembles that of synchrotron sources, stronger at low frequencies and diminishing at higher frequencies, though this noise is generally modulated, or varied, by the creating device in some way. Included in this category are computers and other digital equipment as well as CRT televisions. The rich harmonic content of these generated signals enables them to interfere over a very broad range of frequencies making it impossible to filter it out.

Power line noise

All power-line noise originating from utility company equipment is caused by 60 cycle bleed out, or transmission, and arcing across power-line related hardware. An ionization of the air occurs, elevating ion counts which in turn creates an atmosphere for conduction, and current flows between two conductors in a gap. The gap may be caused by broken or loose hardware such as a cracked insulator. Typically in a 60Hz system the voltage passes through two peaks during each cycle (one positive and one negative) and pass through zero reference twice each cycle. This gives 120 peaks and 120 zero crossings in each second. This results in noise generally occurring in bursts at a rate of 120 bursts per second. This gives power-line noise a characteristic sound that is called hum or buzz. Because the peaks occur twice per cycle, power-line noise has a 120-Hz modulation on the signal.

Lightning, the mother of all spikes, radiates radio energy across all bands from VLF to microwaves. The only good filter for lightning is common ground, meaning to discharge it to ground. Other weather conditions, known as spherics, also generate significant energy which can result in electrical discharges, generating Radio Frequency Interference. While not as dramatic as lightning, significant communication interference can result.

RFI can also be the source of EVPs. This is why you can place no stock into the gimmicky magical electronic devices that claim to communicate with the dead. These devices use randomly tuning AM radio receiver integrated circuits which catch bits and pieces of voice from broadcasts. They are also completely unshielded, so if the input to the IF section is detuned the bandwidth of the receiver broadens to pick up a great deal of garbage. Then there are the harmonics that get involved, and trust me here, it's just a mess. Consequently, there is virtually no way to determine whether you are hearing your dead relative or a Ham operator with a sense of humor. And if someone is telling you different, it is most likely because you have given him money to do so.

Consequently, when debunking your EVPs you MUST remove RFI as a possible cause of the phenomena. Any EVP recorded in conjunction with a radio transmission is subject to question, therefore must be eliminated as plausible evidence. If it can be readily debunked, it isn't strong evidence. This console set up is designed to monitor as much of the RF spectrum as possible and document the activity in real time, for comparison to other readings and recordings.

As always, devices that cannot be monitored electronically as real time data are monitored in real time on video cameras. So remember the mantra, "Monitor, trace to a source, identify and eliminate". Only by doing this can you end up with something that is truly outside the norm, and paranormal in nature.

EMF Console

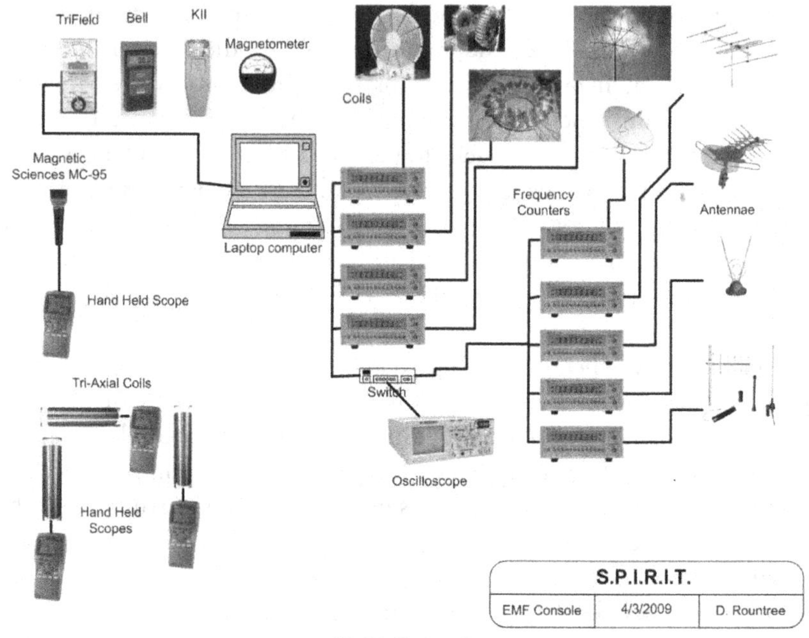

EMF Console

Without a doubt, measuring EMF is probably the most revealing aspect of paranormal research. With the recent discovery of the relationship between EMF and EVP, accurately measuring all aspects of EMF across the frequency spectrum is paramount. Prior to incorporating Data Logging we assembled an assortment of devices to monitor and measure this parameter, and the list is likely to grow larger as more groups expand upon the principle. The lap top is used to record findings from the antenna array using a free program called Right Mark Audio Analyzer. Hand held oscilloscopes are used to monitor the coil array and the MC-95 sensor. Video cameras record the instrument displays. We also employ an Annis magnetometer to monitor any strong magnetic field. The K-II is used as a heads up display, since its lack of shielding and broadband response makes it light up with any present EMF. The flashing LEDs of the KII focus the observer's attention to check the other instruments to make note of any significant deviations.

The MC 95 sensor operates from 25 Hz to 3000 Hz, which pretty well covers the human voice spectrum and below. The hand wound coils cover EMF down to 1 Hz. These coils are hand wound over acrylic tubing that is 3 inches in diameter and are essentially 1600 turn coils. The antenna array covers from about 400 KHz to 2.4 GHz. We also use a frequency counter to identify any stable frequencies.

The Radiation Monitoring Console

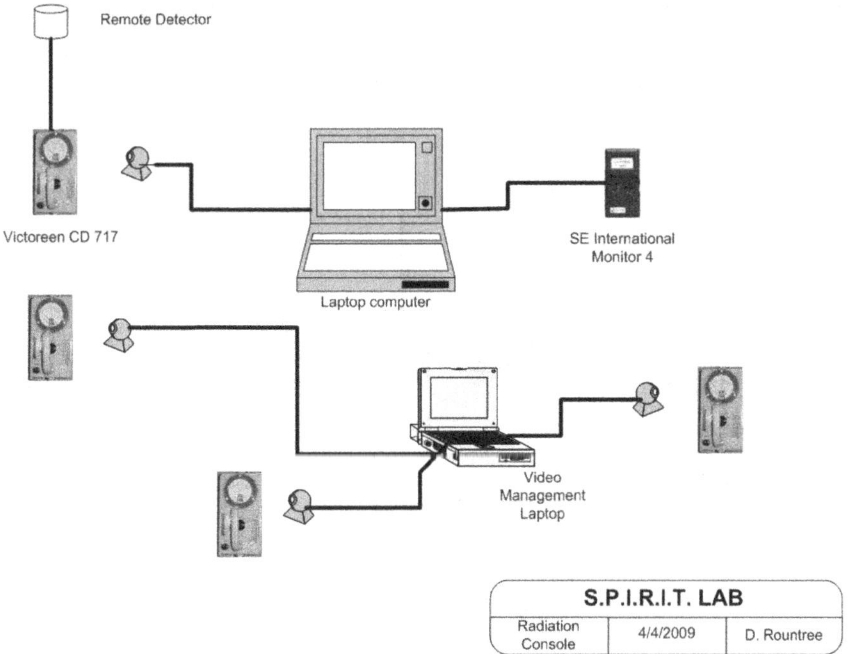

Radiation Console

My first radiation monitoring of a paranormal event took place in 1976. Then, as now, low level radiation spikes (around 100 mR/Hr) in areas that have reported paranormal activity was commonplace. Do I think there is a correlation between these spikes and paranormal activity? You bet! So to provide a continuous data flow during the course of an investigation the meters you are using have to be monitored on a permanent record of some sort. Video recording work perfectly for this, as you can record the instruments, the observer, and any audio present. This not only provides a visual record of the events and data, but may also reveal EVPs that other recorders miss.

I still have my original radiation meters from my early research. In the beginning, the only unit available for civilian use was the Victoreen CD715 and the less common CD717. The key difference in the units is the 715 had a fixed sensor, while the 717 had a removable sensor on a 25 foot tether that allowed for remote placement from the operator. We also employ a modern SE International Monitor 4 with PC interface that allows us to monitor and record readings on a laptop using the SEI's Radiation Alert Observer software. The Victoreen unit is monitored by a modified webcam, and the sensor placed 25 feet away. In this manner we are able to monitor radiation from two different physical places in the room. We can then synchronize the data with other data collected by establishing a time frame with the software for later reference.

The Free Air Conductance Tester (FACT)

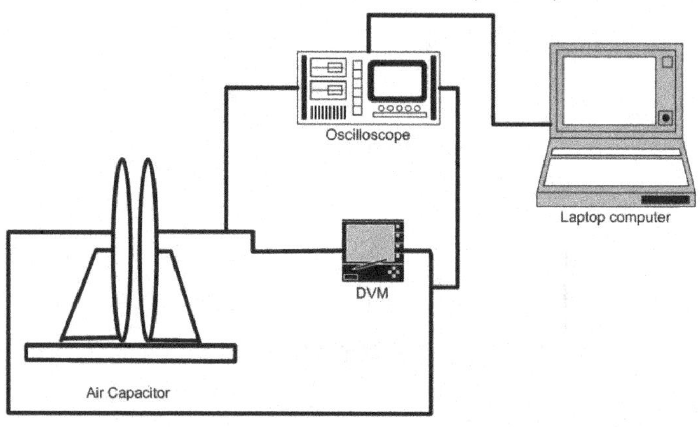

S.P.I.R.I.T. LAB		
F.A.C.T.	4/4/2009	D. Rountree

Free Air Conductance Tester

Unfortunately the potential paranormal environment is not as quiet as one would think. Noise is all around us. I don't mean actual audio noise, but noise of a much higher frequency range, specifically, noise in the radio frequency, microwave and light bands of the electromagnetic spectrum. This noise is around us all the time, and increases as well as decreases depending on conditions and contributors. Collectively it is known as the "Noise Floor" and much of what occurs in a paranormal event resides just above, or often buried in the noise floor. A long time ago I began looking at the EMF spectrum as a whole, with particular attention being paid to the audio and light portions of the spectrum.

Why even look at light?

We look at light because it is associated with many paranormal events in the form of apparitional phenomena.

There is an abundance of high frequency electrical and electromagnetic noise all around us. There are also natural magnetic fields all around us to some degree, depending on the geomagnetic conditions of our locale. Normally, these sources of noise do not interfere with each other but reside collectively in the background. I believe, however, in a paranormal event, they do indeed interfere with each other and could possibly result in some of the phenomena researchers have documented. In order for this interference to occur, the propagation medium that normally separates them must alter to allow the interference to take place. In other words, the air that doesn't conduct electricity so well normally, for some reason increases in its ability to do so, much like what occurs when lightning strikes by traveling through the air from sky to ground (and the current flows from the ground to the sky).

This condition can be enhanced by increased ion counts, as others have previously noted in independent research, which by the way confirms our own observations, so therefore conductivity must increase, allowing the frequencies to blend together. What we are attempting to confirm with this device is the correlation between increases in air conductance, increases in ion count and enhancement of EVP presence. The heart of the device is the sensor portion, a large area air capacitor, which I designed specifically to measure this conductive capability.

We also need to know the frequency of the fluctuations of the air conductance, because that is also a key piece of the puzzle. If the conductance fluctuations are simplistic in nature, then the noise frequencies MUST be complex in nature, and this would indicate that Frequency Modulation is the medium of transport for the noise frequencies. However, should (as I suspect) the conductance is complex in nature, then the noise will be simplistic or Amplitude Modulated. I suspect it will be Amplitude Modulated, because many of the EVPs recorded over the years show evidence of mild amplitude modulation on them. This allows them to move through the air, much like radio waves are transmitted.

Beat frequency is a phenomenon that occurs when you have two frequencies interfering with each other. The result is the difference between the two frequencies. If both frequencies are fluctuating, then the result will be fluctuating, and that result may be an electromagnetic fluctuation in the audio frequency range. You wouldn't hear it, but the coil in your microphone will react to it, possibly generating the recording of an EVP.

A working example of this would be such:

If you have a 1 GHz signal, and a 1.01 GHz magnetic field, the resulting frequency would be 1 kHz, clearly an audio spectrum signal. The next question would be what causes the noise fluctuations to occur with such precision as to generate an intelligible voice, responding to a seemingly just asked question?

That is the question we hope to answer.

EMF-EVP Correlator

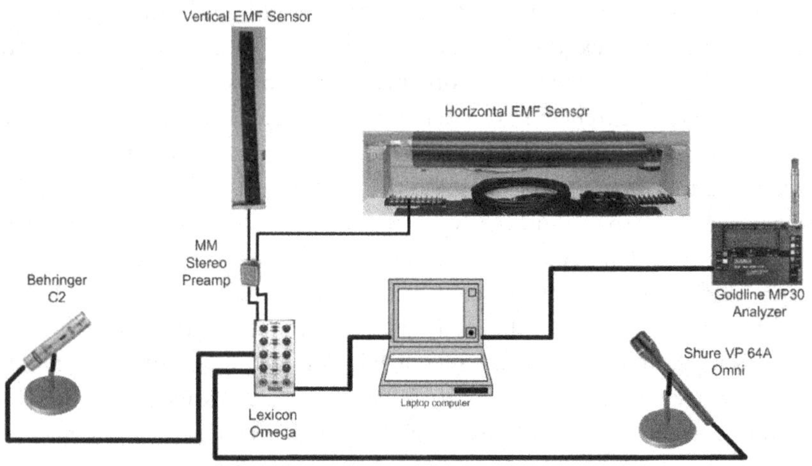

The EVP-EMF Correlation Experiment

S.P.I.R.I.T. LAB		
EVP-EMF	4/4/2009	D. Rountree

EMF-EVP Correlator

As an audio engineer I have been studying Electronic Voice Phenomena (EVP) with much interest for many years, and have relatively recently discovered evidence that EVP is linked closely with Electromagnetic Fields (EMF). After giving this concept a lot of thought, it occurred to me to design an apparatus that would allow the collection of real time correlating data that will link the two beyond any doubt. I am doing this for several reasons. First of all, it will give us a greater understanding of what exactly is going on during an EVP event. Second, it will make "doctoring" the evidence difficult, if not impossible. Since the systems and software I am using create a real time record of the different aspects of the phenomena I am measuring, I would have to hack the program to alter the data. Even if I could do that, I would have to spend a lot of time creating machine code that may or may not work. In essence, it will be impractical, if not impossible, to alter. This will allow the data collected to have a greater impact in research circles. Finally, it will allow me and eventually others to correlate several different types of data and compare them to real time events. While this is primarily designed to work in conjunction with other data collection set ups, it will work fine as a standalone application for the study of EVP.

This device employs some very specialized equipment, such as a Gold

Line 30MP microprocessor controlled 1/3 octave Audio Spectrum Analyzer using a calibrated MK8A condenser microphone. Not only does this device have an LED display, it also has a serial port connection that allows real time monitoring on its software package. Hence, we will have a graphic representation of what we are measuring, that can be saved for future comparison as an image. Additional components we are employing are a dynamic microphone, a pair of studio quality condenser microphones, and of course a laptop computer which will monitor, manage and record the audio and electromagnetic fields using some very specialized software. The laptop is nothing real fancy, a Dell Latitude C-800 with a 1 GHz P-3 processor and 512 MB of RAM. We will also be using a USB mixer as the data interface, and the key requirement for it is the ability to send 4 discreet feeds into the analysis software.

The set up is as follows: The calibrated microphone feeds the audio analyzer, and provides a baseline for all pure audio that is recorded. We employ a condenser microphone as a control because we need a laboratory quality microphone, and also because evidence indicates that Electronic Voice Phenomena may be caused by the result of electromagnetic fields modulated in the audio spectrum and since condenser microphones do not respond to EMF fluctuations, it is the logical choice for documenting the pure audio present, with no EVP interference. Actually proving that Electronic Voice Phenomena is caused by EMF is one of the goals we have underscored as part of the experiment we will be performing with this apparatus. In addition to the external control input, we will also employ a system control input, or a condenser microphone in the actual group data recording system for comparison purposes.

The dynamic microphone will be used as the primary EVP sensor, recording both the audio and any EMF fluctuation that may cause EVP. The USB mixer will allow us to adjust the gain structure to balance the two microphones to achieve an equal intensity or level of operation. Additionally we will also record the output from two different types of EMF sensors for a comparison to the audio signals to see if they correlate in any way. We want to produce a file with four in time sync inputs in order to determine the EMF/EVP relationship.

Feel free to try this at home.

Chapter 18
Weather

"Laws of Thermodynamics:
1. You cannot win.
2. You cannot break even.
3. You cannot stop playing the game."
-Anon-

"In this house, we OBEY the laws of thermodynamics!"
-Homer Simpson-

We study the environment in order to understand what occurs when something reportedly paranormal occurs. As such, the weather is a factor to consider. The weather is essentially the sum total of all the phenomena occurring in a given atmosphere at a given time. Weather phenomena reside primarily in the hydrosphere and troposphere. Weather also refers to current activity, as opposed to the term climate, which refers to the average atmospheric conditions over longer periods of time. When used without qualification, "weather" is understood to be the weather of Earth.

Weather occurs due to density (temperature and moisture) differences from one frame of reference to another. These differences can occur due to the sun angle at any particular spot, which varies by latitude from the equator. Another factor is the strong temperature differential between polar and tropical air gives rise to the jet stream. Weather systems in the mid-latitudes, such as cyclones, are caused by instabilities of the jet stream flow. Because the Earth's axis is tilted relative to its orbital plane, sunlight is incident at different angles at different times of the year. Depending on where you are on the Earth's surface, temperatures can range ±40 °C (-40 °F to 104 °F) annually. Over millions of years, alterations in Earth's orbit have affected both the amount and the distribution of solar energy received by the Earth and influenced long-term climate trends.

Another part of the equation, which is a complex one, is surface temperature differences which lead to pressure differences. Higher altitudes are cooler than lower altitudes due to differences in compressional heating. Compressional heating is caused by the fact that air has mass, it is denser, (more packed) at lower elevations, which create rapid air molecule movement due to compression, which creates heat.

Weather forecasting, while resembling voodoo, is in reality the application of science and technology to attempt to predict the state of the atmosphere for a future time and a given location. Unfortunately, the atmosphere is a chaotic system, so small changes to one part of the system can grow to have large effects on the system as a whole. This is what makes weather prediction so erratic in nature. Human attempts to control the weather have occurred throughout human history, and there is some evidence that human activity such as agriculture and industry has inadvertently modified weather patterns. So, the question is, does the weather influence paranormal activity?

Indeed it does. We know for example that statistically (based on my own record keeping) there is a correlation between certain space weather conditions and the intensity of paranormal reaction, but what normal Earth weather conditions might have an effect on the paranormal? Rationalizing a comparison, the common denominator in Space Weather's effect is energy; the more intense the energy, the more intense the activity becomes. With this in mind, there are several conditions that can also inject a substantial amount of energy into the environment from Earth weather as well.

Wind

Wind is the flow of air or other gases that compose an atmosphere (including, but not limited to, the Earth's). It occurs as air is heated by the Sun which cases it to rise. Cool air, which is heavier than warm air, then rushes to occupy the area from which the hot air has just moved. It can be loosely classified as convection current. Winds are commonly classified by their spatial scale, their speed, and the types of forces that cause them, the geographic regions in which they occur, and their effect. While wind is often a standalone condition, it can also occur as part of a storm system, most notably in a northeaster, cyclone, tornado or hurricane. Winds can carve out landforms, using a variety of Aeolian processes such as wind erosion, transportation, and Deposition. Forces which drive wind or affect it are the pressure gradient force, the Coriolis force (due to the earth's rotation), buoyancy forces, and friction forces. When a difference in pressure occurs between two adjacent air masses, the air will spill from the area of high pressure to the area of low pressure. Between planet rotation and differential heating, little else plays so large a role in global wind generation. In short, the wind is filled with energy.

We all know by watching the events on the news that wind is quickly becoming a preferred alternative source of renewable energy. The advent of huge "wind farms" have made this possible. But turning mechanical generators is just one method of generating power. Additionally, mechanical energy doesn't seem to have any measurable effect on paranormal phenomena based on current data.

However, there DOES seem to be a relationship between static electricity in the environment and paranormal intensity. The wind, while not a direct mechanical cause of usable energy for paranormal manipulation, also generates huge amounts of static electricity, which DOES seem to have an effect on paranormal transients. People have been harnessing this and using it for years to charge batteries on farms and in remote locations. Tesla even developed a power generator from the concept. In fact, the static electricity that is generated on a properly treated insulated wire will produce more than a kilowatt of electricity in a light wind. While some present this as a mystical energy field, or zero point energy, it is neither. What makes this possible is neither mystical nor magical, but due to something in physics we call the Electret Effect. When the surface between a conductor and a dielectric obtains a permanent electric field the Electret Effect manifests. This field has a similar influence on static electricity that a simple magnetic field has on iron filings. To bring this into focus, a treated piece of insulated wire strung out in the wind will act as a Van de Graaf high voltage generator. In some conditions, a 400-foot length of wire can generate 50 kilowatts and even on a bright sunny day with a breeze of 3-4 mph, it will average around 10 kilowatts.

So, how can a small cable extract so much energy from little or no air currents? You would be amazed at how many self proclaimed "scientists" out there working on "alternative" energy projects don't understand the concept involved here. Simply put, the energy collected from the cable is not derived from charge *collection* but from *induction*, as the positive ions in the air rush towards the cable. The Earth's atmosphere is really the electrical equivalent of a gigantic capacitor. At its upper level, air molecules are constantly being ionized and then as the air circulates, the charge is eventually carried to the ground that has a negative charge with respect to the upper atmosphere, and discharges. All the wire does is induce this energy from the ions. And as a foot note here for all you folks who try to elevate Tesla to Godhood, Tesla didn't invent electrostatic induction, nor did he discover it. He merely capitalized off its principles.

Electrostatic induction was actually discovered way before Tesla's birth, by British scientist John Canton in 1753 and independently again by Swedish professor Johan Carl Wilcke in 1762. Electrostatic generators, such as the Wimshurst machine, the Van de Graaff generator and the Electrophorus, are examples of devices that operate on electrostatic induction principles. Personally, I think the confusion lies with novices who are familiar with Electromagnetic induction, but they are in reality two different beasts. But for you folks who need some head ache material, a normal molecule of matter has an equal number of positive and negative electrical charges in each sub part of its makeup. Consequently it is considered to be charge neutral, or it has a net charge of zero. When a charged object is brought near an uncharged electrically conducting object, like metal for instance, the force of the nearby charged matter causes the charges in the uncharged matter to separate. This results in an area of negative charge on the object nearest to the external charge, and a region of positive charge on the part furthest away from it. If the external charge is negative, then the polarity of the charged areas will be reversed. As this is a redistribution of the charges, the object has no net charge. This induction effect is also reversible. If you remove the charged object, the attraction between the positive and negative internal charges cause them to intermingle again. Only the negative charges in matter, the electrons, are free to move about like a band of Gypsies. The positive charges in the atom's nuclei are bound into the structure of the solid matter. All the motion of the charges is the result of the motion of electrons only. However it is important to remember that when a number of electrons move out of an area, they leave an unbalanced positive charge due because of the nuclei, hence the movement of electrons creates both the positively and negatively charged regions described above. Electrostatic induction should not be confused with electromagnetic induction.

Electromagnetic induction is the production of voltage across a conductor placed in a dynamic magnetic field or by a dynamic conductor interacting with a stationary magnetic field. And no, Tesla didn't discover this either. It too predates him significantly. Michael Faraday discovered induction phenomenon in 1831. But I stray off course here.

Ham radio operators will certainly confirm that a coaxial cable strung out, as a dipole antenna, will become highly charged, especially in wet, stormy weather. The *accumulation* of charged ions is not possible in a humid environment. Therefore, the power is derived through *charge induction* rather than from static charge. This is clearly confirmed by the fact that the power generated is directly proportional to the speed of the wind rather than the square of the speed. But hey, slap my face and call me crazy, how can a little wire collect so much energy if it barely intersects the wind?

First, the cross section of the wind from which power is collected is much larger than you might think and second, the electret effect creates an electric field, which attracts charged air molecules much as a magnet attracts iron. The cross section of this electric field can be as great as 2 feet, so a 100-foot cable can intersect as much wind as a 16-foot diameter airfoil, which is a very large cross section. Since we already have some evidence that indicates a relationship between ion levels and paranormal activity, it isn't hard to connect the dots and visualize this viable relationship potential.

But let's return to the static electricity connection. The wind can also generate a static field when blown across the proper material, and this charge can build up to a substantial level without discharging, particularly if the conditions are dry. Low humidity is a vital element in the generation of a static field. Hence, it is conceivable that these conditions can contribute to the intensity or duration of a paranormal event. Perhaps this energy feeds the phenomena in some way. Many researchers are now taking weather data readings prior to an investigation and wind speed and direction are one of these parameters. It can be used to predict where a static field may be building on a structure. And while a naturally caused static field may seem paranormal, it may not be. On the other hand, it may enable or intensify paranormal activity. Either way, it is a parameter we need to document and explore for any possible relationship.

Thunderstorms

A thunderstorm, also known as an electrical storm or a lightning storm, is a form of weather characterized by the presence of a high potential static arcing, (lightning) and its effect: (thunder). It is often accompanied by heavy rain and wind and at times depending on the time of year and conditions, snow, hail, or no precipitation at all. Thunderstorms may line up in a series, coming in phases, and strong or severe thunderstorms may have circulation or rotation. Interestingly, and what few people realize is that if the quantity of water that is condensed in and subsequently precipitated from a cloud is known, then the total energy of a thunderstorm can be calculated. Is that cool or what?

In an average thunderstorm, the energy released runs around 10,000,000 kilowatt-hours (3.6×1013 joule), which just for mention is equivalent to a 20-kiloton nuclear warhead! By comparison, the warhead we dropped on Hiroshima was a 12 Kiloton bomb, and the bomb we dropped on Nagasaki was a 20 Kiloton bomb. So an average thunderstorm packs the same punch as a Fat Man bomb similar to what we leveled Nagasaki with! Frighteningly, a large, severe thunderstorm might be 10 to 100 times more energetic. That is an extraordinary amount of energy!

The lightning discharge can be seen in the form of a bright streak (or bolt) from the sky. In reality it is a huge arc of electricity. Lightning occurs when an electrical charge builds up in a cloud from static electricity generated by supercooled water droplets ramming into ice crystals at approximately 33 degrees F. When a large enough charge accumulates, a rather dramatic arcing takes place, and we have a lightning bolt. The temperature of a lightning bolt can be five times hotter than the surface of the sun (that would be five times 11000°F). Although the lightning is extremely hot, the duration is short and about 90% of lightning strike victims survive. I know, because I am one of them. I have been hit by lightning three times, which may explain a great deal about my psychosis (or lack thereof, you decide). Contrary to the popular myth that lightning does not strike twice in the same spot, skyscrapers like the Empire State Building and other tall structures have been struck numerous times in the same storm. The loud bang that is heard is the super heated air around the lightning bolt accelerating beyond the speed of sound (sonic boom). Because sound travels much slower than light, the flash is witnessed often times a bit before the bang is heard, depending on the distance from the event to the observer, even though both occur at the same instant.

What I find rather fascinating is the notion of investigating during storms is a taboo practice. I read on a lot of investigative sites where teams have established protocols to not investigate during stormy weather, as it could lead to the capture of false evidence. I believe this to be a huge mistake. If rain, dust particles, conditions, etc can create false evidence, then keep that in mind and eliminate it from the data. I think people will find that even by eliminating potential false evidence, they will be left with a substantial amount of viable data. Some of my best experiences and intense evidence gathering has occurred during a terrible weather storm. This area of research needs to be fully explored to discover the exact relationship weather conditions have with paranormal phenomena, but initial findings indicate that there seems to be at least some relationship involved. Is it an artifact, or does the weather raise the spirit's hackles?

Chapter 19
Space Weather

"The most ordinary things are to philosophy a source of insoluble puzzles. With infinite ingenuity it constructs a concept of space or time and then finds it absolutely impossible that there be objects in this space or that processes occur during this time… the source of this kind of logic lies in excessive confidence in the so-called laws of thought."
-Ludwig Boltzman-

Just as we have to take Earth weather into consideration, we also need to look at Space Weather. What exactly IS space weather? I am sure everyone in this field is familiar with the little "Ghost Weather" boxes everyone seems to have plastered on their sites. While this little program shell is helpful, it really only gives you a small portion of the actual data that makes up "space weather". Interestingly, there seems to also be a relationship between space weather and paranormal intensity. Consequently, let's explore the entire spectrum of space weather and what it really does to the earth, so that we can determine what it may be doing to paranormal phenomena. This would qualify, by the way, as another good reason to have a laptop connected to the net while on an investigation. You can get real time space weather info from various sources online.

Solar Wind

The solar wind is simply a stream of charged particles, a plasma form of matter, ejected from the upper atmosphere of the sun and traveling outwards from the sun's surface at various speeds in various directions. It is primarily made up of electrons and protons. These particles escape the sun's gravity in part due to the high temperature of the corona, but also because of high kinetic energy that particles gain through a process that is not well-understood and still one of the unsolved mysteries of Astronomy. I think this makes space weather even more appealing to me…

The solar wind creates the Heliosphere, which is a vast blob in the interstellar medium surrounding the solar system. When Solar wind increases, paranormal activity seems to intensify. Why could this be? Energy, Energy, Energy!

Solar Wind Data

The solar wind data (velocity and proton density) are updated on the net every 10 minutes. The data is actually derived from real-time information transmitted to Earth from the ACE spacecraft and reported by the NOAA Space Environment Center. The location of ACE (at the L1 libration point between the earth and the sun) allows the spacecraft to give about a one hour advance warning of approaching geomagnetic activity. That's right, the solar wind affects geomagnetic activity.

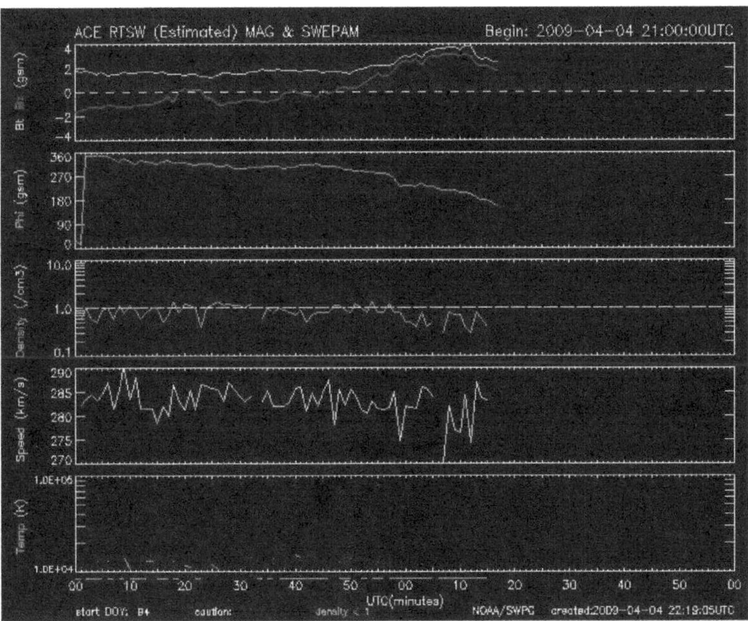

Solar Wind Data

Solar Flares

A solar flare is a sudden, rapid, and intense variation in brightness, often caused by an eruption on the surface of the sun. A solar flare ignites when magnetic energy that has built up in the solar atmosphere is suddenly and dramatically released. Radiation from this type of solar event is emitted across virtually the entire electromagnetic spectrum, from radio waves at the long wavelength end, through optical emission to x-rays and gamma rays at the short wavelength end. The amount of energy released is the equivalent of millions of 100-megaton hydrogen bombs exploding at the same time! It also can disrupt communications on Earth in the form of RF interference.

As the magnetic energy is being released, particles, including electrons, protons, and heavy nuclei, are heated and accelerated in the solar atmosphere. The energy released during a flare is typically ten million times greater than the energy released from a volcanic explosion. On the other hand, to keep things in perspective, it is less than one-tenth of the total energy emitted by the Sun every second.

A solar Flare is typically made up of three stages; first is the precursor stage, where the release of magnetic energy is triggered. Soft x-ray emissions are propagated in this stage. In the second or impulsive stage, protons and electrons are accelerated to very high energies. During the impulsive stage, radio waves, hard x-rays, and gamma rays are emitted. The gradual build up and decay of soft x-rays can be detected in the third, decay stage. The duration of these stages can be as short as a few seconds or as long as an hour.

Solar flares extend out to the layer of the Sun called the corona, a halo type of atmosphere made up of less dense burning gases. This highly rarified gas normally has a temperature of a few million degrees Kelvin. Inside a flare however, the temperature averages 10 or 20 million degrees and can be as high as 100 million degrees Kelvin. While the corona is primarily visible in soft x-rays, it is not uniformly bright, with higher intensities accumulating around the equator as loop like prominences. These bright loops are associated with strong magnetic fields called *active regions*. Sunspots are also located within these active regions and can be a primary source of solar flare activity.

The numbers of flares emitted by the sun are influenced by the Sun's eleven year cycle. When the solar cycle is at its minimum, the active regions are nearly non-existent, but as the sun approaches its maximum intensity these events increase dramatically. The Sun will reach its next maximum period of activity in the year 2011, give or take one year. This activity also coincides with paranormal activity cycles as well. More activity is reported in years of maximum activity. Solar flares are categorized according to their x-ray brightness in the wavelength range between 1 to 8 Angstroms. There are 3 classifications: X-class flares are the big boys, being the major events that trigger planet-wide radio blackouts and long-lasting radiation storms. M-class flares are more common, and are medium-sized events that can cause momentary radio blackouts and primarily affect Earth's Polar Regions. Minor radiation storms (C-Class) often follow an M-class flare. Compared to X- and M-class events, C-class flares are small and have little disruptive effects. Paranormal events seem to be more intense when the flare class reaches M-Class and above. This indicates a relationship that needs further study.

Solar Flare Data

The GOES X-ray Flux plot contains 5 minute averages of solar X-ray output in the 1-8 Angstrom (0.1-0.8 nm) and 0.5-4.0 Angstrom (0.05-0.4 nm) pass bands.

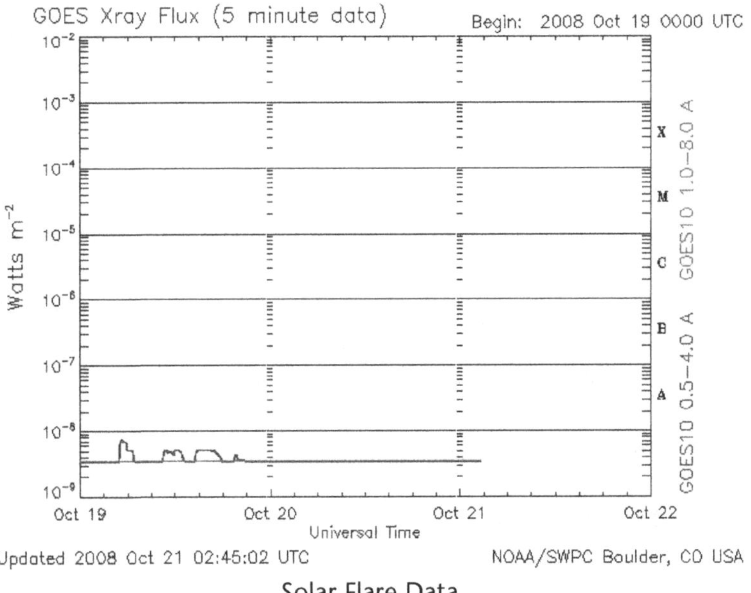

Solar Flare Data

Sunspot Numbers

Scientists document solar cycles by counting sunspots, which are cooler planet-sized areas on the Sun's surface. While it sounds simple, counting sunspots is not as easy as it sounds. If you looked at the Sun through a pair of (properly filtered) low power binoculars, for example, you might be able to see two or three large spots. An observer peering through a high-powered telescope might see 10 or 20. A powerful space-based observatory could see even more say, 50 to 100. So which is the correct sunspot number?

There are two official sunspot number systems in common use. The first, the daily "Boulder Sunspot Number," is computed by the NOAA Space Environment Center using a formula devised by Rudolph Wolf in 1848: R=k (10g+s), where R is the sunspot number; g is the number of sunspot groups on the solar disk; s is the total number of individual spots in all the groups; and k is a variable scaling factor (usually <1) that accounts for observing conditions and the type of telescope (binoculars, space telescopes, etc.). Scientists combine data from lots of observatories, each with its own k factor, to arrive at a daily value. As such, the sunspot number is a calculated average estimate.

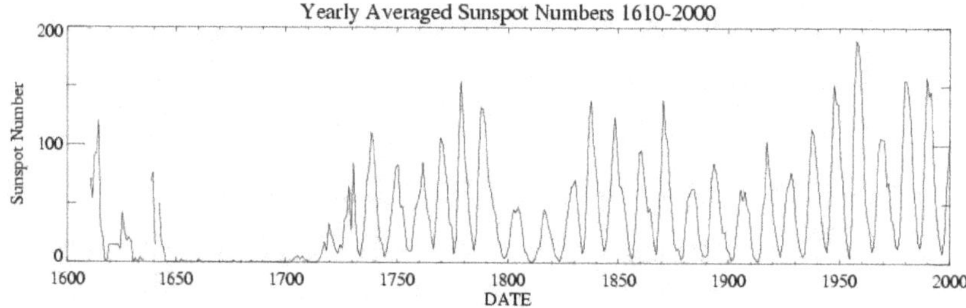

Yearly-averaged international sunspot numbers from 1610-2000

The Boulder number is usually about 25% higher than the second official index, the "International Sunspot Number," published daily by the Sunspot Index Data Center in Belgium. Both the Boulder and the International numbers are calculated from the same basic formula, but they incorporate data from different observatories.

The Planetary K Index

Relationship between Kp and the Aurora

Conceptually, it is a bit of a challenge to explain the relationship between the aurora and geomagnetic activity, and how the 'K-index' or 'K-factor' works. The aurora is officially caused by the interaction of high energy particles (usually electrons) with neutral atoms in the earth's upper atmosphere. These high energy particles can 'excite' (by collisions) some of the electrons that are bound to the neutral atom. The 'excited' electron can then 'de-excite' and return back to its initial, lower energy state, but in the process it releases a magic photon (a light particle). The combined effect of many photons being released from many atoms results in the aurora display that you see. So by bouncing violently into to each other, particles hitting particles create more particles.

The details of how high energy particles are generated during geomagnetic storms constitute an entire discipline of space science in its own right. The basic idea, however, is that the Earth's magnetic field ('geomagnetic field') is responding to a disturbance from the Sun and as the geomagnetic field compensates for this disturbance, various components of the Earth's field undergo a sort of "metamorphosis", releasing magnetic energy that accelerate charged particles to high energies. These particles, now having a charge, are forced to stream along the geomagnetic field lines based on their polarity. Some end up in the upper part of the earth's neutral atmosphere and the auroral display is triggered.

The disturbance of the geomagnetic field may also be measured by an instrument called a magnetometer. We use a magnetometer in the course of our investigations, so it is really important to understand what the current natural levels are so as not to confuse them with paranormal activity. The K-index scale uses a range from 0 to 9 and is directly related to the maximum amount of fluctuation (relative to a quiet day) in the geomagnetic field over a three-hour interval. As such, we can go to NOAA and get the current readings on a laptop, and use this as a reference for the readings we encounter. Large deviations from the background Magnetic field are documented, and other influences are sought out and eliminated, such as localized ferrous material, underlying rock outcroppings or other natural causes.

The K-index is updated every three hours at NOAA. This requires a post investigative analysis of the data to determine any deviations caused by a natural occurrence, an earth based occurrence, or a paranormal event. The important take away here is not to understand the K-Index, but to accept it as a base line from which other magnetic data must be compared to and evaluated.

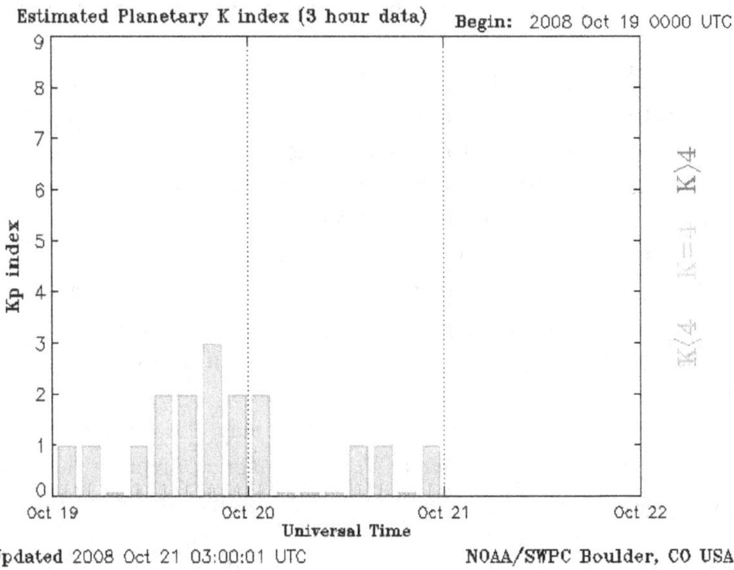

Planetary K Index Data

Planetary Index Data

This is the estimated 3-hour Planetary Kp-index plot. This is derived at the U.S. Air Force Space Forecast Center using data from ground-based magnetometers: Meanook, Canada; Sitka, Alaska; Glenlea, Canada; Saint Johns, Canada; Ottawa, Canada; Newport, Washington; Fredericksburg, Virginia; Boulder, Colorado; and Fresno, California. This data is made available through the cooperation of the Geological Survey of Canada (GSC) and the US Geological Survey.

Other SWPC Real-time Monitors

Kp-indices of 5 or greater indicate storm-level geomagnetic activity. Geomagnetic storms have been associated with satellite surface charging and increased atmospheric drag. Note also as previously "beaten like the dead horse" it is, geomagnetic field disturbances have been associated with paranormal activity. The meaningful measuring of the geomagnetic field is a highly complex and confusing system that can vex the layman's understanding of the current environment. Suffice to say, it is important to be aware of the forecasted activity, the current levels, and the levels encountered on the investigated site. It is also helpful to compare the site with known geomagnetic activity from the USGS magnetic anomaly map. The map can be found online via the U.S. Geological Survey Site, and must be factored into your base data to understand if elevated magnetic activity is natural, or the possible result of paranormal activity.

The Interplanetary Magnetic Field

The Sun is essentially a HUGE magnet. During the condition known as the solar minimum, the Sun's magnetic field, much like Earth's, resembles that of an iron bar magnet, with great closed loops near the equator and open field lines near the poles. Remember when you were in school in science class and you sprinkled iron shavings on a piece of paper with a bar magnet underneath it? Scientists call this type of field a "dipole." The Sun's dipolar field is about as strong as a refrigerator magnet, or around 50 gauss. Earth's magnetic field is 100 times weaker than the sun's. We are talking about very low levels here.

On the other hand, during the years around solar maximum (2000 and 2001 are good examples) spots pepper the face of the Sun. Sunspots create fields that are hundreds of times stronger than the ambient dipole field. Sunspot magnetic fields completely overwhelm the underlying dipole field. The result is a tangled and complicated field of helter-skelter magnetism that creates conditions that potentially feed anomalies here on Earth. Paranormal activity may be one of those anomalies.

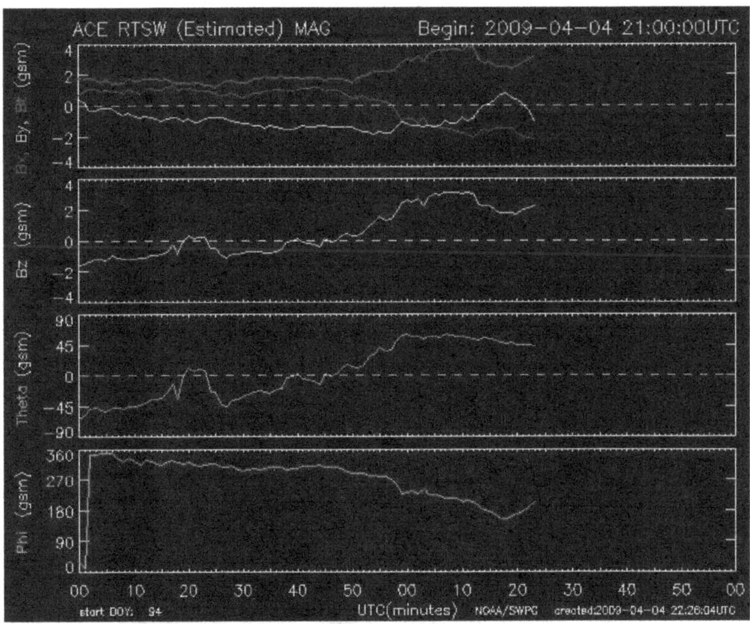

Space Weather Data

The Sun's magnetic field doesn't get contained just around the sun. The solar wind "blows" it throughout the solar system. Out among the planets we call the Sun's magnetic field the "Interplanetary Magnetic Field" or "IMF." Because the Sun spins on its axis (a solar day is 27 Earth days) the IMF has a spiral shape, named the "Parker spiral" after the scientist who first defined it.

As mentioned, Earth has a magnetic field too. It forms a spheroid around our planet called the magnetosphere, which protects us largely by deflecting solar wind gusts. Mars for example, has no protective magnetosphere, and has lost a lot of its atmosphere due to solar wind erosion. Earth's magnetic field and the IMF come into contact at the "magnetopause". No, this isn't a middle age crisis; it is simply the point where the magnetosphere meets the solar wind, much as the "rubber meets the road". Earth's magnetic field points north at the magnetopause. If the IMF points south, (a condition scientists refer to as "southward Bz"), then the IMF partially cancels Earth's magnetic field at the point of contact. When Bz is south, or opposite the Earth's magnetic field, the two fields align. At this point it is possible to follow a field line from Earth directly into the solar wind, or consequently from the solar wind to Earth. South-pointing Bz's are unique in that they cheat the magnetosphere by opening a portal through which energy from the solar wind "pours" into the Earth's atmosphere. It is all a matter of flux relationships. Southward Bz's generate widespread intense auroras, triggered by solar wind gusts or coronal mass ejections that are able to inject energy into our planet's magnetosphere. As such, this energy bleeds down into the atmosphere, and on to the surface of the planet. This bleedover can cause increases in reported paranormal activity. Why? Energy, Energy Energy!

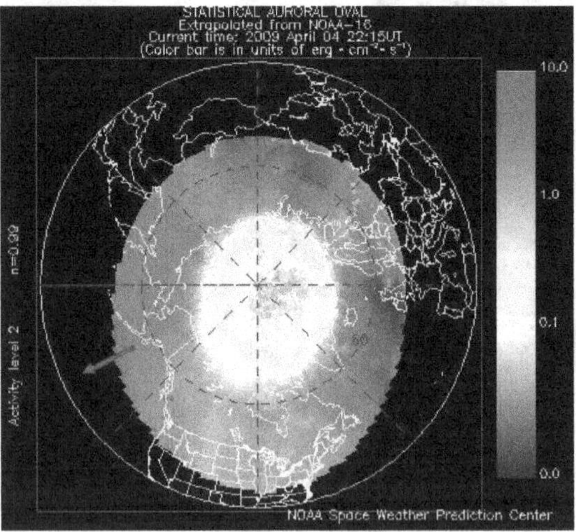

Auroras Range

Geomagnetic Storms

While a thunder storm is cause by a transitory disturbance in the Earth's atmosphere, a geomagnetic storm, or solar storm, is a temporary disturbance of the Earth's magnetosphere, which in turn is caused by a disturbance in the space weather. Linked with solar coronal mass ejections (CME), coronal holes, and solar flares, a geomagnetic storm is the result of a solar wind shock wave which typically impacts the Earth's magnetic field 24 to 36 hours after the originating solar event. Of course, this only occurs if the shock wave heads toward Earth. This being the case, the solar wind pressure on the magnetosphere fluctuates depending on the Sun's magnetic activity. Solar wind pressure changes alter the electric activity in the ionosphere. Lucky for us, magnetic storms generally last 24 to 48 hours, but some have been known to last for days or weeks. In 1989, an electromagnetic storm disrupted power throughout most of Quebec and caused auroras to penetrate as far south as Texas. I was living in North Florida at the time and actually filmed the aurora activity from Gainesville. There is statistical evidence that indicates reported paranormal activity may be more commonplace and increases in intensity when a magnetic storm's effects are present on Earth. All of these factors must be taken into consideration when researching and investigating a site with reported paranormal activity, as they can lead to increased or decreased data opportunities. The vital take away here is more available energy seems to stimulate paranormal intensity. Additionally, the more statistical data that backs this theory up the closer we may get to understanding how paranormal events take place. No stone should be left unturned or energy source neglected in the search for source and cause.

Chapter 20
Instrumental (or Interdimensional) Trans-Communication

"The tendency has always been strong to believe that whatever received a name must be an entity or being, having an independent existence of its own. And if no real entity answering to the name could be found, men did not for that reason suppose that none existed, but imagined that it was something peculiarly abstruse and mysterious."
-John Stuart Mill-

Instrumental Trans-Communication (ITC) is a highly controversial methodology that purported allows communication between spirits or other discarnate entities and the living using electronic devices such as fax machines, television sets, special "magical ghost boxes", telephones or computers. ITC includes not just voice, but visual phenomena and other anomalies. Physicist Professor Ernst Senkowski, of the Faculty of Engineering in University of Mainz, Germany, first came up with the term.

Regardless of what some would lead you to believe, Instrumental Trans-Communication is not accepted by the scientific community as anything but junk pseudo-science, and there are a multitude of reasons for this. The claims made by ITC practitioners are incredible, too good to be true, such as the one made by ITC "expert" Claus Schreiber, concerning an event he claims occurred at exactly 13:22 on October 21, 1987 in which the image of EVP enthusiast Friedrich Jürgenson (whose funeral was held that day) appeared on a television in the home of a colleague, which had been purposefully tuned to a vacant channel. My question would be, with all the channels available, how did they know which one to tune to? It is also claimed that similar effects can be achieved using a TV and video camera via the Droste effect. The Droste Effect involves aiming a video camera at the television and feeding the output of the camera back into the TV, in order to achieve a feedback loop. These people have a general lack of understanding of RF broadcasting, Video broadcasting, and video technology.

Punch me, Guido...

If it is going to be possible to communicate with the dead, other beings from parallel universes, or any type of trans-communication for that matter, there are about a million things between the source and proposed destination. To say this ITC methodology is talking to the spirits is an assumption or opinion based on belief, or the consumption of mass quantities of Kool-Aid. To take a box, TV, recorder, blender, food processor microwave oven or whatever and carry on a conversation with the dead is certainly a hit and miss type of thing at best, assuming you really are talking to the dead and not someone or something else entirely. No where have I seen any effort to debunk this type of research by the researchers themselves. They simply accept that they are talking to the dead.

In order for ITC to ever be taken seriously, an established protocol must be designed in order to insure a successful communication and eliminate the explainable causes for the phenomena perceived. In spite of everything you may have read on the subject, this protocol does not exist. This brings up another important point that is applicable to all paranormal research; it is up to every one of us, as serious paranormal researchers, to discover and establish these protocols, not just for ITC research, but for ALL paranormal research. In order to do that, we have to know a whole lot more than we do now about what exactly is really going on in a real paranormal event. But let's stick to the subject at hand, ITC.

I have reviewed all of the current methods of ITC and I can duplicate all of the results reported without a shred of paranormal activity present. Therefore, there is absolutely no guarantee, that what is currently thought to be ITC is the result of a completely unnatural explanation. The problem is, someone gets an effect, then believes it is paranormal without searching for what it possibly could be. In other words, Mr. X decides he is going to build a device to talk to the dead. He builds the device, turns it on, and sure enough, he gets a voice. He is firmly convinced that since he built the device to speak to the dead, it must be the dead he is speaking to. This is a highly subjective way to do research.

To HELL with the scientific method…

Only when all natural explanations have been eliminated do we have a *possible* paranormal explanation. Current methods, as I have said, fall very short of establishing a paranormal connection.

For example, let's look at a few of the methodologies employed in ITC and some EVP research. There is a great deal of buzz going around about the use of white noise to enhance one's abilities in capturing EVPs, because the energy helps the spirits come through. This has been made even more preposterously popular by recent movies offerings such as "White Noise". My response to this craze is if you can capture perfectly good EVPs without white noise, why use it in the first place? By injecting noise into the environment, you are altering the medium of recording upfront, changing the noise floor dramatically, so anything you get will be dismissed scientifically as Pareidolia, the product of the noise, your mind and your hearing anomalies.

Another example is the spirit talking boxes that have been going around for decades. Of course these devices are going to pick up voices and noises that are perceived as voices. Any close examination of the schematics of these devices will reveal they will be able to pick up commercial radio broadcasts, cordless telephone conversations, GPRS radio, Wi-Fi VOIP and much more.

To leap to the conclusion that it is a voice from the dead would be irresponsible as a serious researcher and based on the data, an impossible conclusion to reach based on science. With a million potential sources for the audio coming through, how does one determine which one is from a dead person, and which one is from an accomplice a block away on a portable radio transmitter? Without very sophisticated equipment, such as an RF Spectrum Analyzer, you can't. Since no ITC researchers have included this data in their findings, Science laughs at these reports.

In order for ITC to have any weight at all, we have to know every frequency present at a paranormal event. Weather radio, police and fire radio, Wi-Fi, blue-tooth, cell phones (which are terrible sources of interference, bleeding through everything) as well as audio and infrasound must be eliminated from being possible sources. We must know the source of every signal present. Only after identifying the sources can we eliminate the normal, and focus on the *possible* paranormal. I am not saying ITC is impossible, I am saying we don't have enough information to know one way or the other. Only through research will we discover the possibilities. Just listening to EVPs or recording multiple images with a camera and monitor isn't going to tell us anything definitive.

Using Occam's razor, (sometimes spelled Ockham's razor, a very over used term in the paranormal community) which is a principle attributed to the 14th-century English logician and Franciscan friar William of Ockham, (the principle states that the explanation of any phenomenon should make as few assumptions as possible, eliminating those that make no difference in the observable predictions of the explanatory hypothesis or theory. Or in simpler terms, "All other things being equal, the simplest solution is the best." In other words, when multiple competing theories are equal in other respects, the principle recommends selecting the theory that introduces the fewest assumptions and postulates the fewest entities. It is in this sense that Occam's razor is usually understood) the simplest explanation is often the correct one. However, a famous physicist one told me that at the quantum level, Occam's Razor no longer applies. So what is the path we must take? We must eliminate the normal from the equation scientifically. Only then will a paranormal explanation be probable and hold any weight. So how do we do this?

Frequency Mapping is one possible solution. We have to map everything. We have to have real time continuous data that is in sync with every recorded activity. Not every group out there will be capable of doing this, in fact, few will. Some, however, will do it and they will make discoveries. It will require a laptop computer, data loggers and sensors, logging software, as well as an assortment of cameras, recording devices and sound gear and the vision and know how to arrange them properly. There will have to be universal time references. Every team member must be wired for sound, and periodic reference points (such as audible time checks) must be added to reference the data. Photo-optic sensors should be employed to record the flash from cameras (photon bombardment), to reference them into the data, as well as microphones and EMF sensors.

Additional environmental sensors for temperature, barometric pressure, and humidity, as well as infrasound, vibration should be recorded in sync with the other data. Personal experiences should be commented on so they too will be referenced with the data. There are a few groups out there capable of doing this, and I challenge them to do so when they can. To prove anything it takes a preponderance of evidence. Currently, there is not a lot of preponderance and a lot of assumption. If ITC is indeed possible, the assumptions must yield to facts. And the facts will enlighten us all. But let us take a brief detour into the realm of ghost talking devices.

Many years ago, an article appeared in an un-named magazine that went something like this:

"In a stunning breakthrough, two different teams of researchers, one in the US and the other in Germany, have both developed devices that let them talk with

the dead. So far, they are said to have actually held conversations with at least nine "dead" people."

Really? Why do you suppose a breakthrough as revolutionary and earth shattering as this, failed to make the nightly news or front page headlines in every major world newspaper?

The article went on to make great claims, using words like "This is undeniable proof that there is life after death,"

"They have shown us wit, personality, memory and an active mind. They are as much 'alive' now as when they had physical bodies."

"Our findings give us undeniable proof that the dead ARE TRYING to contact us."

Amazingly, when other researchers attempted to repeat the experiments, they found they were unsuccessful. But in response to the failure of other researchers to achieve similar results, there was an answer hastily supplied for this:

"The voices of the dead are about twice the speed of normal human speech and they have a rhythm that is different from our own - almost a flat monotone,"

Really? So all the standard EVPs collected over the years are chopped liver? In reality those voices captured sounded a lot like an electronic voice box similar to what Peter Frampton used when he recorded "Do you feel like I do" or what would eventually become known as an Artificial Larynx. Of course I am referring to the "work" of George Meek whose "team" developed a NAVY surplus radio based system which they called SPIRICOM. It used a self proclaimed medium (psychically sensitive Bill O'Neil) with technical skills to operate an electronic arrangement of signal generators which produced 13 simultaneous audio signals. The "departed" supposedly could somehow manipulate those signals in such a way as to magically generate intelligible speech. As the machine was being tuned for the best operation, the technician was being "guided" by voice from the other side. A most interesting arrangement adding a medium, as this eliminated any type of scientific duplicability.

One of the spirits Meek's team supposedly talked to numerous times identified himself as Dr. George J. Mueller, an electrical engineer who died in 1967 of a heart attack.

"Dr. Mueller told us where to find his birth and death certificate records. He told us he graduated from Cornell University with a degree in Engineering and that he taught there," claimed Meek.

But to back up a bit, in 1979, George Meek and his colleague and accomplished con artist Bill O'Neil developed the Spiricom device, a set of 13 tone generators spanning the range of the adult male voice (Why not female? Because O'Neil was the source of the voices). O'Neil claimed to be psychically gifted, and also claimed that he collaborated with his spirit friends while developing the large radio-like apparatus, which gave off a hypnotizing droning buzz that filled the room. When O'Neil finally managed to tune in a voice, everyone went crazy. Unfortunately, the voice sounded suspiciously like the Mechanical Larynx, which oddly enough, O'Neil just happened to have handy.

Was this the voice of a spirit, or the sound of one of the largest hoaxes in the history of paranormal research? I vote for the later as being the truth and the evidence for fraud is overwhelming.

The SpiriCom

I was one of the rubes who bought into the "Spiricom" concept: I paid my money, I got the block diagram and pseudo-schematic, bought the components and assembled an AM low power radio transmitter and AM receiver and drove the transmitter with 13 frequency specific oscillators. The transmission signal was a composite wave form composed of 131, 141, 151, 241, 272, 282, 292, 302, 415, 433, 515, 653, and 701 Hz. That's right 13 waves, count em', the magic number (Twilight Zone Music please...).

I fired it up, talked into the microphone and fired up the recording device (in those days I used a Teak Reel to Reel) and waited for the voices from the dead to answer me.

I waited a long time.

After several weeks of listening to noise I never received one voice. Oh, excuse me, I did manage to hear a trucker tell me he was south bound with a load of manure, and I somewhat related to his plight. His CB transceiver was running a linear amplifier, and I am sure it bled through every receiver within five miles of the highway. Naturally, I tried to find out what I did wrong. I contacted the Metascience Foundation and I got this cryptic reply back:

"Mr. Rountree,
Thank you for your interest in the Spiricom, but a word of CAUTION;

- *Tens of thousands of hours spent over 25 years by hundreds of EVP (electronic voice phenomenon) researchers in Europe have clearly shown that some form of supplemental energy must be utilized to permit even individual words or short phrases to reach a level of audibility detectable even by a researcher with a highly acute sense of hearing.*
- *Eleven years of effort by 'Metascience researchers has established that the energies involved in the different levels of the worlds of spirit are not a part of the electromagnetic spectrum as science presently knows it. To have any chance of sensing or detecting such energies it is necessary to create some means of coupling the spirit energies to the devices at our disposal - transceivers, speakers, microphones, tape recorders, oscilloscopes, etc. Hence it seems that some form of transformer, coupler or transducer must be utilized to serve as an interface between the energies of the "dead" and the energies used in our electronic devices.*
- *Of the five different system design concepts explored by Metascience researchers, only one has so far resulted in prolonged, two-way, normal voice conversation. That system, which we call Mark IV, uses the energy input from 13 different audio tones in what seems to be a more effective and constant energy source than the miscellaneous energies used by EVP researchers past and present. It also seems to use the auric energy field of one of our technicians who is such an advanced psychic that his clairaudient and clairvoyant abilities have on occasion allowed him, to converse with and see the " dead " person. His energies have, on at least one occasion, been utilized in a full body materialization of a spirit form. To date, our only extensive two, way conversations have been obtained when this technician is present in the room in which the equipment is located.*
- *Because of the above fundamental factors, we caution that merely building equipment according to the diagram for Mark IV may result in a waste of effort and money unless there is some form of highly charged human energy field available for use in combination with the mixture of 13 audio tones.*
- *In an effort to eliminate the need of a human energy field, three other types of transducers are already being investigated by Metascience Foundation researchers - electrically activated quartz crystal utilizing ultraviolet light, living plants and the plasma of an open flame.*
- *One of the principle reasons for releasing this information now is to encourage you and other researchers throughout the world to use your inventive talents to explore and solve the many mysteries which still separate us from the desired quality of communication.*

They were kidding me, right? Hey this wasn't part of the come on when

I started this journey, now suddenly in order for this to work I have to have some kind of unquantifiable energy? I couldn't believe this malarkey was coming from a person who was supposed to be an electrical engineer. It was pure hogwash.

At this point, two things struck me right between the eyes where my gray matter should have been.

1. If a medium can already talk to the dead, why does he need a machine to do the same thing?

2. Why did the sound files sound suspiciously like an artificial voice box, which by the way was not typical of EVPs captured up to that time?

I did some more digging. It turns out that the ONLY "researchers" that had any success with this device at the time were George Meek and his colleague Bill O'Neil. Big surprise! Additionally, the design for the device was supposedly communicated to them from a Dr. George J Mueller, PHD, who was supposedly born on September 1, 1906, and died May 31, 1967. His resume' is impressive, to say the least.

Dr. George J Mueller, PHD
LAST POSITION HELD
Associate professor of engineering and mathematics, Orange Coast College, Costa Mesa, Calif., 1964-1967.
ENGINEERING EXPERIENCE
Manager, research and development center, Cannon Electrical, Co., Anaheim, Calif., 1962-1964.
Chief of development and planning, Nortronics Division, Northrop Corp., Anaheim, Calif., 1960-1962.
Senior staff member, Ramo-Wooldridge Division, Thompson Ramo Wooldridge, Inc., Canoga Park, Calif., 1959-1960.
Director of engineering, technical products division, Packard Bell Electronics Corp., Los Angeles, Calif., 1956-1959.
Chief, test support department, Ramo-Wooldridge Corp., Los Angeles, Calif., 1955- 1956.
Consultant in engineering and physics, Douglas Aircraft Co., 1953-1955.
Technical director, Dumont Labs, Inc., Los Angeles, Calif., 1952-1953.
Supervisory physicist and chief, technical services division, Patrick Air Force Base, Fla., 1950-1952.
Physicist and chief, research laboratory, Picatinny Arsenal, Dover, N.J., 1935-1950.

ACADEMIC POSITIONS
Research fellow, Cornell University, Ithaca, N.Y., 1933-1935.
Physics instructor, Cornell University, Ithaca, N.Y., 1931-1933.
Physics teaching assistant, 'Cornell University, Ithaca, N.Y., 1929-1933.
EDUCATION
B.S. Electrical Engineering University of Wisconsin 1928
M.S. Physics Cornell University 1930
Ph.D. Experimental Physics Cornell University 1933
PUBLISHED WORK
Mueller, George J. Introduction to Electronics, 1947.
Also contributed to various professional journals in physics.
MEMBERSHIPS
Institute of Electrical and Electronics Engineering (Senior member)
American Association for the Advancement of Science
The Franklin Institute
Institute of Radio Engineers
The Physical Society
Society for Engineering Education
Society of Motion Picture and Television Engineers

I live right down the road from Picatinny Arsenal. I thought I would check to see if there was a record of him working there. For those of you who are not familiar with Picatinny arsenal, Google it sometime. It has been there a very long time and they make munitions including ammunition, among other things. Today they have several projects including robotic field devices to help the ground soldier, acoustic weaponry and other things. But what they don't have is a record of George J. Mueller. Published photos of Dr. Mueller have several identifying components that link the likeness to a Dr. E. Mueller, who worked for N.A.S.A. and was a manager of the Apollo project. He died in 2002 and could have very easily told them how to build the device, because he was very much ALIVE in 1979. There are a lot of other mysteries about this man, the team and the device, and for a complete report go check out http://www.audiomedium.com/spiricomstudy/. It seems that Dr. Stephen Rorke found out some similar info that I discovered, only he took it quite a bit further. After years of research, Dr. Rorke has uncovered possibly the largest hoax ever perpetrated on the paranormal public. To me, Dr. Rorke is far more believable than Mr. O'Neil or any of the modern claimers of ITC using this technology. Dr. Rorke is a physicist and an academic, and an established scientist. The equipment used was Naval Surplus Radio equipment, the kind used for years by ships at sea to communicate. Strangely, the NAVY never talked to ghosts with the gear, although today the equipment is very popular with HAM radio operators world-wide. They also don't seem to be talking to ghosts either.

The point to all of this is, the Spiricom was a fake and it is still being peddled on the web as the Real McCoy even today. This is a prime example of why when someone tells you they have found a way to talk to the dead, you should hold onto your wallet with both hands and run in the other direction as fast as you can go.

But don't take my experiences or word on this. Let's look at it with pure logic and common sense. First of all, how in the world could you possibly know you were talking to the dead and not some HAM operator having a good time? The content of the message may seem compelling, but is it specific enough to identify it with the dead? How do you know you are not picking up un-modulated audio, interference, cell phone conversations, or a simple prankster who knows information about you? Of course there is no way to know. Not unless as part of your experimentation, you eliminated those potential causes. They did not. In fact there is extremely strong evidence that suggests O'Neil and others purposely pulled off the stunt to defraud Meeks and corporate sponsors out of their money.

This is why I am against any research that uses TV, Radio, White Noise, etc. If you are using this, and you receive something, you HAVE to check to see if it is an RF signal you are receiving. RF field strength meters, RF spectrum analyzers, etc are required to eliminate this as a possible cause. In the end, I just don't believe that when we die, we suddenly sprout an RF modulation unit and transmitter, and speak in the RF spectrum. If this were the case, we would be hearing the dead every day on our way to work, listening to the radio. There are too many viable explanations for the material these devices receive. It is too easy to debunk. I don't know about you, but If I COULD talk to the dead, and no one believed me, what good is it?

Everything you do must be backed up by evidence that stands up to scrutiny. Otherwise it does more harm than good. Spiricom inspired the modern ITC movement, and it is all based on a hoax. Yet no one from the ITC movement has discovered this, or even seen the original equipment. If they had, and understood the electronics, they would have known instantly they were being deceived. This speaks volumes about the modern ITC movement. They either know this and are intentionally perpetrating a fraud, or they are ignorant and in bliss. I propose the field is made up largely of both. It is a multi-million dollar industry. I suspect that is where the real truth lies. Greed…

The PsychoPhone

First of all, I realize there is a whole cadre of researchers devoted to using background noise as an aid to recording EVPs. I personally reject those notions as opening the door for your work to be debunked. I can't repeat this enough. I also realize that my stand on ITC is going to make some enemies. But I have been making enemies for years now. Eventually, they simply fade away, much like the "ghosts" they reportedly talk to. The fact is I base my stance on my education, experience and science. They base their work on... well I am not sure what they base it on.

Franz Seidl, a self proclaimed EVP-pioneer, "invented" the Psychophone, self hailed as a revolutionary new device that practically guarantees the user success in contacting the Spirit World.

Uh-huh, yeah. So where is the Nobel Prize for physics? Excuse me if I don't fire my electron guns in the air and dance around in celebration. Well there is one accurate part to this scam: the "Psycho" in the phone.

"The Psychophone integrates several electronic devices e.g. an oscillator (a small radio transmitter) that generates energy/carrier waves for transcendental voices to modulate. Secondly a radio-receiver for the reception of electromagnetic waves that may be influenced by the voices. Furthermore there is a microphone-preamp onboard to enable the use of a microphone to capture voices."

What this really states is that there is a radio transmitter that broadcasts to a receiver. All other statements are pure conjecture not backed up with facts. I have carefully studied the schematic of this device and built a test unit, I have noted a few things. First, not every oscillator is a radio transmitter. It is only a radio transmitter when the carrier frequency is in the Radio Frequency Spectrum. Otherwise it is a small EMF transmitter. Second, the oscillators in this device are highly unstable circuits, and have adjustable potentiometers that will literally allow you to make it talk. By rotating the knobs you can alter pitch and cadence. As for "transcendental voices to modulate" I have yet to see that proof. What this device will do is allow any frequency present in the audio range to modulate the carrier. Twisting the knobs will also modulate the carrier. This thing is a win/win situation. If you don't detect an EVP, you can generate one. I could do the same thing with a MOOG synthesizer. It too is made up of oscillators, wave generators and the like. You can make a violin sound, an electrical sound, or even an electric voice.

The best part of these "boxes" is the antenna the designers add to them. They tend to use whatever they have laying around to make it "look functional" and in this case the builder used a mobile scanner antenna that is cut to the wrong wavelength for the frequencies this thing is operating at. To his credit, he also added a long wire antenna called a "dipole". Its length is critical and must be cut for a specific frequency. At best this device will pick up AM station bleed-over, if it's close enough to the radiating tower. Then again, so will your bathtub if filled about ¾ of the way full of water. Most of these people are crackpots who demonstrate a general lack of knowledge about electronics and engineering. Or again, they do know and are purposefully defrauding the public. (I report, you decide).

The device also requires some specially modified equipment and special software. In his case he used a BASF type 9210 automatic cassette recorder modified with a 100 K ohm potentiometer attached to the motor power feed to regulate the speed of the motor. He also recorded straight to his PC from the device using the old Cooledit 2000 software. Amazingly, the dead hang around his house just waiting to be a popping jay.

Well let's remove all chance of it being a message from the dead. Cooledit can do a lot, including making EVPs from noise in the hands of the trained engineer. Adjusting the motor speed can also make something sound quite different from what it really is. Apparently, tampering with the recording isn't a breach of scientific protocol to these "engineers". But here is the disclaimer that sold me on the device. This claim makes it a lead pipe cinch!

"If you are using the psychophone it is advisable to create inner peace and tranquility for this increases the chances of good contacts with the other side. There is no need to act mysterious like sitting in a darkened room in the middle of the night burning incense. You may as well do it during the day in full light at the time of your choice. Do try to repeatedly pick the same time of day for subsequent recording sessions. It has proven to increase the number of contacts and their quality. If a contact has been established, always bear in mind that it is not only your apparatus that is responsible for it. Your participation level is high, you are the conductor. They use your energy to be able to communicate (aura or magnetic radiation). That is why you may feel tired after having done several subsequent recording sessions."

That must have been my problem. Forget that this is about as scientific as a toilet. I was so angry at the designer, I had no inner peace. Or maybe my participation level wasn't high enough. These people should be jailed for fraud, or better yet, tarred and feathered and run out of town. Anytime someone tries to sell you on a "scientific" instrument that requires peace of mind, a good measure of tar and feathers should be applied liberally.

By using a device that generates noise, any noise, including white noise, pink noise, sweep oscillations, etc. you are opening up your work to be debunked, period. Nothing you do, claim or discover will ever be taken seriously by anyone in the scientific community. Furthermore, using these devices and methods allow you to pick up the voices from thousands of non-paranormal sources, including but not limited to un-modulated audio, resonant audio, subcarrier detection, microwave harmonic reception, and the list goes on. The idea is to REMOVE these possibilities, not add them. It is also a prime recipe for Pareidolia.

You want your work taken seriously by the scientific community? Get a good dynamic microphone, a good recorder, and go ask questions in a place that has reported activity. Good people are wasting good money and valuable resources on junk, and the only thing they are discovering is that they are making other people rich. Stay away from devices that require your proper peace of mind to function properly. By the way, if you have peace of mind, I can change that with some swamp land in Florida I'd like to unload…

Frank's Box

Having debunked such devices as the Spiricom, and the Psychophone as devices that easily receive interference and due to the meshing of unstable frequencies, create beat frequencies in the audio range, that often make some sense as being quackery, I thought I had seen the end of this foolishness. Not so. What I really find fascinating is why do people try these things? I have heard the "voices" these boxes produce, and they are more often than not electronic signatures, not real voices. So when you can capture a clearly understandable EVP (one to which all who hear it agree to its content) with a microphone and a recorder, why add all of these opportunities for a scientist to debunk your work by using unstable oscillators and varying the bias on the control amplifier or randomly tuning an AM radio receiver? Why, to talk to the dead of course! And to make $200.00 a whack from other people's sorrow. This is an overwhelming reason why there is reluctance among mainstream scientists to get involved with scientific research of the paranormal.

These boxes are essentially a crude form of synthesizer, very similar to the one invented by MOOG in the early 1960's. In fact I have an old synthesizer here in the lab and as I have mentioned earlier, I can make it say whatever I want. Better yet, I can manipulate to say anything YOU want. It certainly is no proof of voices from the dead, although I could make it seem as such. I can also use simple voice emulation software, or a text to speech engine to make an amplifier and a speaker talk to you from the great beyond. It has nothing to do with the dead, but I can make it seem so. Unfortunately, the evidence points to this being the case with all of these "hi-tech" devices.

Like the few scientists who do research paranormal phenomena, I want to believe it is possible to build an electronic device that will enable us to communicate with the dead. I really do. But on the other hand, I have to be able to quantify this action with documental proof. I am sorry to say that eye witness accounts are weak proof, anecdotal at best in the scientific community. A person can easily be manipulated by a trained charlatan. So, bearing this in mind, I built a model of Frank's Box, a copy of one of the devices that is currently becoming the rage among paranormal circles and making certain individuals a lot of money. We secured the plans, schematics and "theory" of operation, and we built it. We operated it and analyze it. I spent a day with my Father-in-Law and we dissected the schematics. Let me add a little background.

My father-in-law works for a lab in the Northeast and is literally a rocket scientist. He has been a great inspiration to me in the debunking of some, and investigating the reality of other paranormal phenomena. He has forgotten more than I will ever know and his assistance and input has been greatly appreciated. The two of us noted that the current device shares a lot with its infamous predecessors, the Spiricon er com, and the Psychophone.

First of all we were highly entertained by the technical write up. The author claimed to have little technical knowledge, and we believe him. The term "Random Voltage Generator" is a hoot. The correct term should be Gaussian noise generator. He employs a simple reversed bias transistor circuit that generates not only harmonic distortion, but causes an AM tuning chip to randomly tune along its bandwidth, capturing tidbits and words and stringing out basic sentences on occasion. It is then amplified, run through filter circuits that effectively enhance the audio spectrum response. There are many paragraphs dedicated to this circuit, but the simple reality is, it's a noise generating word randomizer using commercial broadcasts as the dictionary. It starts oscillating based on the first noise that it picks up, which can be a goose fart. Then the whole circuit continues to randomly oscillate, with no particular order to its wandering. The AM tuner picks up random words from all the various commercial broadcasts and you get a metallic robot like voice sound from it. Additionally, the speaker is mounted in an "Echo Chamber". The box is very small, so the echo is more imaginative than quantitative. I guess it was cheaper than adding a small delay circuit.

My father-in-Law by now is laughing so hard he has tears rolling down his cheeks. In fact, my Father-in-Law believes it will produce voices anywhere, haunted or not. And amazingly, it does. But are they voices from the dead?

The antenna employed once again, is also problematic. It is too small to receive audio from the spirits, as a quarter-wave antenna for the audio spectrum would be in the neighborhood of 68,000 miles long. It is also far too short for the AM receiver built in. It is about the size required to be a quarter wave length for 2.4 GHz, which is the densest frequency band in the RF band. This band contains wireless microphone transmitters, Cordless phones, WiFi networks, and essentially everything covered by FCC regulation 802.11. Consequently we are both deadly certain people are hearing voices from this box. It is also unshielded. It has the potential to be a broadband radio receiver. So I built one. Fired it up. Twirled some knobs and heard voices. Really!

The kid up the street with his GFRS Walkie Talkie comes through clear as a bell. My neighbor's cordless phone revealed their pizza order. I heard random words from various broadcasts. This device can and does pick up everything. It is the KII meter of the ghost box world! By twirling the knobs, we can make it talk. It certainly is a lot of fun, but so far, I haven't heard from a single dead relative. I do however know my next door neighbor is rather fond of pepperoni and mushroom pizzas, and THAT is a revelation.

On a more serious note, is it possible, that mixing random audio noise with an unknown quantity of RF could open a portal and allow something to come through? This is highly unlikely, as equipment of varying designs have been operating all over the world with no voices from the dead interfering with that operation on a daily basis and have been doing so for years. Additionally, any experimentation into the realm of electronics, particularly by someone who claims Edison gave him the design (my question is, if you can already talk to Edison, why build the damn box?) is dubious at best. Vacuum tubes were in their infancy when Edison was alive, and the transistor didn't exist. Commercial radio broadcasts didn't exist. Radio transmissions were all done with a telegraph key using Morse code for communication. But amazingly, a magical thirty people as claimed by one of the devices users are able to talk directly to the dead. The basic difference between this and a bucket of manure is the bucket.

Many serious scientific based groups have built copies of this device, and have had a similar success or lack thereof that we experienced. And what was the magic reply to explain this lack of success?

Apparently, we were not one of those 30 special individuals in the world.

Ok, now I am screaming, pounding my fists on the wall, and laughing maniacally. Apparently, this common circuitry is so fantastic it is able to selectively apply the laws of physics to specific individuals and deny them to others. Do you see how utterly ridiculous this sounds? If you don't, then this book will be wasted on you. But the truly astounding thing is I have talked to witnesses that are firmly convinced that they spoke to a dead loved one. I have spoken to others who claim to operate these devices and are communicating with the dead on a regular basis. It is my belief, that the ability of the operator is responsible for this more than the device is. The same results could most likely be achieved using a white noise generator, a Magic 8-Ball, a deck of Tarot cards or a partridge in a pear tree.

Another device that was popular for a time was the "**Raudive Recorder**", in which a regular tape recorder was employed using a germanium diode as the audio input instead of a microphone. When plugged into the jack and the volume turned up to the highest it will go (11 if you are a Spinal Tap fan), the diode picked up a very wide range of frequencies because it was essentially demodulating every RF broadcast in range. Will you hear disembodied voices? Absolutely! Are they from the dead? Absolutely NOT!

Other devices have recently appeared on the market that claim to communicate with the dead. The **Ovilus** is one of these devices that have become incredibly popular by its appearance on certain popular TV programs. Built by Digital Dousing LLC, the Ovilus, AKA the Puck, is hailed as a technological wonder. It is designed to replace all the other ghost hunting equipment available to the paranormal researcher. It is of course, a hoax.

The Ovilus uses environmental detectors that feed a processer to mathematically produce preset responses. Those responses are programmed into a memory chip and determined by the builder. Its vocabulary is limited to the 1024 word list added by the manufacturer. Any sensor input will trigger a word or series of words. The outcome is dependent on chance. This is akin to rolling the spiritual dice. The problem is, you don't know which sensor input triggered the response, or whether the frequency of the EMF is 60 Hz from the wall outlet, or from something else. In addition, because the vocabulary is custom designed to provide the maximum paranormal interface capability, you are dealing with a loaded set of dice. This is a "novelty item" only. In other words, expensive garbage.

Other items worth mentioning are software packages that detect EVP, which are essentially word randomizer protocols, Radio Hack scanning, Infrasonic Descramblers, and the list just goes on and on. The only things these devices do is make money and fame for their manufacturers, and make gullible researchers look even sillier than they normally would and poorer for their effort.

So, do I believe you can build a box that can talk to the dead? Well, first of all, I am not ready to say it is the dead we are talking to, but I do believe a communication device is possible. As such, I have employed some off the shelf equipment to make my own ITC device, and I call it Dave's Improbability Audio Pile. And the best part is that anyone can employ it with little or no skill.

EVP is an electromagnetic field. You are recording it with a transducer (Microphone) that responds to the electromagnetic field. IF it is communication from the dead, and they are using EMF to communicate, it stands to reason that EMF can be used to communicate back. So try this out next time.

The first system is the budget, or low cost system. Radio shack makes a small personal amplifier that has been picked up and marketed by several companies. The kit below is available from the EMF Superstore. Links are provided. An inexpensive microphone is also identified below.

The Budget Dave's Improbability Audio Pile (Cheap Version 1.0)

EVP Listener (Cat. #A175-C) $19.95
http://www.lessemf.com/ghost.html#Other

Multipurpose microphone. Black ABS housing. Dynamic, moving-coil element. Unidirectional cardioid pattern. 600 Ohm impedance. 8' shielded cable. 1/4" phone plug. Sensitivity: 76dB plus or minus 3dB. Frequency response: 80-12kHz. CAT# MIKE-100

Your Price: $6.50 each
http://www.allelectronics.com/cgi-bin/item/MIKE-100/390/BLACK_MULTI_PURPOSE_MICROPHONE,_600_OHM_IMPEDANCE_.html

By purchasing two of these kits and two microphones, you can start communicating with the dead tomorrow! Simply hook the microphones up to the units, place one of them in front of you, with the speaker facing away from you. This will allow you to talk into the microphone and have the audio of your voice amplified and broadcast into the room away from you. This is your "transmitter" The speaker in the amp is also generating an EMF field of your voice. Now set the other one up in an opposing fashion, with the microphone pointing away from you, and the speaker facing you. This is your "receiver" and now you have a real telephone to the dead. Instead of listening to the speaker, you can plug a small recorder into the earphone jack of the amplifier, and record the responses, if any.

Total cost of the rig is around $60.00 bucks with the adapter required to connect the microphone to the amp (1/4 phone plug to 3.5mm mini phone plug)

The High Tech Dave's Improbability Audio Pile (Pro Version 2.0)

Behringer XENYX-802
List Price: $79.99

8 Input 2 Bus Mixer w/EQ
http://www.bswusa.com/proditem.asp?item=XENYX-802

Behringer XM1800S
List Price: $49.99
3 Pack Dynamic Microphones

Proco SMM5
List Price: $11.99
5 Foot Audio Cable (XLR To XLR)

AudioSource AMP100 - Stereo Power Amplifier with A/B Speaker Selector - 50 Watts at 8 Ohms
Price: $ 84.50
http://www.bhphotovideo.com/c/product/356256-REG/AudioSource_AMP100_AMP100_Stereo_Power.html

DB Technologies M50T 4 Speaker – Black (Item # M-50T-B)
List Price: $49.95
http://www.guitartrader.com/DB-Technologies-M50T-4-Speaker---Black

This system is way more powerful, and could possibly transcend multiple parallel universes (just kidding). In this system, you can hook the speakers to the amp, the mixer to the amp, and the microphones to the mixer. Put one microphone in channel 1 of the mixer, and pan it far left. Put another microphone in channel 2 and pan it to the far right. You can now use one channel for transmit and one for receive, as well as attach a recorder to the aux outputs.

You can use any equipment laying around to do this, old stereo amplifiers or receivers, old garage band mixers, whatever you have lying around, the point will be the same. Listen for an EMF field after transmitting one. We are going to experiment with this set up in the next few months and we will share our findings.

And please, if you hear from a dead relative, drop me a line.

Chapter 21
Sensitive's, Psychics and Mediums

"What lies behind you and what lies in front of you, pales in comparison to what lies inside of you."
-Ralph Waldo Emerson-

This work would be incomplete if I didn't have a chapter on Sensitive's, Psychics and Mediums. Not because they are technology or a scientific tool, but they are a tool none the less when used properly. How analytical I must come across making this statement. As a scientist, it is true. People who sense things have a valuable place in paranormal investigating. If one accepts eye witness accounts as evidence, and data to be analyzed, then we certainly must evaluate mental witness accounts, or the input from sensitive individuals. While it is anecdotal evidence, it is clearly a part of the mystery we call paranormal. Like the rest of the evidence we have explored in this book, psychical evidence is pretty weak standing alone. But when placed in context and correlated to supporting scientific data, psychic evidence is important, both in gaining a keener understanding into the nature of the paranormal phenomena being investigated, as well as providing insights to the mystery of precognition, clairvoyance and clairaudience. By understanding one, we understand the other, to a degree and gain insight into the workings of the psychic mind.

Over the years I have had the opportunity to work with many mediums and psychics in the course of paranormal research. In a way, they come with the territory and traditionally, people seek out psychics and mediums to help them with hauntings. Some of these people are very good at what they do. Some are charlatans. But the people that consistently score high in their work are fascinating to me. How do they do what they do? Well I have a theory on this, based on experience, knowledge of Quantum Mechanics and human nature.

IF paranormal communication is indeed electromagnetic radiation, as the evidence seems to indicate, then sensitive individuals must be sensitive to these radiations. They call it vibrations (frequency) and this makes complete and total scientific sense. If they can read these frequencies, then they are literally receiving EVPs in their heads! This is not so farfetched.

In the 1980's, Dr. Michael Persinger performed a series of experiments with what became known as the *"God Helmet"*. The term God Helmet refers to a controversial experimental apparatus in neurotheology. The apparatus, placed on the head of an experimental subject, stimulates the brain with magnetic fields. Some subjects reported experiences similar to spiritual experiences. Persinger used a modified snowmobile helmet or a head-circlet device nicknamed the Octopus that contains solenoids which created a weak but complex magnetic field over the brain's right-hemisphere parietal and temporal lobes. Persinger reported that at least 80 per cent of his participants experience a presence beside them in the room, which they variously say feels like God or someone they knew who had died.

While there is significant controversy as to whether Persinger measured actual effects or just led his subjects into believing they experienced an electronically-induced epiphany, the experiments are interesting none-the-less and certainly bear repeating in a more controlled study. In December 2004 *Nature* reported that a group of Swedish researchers, replicating the experiment under double-blind conditions, could not verify the effect. Susan Blackmore, experimental psychologist and experienced researcher of 'paranormal' experiences, was reluctant to give up on the theory just yet. She said "When I went to Persinger's lab and underwent his procedures I had the most extraordinary experiences I've ever had….I'll be surprised if it turns out to be a placebo effect." Persinger, however, takes issue with the Swedish attempts to replicate his work. "They didn't replicate it, not even close," he says. He argues that the Swedish group did not expose the subjects to magnetic fields for long enough to produce an effect. He also stresses that some of his studies were double blinded.

Interestingly, from my experience, people who report ghosts in their homes tend to live in an environment rich with electromagnetic fields that seem to occur at very low frequencies. Even standard wall electricity produces EMF at 60 cycles, which, if at a high enough intensity, gives me the feeling that my skin is crawling, or that I have walked through a cobweb. Over the years, different members of my various teams have experience similar feelings related to EMF levels. I propose that sensitive's, psychics and mediums are sensitive to a specific type of EMF, what I call low frequency paranormal radiation. There is some evidence to support this.

A few years ago I ran an experiment on a psychic friend of mine. By using transducers, I stimulated her temporal lobes with different EMF frequencies, all 60 hertz and below. She actually got several hits while I was stimulating her brain, in the range of 12, 16 and 24 Hz EMF frequencies. Each one of these frequencies opened a door for her. This is certainly something I want to study further, but let's move on. To her, she was watching TV in her head, and I was changing the channels.

For whatever reason, true psychic individuals can be very helpful in knowing where to record EVPs, where to take photographs, picking up names of former occupants that can be verified historically, and generally proving information specific to an individual associated with the house. By cross checking the information, verifying historic research, and producing active evidence based on psychic suggestions, we have done two things; we have shown a correlation between an individual's perception and the paranormal phenomena, and revealed a common thread, energy or power that binds the two together.

If there is such a thing as life after death, and if when we die we shift to a higher frequency, we may enter a parallel universe. This universe, because it resonates at a different frequency than our own, can occupy the same spatial area as our universe, yet neither interfere nor react with it, except under very special situations or circumstances. One of these circumstances could be a portal or wormhole. The other could be psychic perception.

We are made up of energy. Our consciousness has its own frequency and our thoughts have their own level of radiation. When we die, that energy continues on. In physics, the law of conservation of energy states that the total amount of energy in an isolated system remains constant. A consequence of this law is that energy cannot be created or destroyed. The only thing that can happen with energy in an isolated system is that it can change form, that is to say for instance kinetic energy can become thermal energy. Now, think about this next statement very carefully, because scientifically, it is true.

The law of conservation of energy proves that something of us continues after our death.

Interestingly, ancient philosophers such as Thales of Miletus had ideas concerning the conservation of some underlying substance of which everything is made. In those days it was accepted notion that there was a "life force" but, there is no firm evidence identifying this with what we term today as "mass-energy" (for example, Thales thought the life force was water). In 1638, that rebel Galileo published his analysis of a lot of mysterious phenomena, including the celebrated "interrupted pendulum", which conservatively converts potential energy to kinetic energy and back again. However, Galileo did not state the process in scientific terms and cannot be credited with this crucial insight. It wasn't until Gottfried Wilhelm Leibniz came along (1676–1689) that a mathematical formulation of the kind of energy which is connected with motion (kinetic energy) was published. Leibniz observed and noted that in many mechanical systems (of several masses, mi each with velocity vi),

$$\Sigma\ miv^2i$$
$$i$$

energy was conserved so long as the masses did not interact. He called this quantity the living force of the system. The principle is an accurate representation of the conservation of kinetic energy in conditions with no friction applied. The common view at that time held that the conservation of momentum, which holds even in systems with friction, as defined by the momentum:

$$\Sigma\ mivi$$
$$i$$

was the conserved "living force". It was later demonstrated that, under the right conditions, both forces are conserved simultaneously such as in elastic collisions.

It was due to questioning engineers, not physicists that objected to the notion that conservation of momentum alone was not adequate for practical calculation and who made use of Leibniz's principle. Those wild and crazy throwers of the proverbial monkey wrench were John Smeaton, Peter Ewart, Karl Hotzmann, Gustave-Adolphe Hirn and Marc Seguin as well as academics such as John Playfair. Collectively they pointed out that kinetic energy is clearly *not* conserved. This is obvious to a modern analysis based on the second law of thermodynamics but in the 18th and 19th centuries, the fate of the lost energy was still a big mystery.

Gradually it came to be suspected that the heat inevitably generated by motion under friction, was another form of living force. In 1783, Antoine Lavoisier and Pierre-Simon Laplace reviewed the two competing theories of "living force" and "caloric theory". Count Rumford's 1798 observations of heat generation during the boring of cannons added more weight to the view that mechanical motion could be converted into heat, and (as importantly) that the conversion was quantitative and could be predicted (allowing for a universal conversion constant between kinetic energy and heat). "Living Energy" now started to be known simply as energy, after the term was first used in that sense by Thomas Young in 1807.

Thus the recalibration of "living energy" to

$$\frac{1}{2}\sum_i m_i v_i^2$$

which now can be understood as finding the exact value for the kinetic energy to work conversion constant. This brain fart was largely the result of the research performed by Gaspard-Gustave Coriolis and Jean-Victor Poncelet between 1819–1839. Coriolis called the quantity "quantity of work" while Poncelet named it mechanical work, and they both advocated its use in engineering calculations.

In 1843 James Prescott Joule discovered the mechanical equivalent in a series of experiments, on his own. The device of course that will always be remembered is the "Joule apparatus", which was made up of a descending weight attached to a string that caused a paddle immersed in water to rotate. Joule demonstrated that the gravitational potential energy lost by the weight in descending was equal to the thermal energy (heat) gained by the water by friction with the paddle. Hence energy conservation was proven to be a very real phenomenon. Similar work was carried out by engineer Ludwig A. Colding from 1840–1843, but little was known about this work outside his native Denmark.

The fields of Science are dynamic, as has been demonstrated time and time again, and yet its practitioners often anchor themselves in a static point of view. We have learned little in that aspect as just like new theories and discoveries today, both Joule's and Mayer's work suffered from resistance as well as neglect. In the end, however, it would be Joule's work that would be the primary work accepted by science.

The point I am trying to make here with this science history lesson is that we are made up of energy, and our energy exists forever. So while we know now that our brainwaves, nerve firing and essentially all electrical impulses radiating internally in our bodies continue after we breathe our last breath. The question remains, do we maintain the totality of ourselves after death and keep our consciousness? There is a great deal of anecdotal evidence that suggests that this may be so. All we have to do is find the physical evidence to demonstrate this. However elusive this may be, it is out there waiting to be discovered!

If you have the good fortune of having a psychic person on your team, use their talents. Monitor the environment around them to see if you can correlate what they report and what you measure. Check the history of the home to verify any information the psychic picks up. Establish a correlation between the psychic's data with the scientific data. These findings add yet another piece to the puzzle and add depth to the preponderance of evidence you must build to prove that we continue to exist after we die. We not only wire up our team members to voice recorders, we even wire up our sensitive in order to monitor her as well as record what she says and keep it all in perspective with the rest of the data being collected. I also believe that a greater understanding of how a psychic works will also lead to a greater understanding of what we are dealing with across the veil. This also may be a manifestation of the Observer effect in quantum mechanics. While arguably using a psychic isn't a part of the scientific method, it can be and may reveal new data if it is done in a scientific manner. We are just now learning how human interaction via the power of intention can affect the physical world in life, at least the data collected by Dr. Robert Jahn of Princeton P.E.A.R. lab and seed growth experiments performed by Dr. Lynne McTaggart offer strong indications that this is true, and I know it must be, since modern science today is reluctant to admit there is this connection. Thank goodness for the rogue scientists of today, because we are making progress in solving the mystery.

An interesting footnote to this chapter is that just prior to submitting the manuscript for publication, I had the opportunity to record a séance held at a client's house with medium Jane Doherty. I got Jane's permission to make the audio record of the séance, but I did not tell her I would also be running an experiment to test out an aspect of my hypothesis. On arrival, I set up recording devices in the area where the séance would be held, as well as an EMF sensor monitored by an oscilloscope and the data logged onto a laptop. Jane wasn't aware of what I was specifically doing until well into the séance when I commented on the data being collected.

At the onset, the EMF detector indicated a flat line response, or no EMF present. However, once Jane closed the circle of attendees by getting them all to hold hands, she verbally invited the spirits to enter the circle. At this point, a low frequency EMF (under 10 Hz) appeared on the monitor. This wave form fluctuated indicating there was some type of modulation on the fundamental wave. Jane immediately began to receive information and relay it to the attendees. Now at this point I am telling myself it is coincidental. But over the course of the evening, we would break and resume 7 or 8 times, and each time we broke the circle, the wave form disappeared, and the instruments flat lined. Each time we started again, as soon as she would invite spirits to enter the circle, the wave form returned. This continued during the course of the evening with a 100 % response rate. This was way above normal odds for coincidental occurrences. To me, at this point, I think the evidence is very compelling that low frequency EMF has some type of relationship with the event. Now at this point I don't know the source of the EMF. Was it generated by the medium? Was it a product of the attendee's intent? Was it from an outside source and did it carry the information to Jane in the form of modulation on that waveform? Did Jane act as a TV set and see and hear in her mind what that information was? Certainly these questions beg for a follow up series of experiments that I will have to design in the future. The results of these future experiments may offer a litmus to test psychical claims, and verify whether a person is actually psychic, or acting. It may also reveal the nature of the universe itself, and give us insight into the possible Theory Of Everything!

Chapter 22
The Theories

"Penetrating so many secrets, we cease to believe in the unknowable. But there it sits nevertheless, calmly licking its chops. "
-H. L. Mencken -

Author's Note: Warning! The following chapter contains mind numbing verbiage, raw theoretical mumbo-jumbo and quantum mechanical nudity. Read at your own risk! I will NOT be held responsible for confusion and dismay.

Just kidding. This chapter is not so much about equipment, but more about what is really going on with paranormal phenomena, or at least what I think it may be. It gets rather deep and abstract in places, but I will try to explain it as simple as possible. I will leave in some of the high tech stuff for those out there who may have a keener insight into Quantum Mechanics that the average Ghost Hunter. And for those of you who don't understand some of the things that follow don't worry; sometimes I don't understand it either.

I won't go into detail on the Many World's Theory of Hugh Everett, or other theories of a multi-verse, as entire books are dedicated to them. If you are not aware of these theories, Google them and read about some pretty mind bending physics. Picking up from there, let me build upon the foundations of those much greater than I.

A lot of people are talking these days about how scientific research in the paranormal is a waste of time because they believe we will never find the answers with science. Well I say poppycock! To them I would quote Dr. William James, M.D.:

"In order to disprove the law that all crows are black, it is enough to find one white crow."

And this is what I seek: The White Crow.

I have been researching paranormal phenomena as related to "ghosts" since 1976. Over the years I have pooled all the data I have collected while working with various groups, analyzed it, and starting to reach some conclusions. First of all, here is what I know. During active paranormal activity, Electromagnetic field energy increases, or spikes during an event. This energy often fluctuates at specific frequencies; these frequencies are often in the audio spectrum and excite the microphone coils and magnetic tape of local recording devices, resulting in a disembodied voice being recorded, or an EVP.

An amorphous shaped area of extreme temperature differentiation, more commonly lower than the ambient temperature, but occasionally a higher temperature is experienced during a paranormal event. A slight decrease in atmospheric pressure commonly occurs prior to an event. This can be from 1 to 5 millibars (100 to 500 pascals). I know that the ion count increases dramatically, most often the negative ion count, which generally increases by 3 or 4 thousand ions/CM^3. We also know, on occasion, the positive count increases, but generally to a lesser extent. I also know that if I increase the ion counts artificially in an area that is active, it has no measureable effect on that activity.

Magnetic fields increase, sometimes significantly during a paranormal event. Background noise levels increase all across the spectrum, from audio to light. Static electricity strength increases in the positive or negative range, usually 250 to 500 volts but sometimes as much as 5000 volts. Air conductivity increases prior to activity, and can generally be used to predict an outbreak. The conductivity fluctuates at various frequencies, generally below 100 Hz.

By artificially injecting energy (with a Tesla coil or even a Van De Graaff generator) into the environment during an event the activity increases rather dramatically. Activity increases when there is increased activity in the earth's magnetic fields. There is increased activity when the sun is more active. In some cases, batteries are drained during paranormal activity. On occasion paranormal activity has interrupted power to certain devices or lights. During and at the end of the event, there is alpha, beta and gamma radiation present from 200 to 400 mR/hr and it comes and goes, as if "blinking" in and out. There is significance evidence that cold plasma may be a byproduct of this action, creating a measurable ball of UV radiating plasma that some people call orbs. And while most orbs caught on camera are dust, some are definitely

NOT dust, unless dust discharges 35,000 volts upon impact with a good ground. There are measurable time anomalies associated with paranormal activity. So where does this come from?

My theory is a complex one, and like a fine jewel it has many facets to it. I will start with saying that interaction with a parallel universe is the most probable root source of these phenomena. It is even possible that the effects are due to a non-catastrophic transference of matter from one universe to the other. This may explain the physical measurements taken during these events. While I am not yet ready to say that ghosts are communicating with us, I am will to state that something with intelligence is trying to communicate, and there is a significant amount of evidence to indicate there is a space-time anomaly involved. The trick is going to be making the connection with this parallel universe in such a way as to gather direct evidence supporting the reality of the concept.

Part 1 – The Fundamental Frequency and Parallel Universe Theory

Many of my colleagues have noticed that I have a preoccupation with frequency. Actually, I don't have a preoccupation with frequency at all; The Universe does. I just seem to notice it all the time. Consequently I have proposed a new theory on paranormal activity, **The Frequency Theory**. In order to explain it, there are other things we need to explore.

The first thing to bear in mind, is that our Earth is encased in a donut-shaped magnetic field. Magnetic flux continuously descend into the North Pole and emerge from the South Pole, much like a huge bar magnet. Inside this field, the Ionosphere, resides, approximately 62 miles above the earth. This electromagnetic-wave conductor consists of a layer of electrically charged (ionized) particles that acts as a shield from solar winds. This is why we are able to live here. Without that protection, little life would exist on Earth.

Earth Resonant Frequency

Natural waves are created by electrical activity in the atmosphere. These waves are believed to be the result of multiple active lightning storms all over the planet. These waves are referred to as "The Schumann Resonance", with the highest energy level registering at 7.8 Hz. These are quasi-standing [scalar], extremely low frequency (ELF) waves that naturally exist in the earth's electromagnetic cavity, a layer between the surface and the Ionosphere. These "earthwaves" are identical to the frequency spectrum of some of our human brainwaves.

Reference notes:
Frequency nomenclature:
1 Hertz = 1 cycle per second,
1 KHz = 1000 cps,
1 MHz = 1 million cps.

Wavelength:
A 1 Hertz wave has a wavelength that is 186,000 miles long;
A 10 Hz wave is 18,600 miles long, etc.
Radio-waves move at the speed of light (186,000 miles per second).

Geomagnetic Waves

Geomagnetic waves are ultra-low-frequency (ULF) waves from roughly 1 millihertz to 1 hertz. Geomagnetic frequencies were first discovered in the ground-based measurements of the 1859 Great Aurora events (Stewart, 1861). Geomagnetic waves are believed to be the lowest frequency and longest wavelength electromagnetic waves in the universe. They are generated by movements in planetary structures that modulate a planet's magnetic field to create the wave.

The Brainwave connection

In 1963, Dr Robert Beck explored the potential effects of external magnetic fields on brainwaves and discovered a relationship between psychiatric hospital admissions and solar magnetic storms. He set up a series of experiments in which he exposed volunteers to pulsed magnetic-fields similar to magnetic-storms, and produced a similar response. The 60 Hz electric power ELF waves we use for power in the United States for example, vibrate at the same frequency as the human brain, in the range known as Beta. Beta waves are emitted when we are consciously alert, or we feel agitated, tense, or afraid.

Beta frequencies range from 13 to 60 pulses per second in the Hertz scale. In the United Kingdom, domestic power is 50 Hz. Studies in Europe indicate electricity emissions can in some cases depress the thyroid gland. So brainwave frequencies artificially generated may affect a person's physical being and perception if the field is strong enough, or in close enough proximity to the subject. Naturally occurring EMF can also affect the perception and physical body. As such, we need to keep in focus the potential of EMF influencing perception.

Additional studies performed by Dr Andrija Puharich in the 1950's and 60's indicated that clairvoyant's brainwaves stabilized at 8 Hz when their psychic powers were engaged. He reportedly witnessed an Indian Yogi in 1956 controlling his brainwaves, reportedly deliberately shifting his consciousness from one level to another. Puharich set about to train people with biofeedback to do this consciously, syncing their brains to the 8 Hz wave. A healer reportedly made 8 Hz waves pass into a patient, healing their heart trouble, while her brain was recorded emitting 8 Hz. These studies also indicated that one person emitting a certain frequency can create a resonance with another subject, syncing their brain to the same frequency. Puharich's experiments discovered that 7.83 Hz (earth's resonant frequency) made a person feel elated, producing an altered state of consciousness. Additionally, he discovered that 10.80 Hz caused riotous behavior and 6.6 Hz caused depression. Puharich supposedly made ELF waves change RNA and DNA, breaking hydrogen bonds to make a person have a higher vibratory rate. He wanted to go beyond the psychic 8 Hz brainwave and attract psi phenomena. James Hurtak, who once worked for Puharich, also wrote in his book "The Keys of Enoch", that ultra-violet radiation caused hydrogen bonds to break and this raised the vibratory rate. My own research from 1979 to 1984 on EMF on test subjects confirmed this phenomenon.

Nikola Tesla wrote in 1901 that power could be transmitted through the ground using ELF waves. He added that nothing could stop or weaken these signals. The conclusion was that a human brain functioning at beta-level (above 13 Hz) is agitated and can't change its perceptions, if it is artificially maintained at that frequency. It is possible then, that by artificially altering a person's brainwaves, you could not only alter perception, but stimulate psychic ability.

Hundreds of inmates at the Gunnison Facility of the Utah State Prison, and the State Hospital were subjected to behavioral modification experiments in order to test the concept for possible battle field use, as well as population control in a prison environment. In the early 1970s, this was brought out in the Utah U.S. District Court, because inmates who had been subjected to this supposed Tesla-wave mind-control in prison had tried unsuccessfully to fight its use in a highly publicized court case. The University of Utah researched how Tesla-waves could be used to manipulate the mind into hearing voices, overriding and implanting thoughts into the mind, and reading the thoughts, as well as developing eye-implants. While this story is widely reported and quoted upon from various sources, I have not been able to access any information or data on its actual use. I can say that my own research indicates that you can affect the perception in many different ways depending on the areas of stimulation, and the stimulating frequencies, or combinations thereof. And of course, no study on potential mind control would be complete without the mention of Dr. Michael Persinger. During the 1980s Dr. Persinger stimulated volunteers' temporal lobes artificially with a weak magnetic field to see if he could induce a religious state. The device he used was called The God Helmet. He claimed that the field could produce the sensation of "an ethereal presence in the room". Persinger's work certainly has its fair share of critics, and perhaps his controls weren't as strict as they should have been, but I can tell you that while I haven't experimented with magnetic fields, I have experimented with Electromagnetic fields of various frequencies, and not just at the temporal lobes, but on all surface regions of the brain. While the experiments were limited, there were indications that perceptions could be induced in this manner.

Maxwell's 'Hidden' Etheric Component

Evoked-potentials don't "officially" exist in physics, but in 1873 James Clerk Maxwell discovered that electromagnetic waves have 3 components. He found waveforms which existed at a certain number of right-angled rotations away from the primary electromagnetic-field. These hyper-spatial components are subsequently not affected by the constraints of time and space. He claimed that electromagnetic radiation waves were propagated by the *aether* and the aether consequently was "disturbed" by magnetic lines of force. This supposedly hidden component is now referred to as "*potential*" and the whole concept of Aether as envisioned in the past has since been discounted. However, various studies hint that approximately one person in 3000 may be naturally sensitive to this potential magnetic waveform component, and additionally that it may have a fundamental relationship with Psi ability in humans, but there is also sufficient evidence that indicates we may all be capable of tuning into this magnetic component by focusing our sub consciousness on it. Some researchers after Maxwell associated these potentials to mysticism (mysticism was coming into rage at the time), because of their antiquated beliefs that fields contained mass which cannot be created from "nothing", which is what potentials are, both literally and mathematically. A potential is an accumulation or reservoir of energy, in other words, an energy potential; but this hasn't been taught in mainstream physics. Interestingly from a sociological perspective, there are parallels in shamanism that support this notion. While the concept of the Aether may be obsolete, the Zero Point Energy Field may be its successor in modern Quantum Mechanics.

****Please note that some of the information posted below is based on purely logical and mathematical speculations and have not been proven or tested with experimental equipment and test results. However, when the theories stated have been backed up by experimentation, it is noted as such. The information is*

intended to encourage new mathematical and computational models which may encourage new theories and experiments based on the collected data and analysis.
***

There are several types of directed energy waves, particles, plasmas, and media that may come into play as associated with potential paranormal activity.

1. Radio and electrical magnetic radiation which are transverse waves that oscillate up and down or north to south. These waves include the cosmic, ultraviolet, infrared, ordinary TV and Radio waves, and extremely low frequency or ELF waves. All of these along with commercial power are the most common manifestations of ambient noise in our environment, and makes up the majority of the noise floor, or background noise we encounter in paranormal or any other type of environmental investigation.

2. Nonhertzian electrical and sound waves, which here are defined as longitudinal waves that propagate sideways, back and forth or east and west. These waves include pure electrical waves, and all sound waves including sonar and ultrasound. Tesla believed that energy could be transferred by means of waves of 'current energy' rather than Hertzian waves, and the term non-Hertzian wave "stuck to label this proposed phenomenon. However, modern Physics doesn't recognize any other interaction between charge apart from EM. In other words, there are no extra paths of communication between charged particles until you start to take into account the other fundamental forces (lesser nuclear force, greater nuclear force and gravity).

On the other hand, we do accept two different types of EM fields, and the relationship is important because we can then analyze any EM wave and determine it to be a mixture of the two kinds in some proportion. This is referred to as the "near-field" and "far-field". When you examine an EM wave that is a significant distance from its source, its E and H components have amplitudes close to the ratio E/H = 376.73 ohms. This "mystical" value is essentially due to the impedance of empty space. In fact, the further a passing EM wave is from its source, this value for its E/H ratio will be nearer to this "mystical" value.

This Far Field causes the E and H to oscillate up and down in phase with each other and represent a very real flow of energy away from the source. A proximity effect is also in play as components E and H fall off in amplitude in proportion to 1/range and the power density falls of as 1/(range squared). Consequently, these longitudinal waves are perpendicular to transverse waves and thus, "different". It is possible that these waves are also created by using nonlinear parametric EM circuits which could presumably cancel out the magnetic energies from the EM wave, creating pure electrical energy or even voltage wave oscillations by using a capacitor and a series of magnetic coils placed perpendicular to each other in all three x, y, and z axis.

3. Scalar or holographic waves, which may be a combination of two waves from the above, which interfere, intertwine and combine to form a complex holographic wave or potential wave which has no energy that can be detected until it reaches its destination point and discharges. Detecting these waves require the use of two conducting surfaces placed at a distance apart to measure both of the scalar waves if present. Scalar waves may be the most common wave propagation associated with paranormal events, as the alterations of the environment seem to appear out of nowhere.

4. There may also be subatomic particle beams, waves, and radar ionic gas plasmas such as electronic ion plasma clouds, neutrino's that are nonelectric or magnetic, tachyon *time particles/waves*, and gravity particles/waves influencing paranormal activity. These waves can be artificially created by magnetic accelerometers, atomic lasers, or even employing a simple Jacob's Ladder anode and cathode plasma antennas, and placing them into a directed energy beam. Subatomic particles may be rotated up or down, to change the properties of the subatomic particle to be antigravitational, antimatter, or reverse in time. We know that time anomalies are present at a paranormal event because we have detected them. Recent discoveries by NASA have added some unexpected fuel to this notion. Designed to hunt the universe for Gamma Rays, the Fermi Gamma-ray Space Telescope picked up some intriguing data from Earth while undergoing its testing. During its first 14 months of operation, the flying observatory detected 17 gamma-ray flashes associated with terrestrial lightning storms and some of those flashes have contained a surprising signature of antimatter! In at least two of those lightning storms, Fermi recorded gamma-ray emissions of a specific energy that could have ONLY been produced by the decay of energetic positrons, the antimatter equivalent of electrons. The observations were the first of their kind for lightning storms. So for those of you out there who think anti-matter doesn't exist? Think again.

Here is something else to take into consideration. A typical atomic particle or wave may be viewed as a holographic vortex which has 137 rings wrapped around the "eye" traveling at 13 times the speed of light, and 2 rings in the "eye" traveling at 2 times the speed of light. This potential to alter perceptions or influence perceptions of time may offer the foundations for what we term a *"residual"* haunt. We actually may be glimpsing something that occurred in the past. This voodoo demonstrates why I study all aspects of quantum mechanics with a passion. It is my firmly held belief that the key to unlocking the mystery of paranormal phenomena will be determined by its analysis at a subatomic level. But enough of this brain straining tangent. Let's get back on course.

So what is Frequency?

To review, frequency is a property of a wave that describes how many full wave patterns or cycles pass by in a period of time. Frequency is now measured in Hertz (Hz), where a wave with a frequency of 1 Hz will pass by at 1 cycle per second. Originally frequency was measured in cycles per second. Let's begin our journey of frequency discovery in the grand scale of things, and work our way down to the subatomic level.

Resonances in the universe

It has been surmised that the fundamental frequency of the Universe is approximately 1934.765 Hertz. Ok, so the Universe has a frequency. Let's continue...possible resonant frequency of Neutron Stars has been suggested to be about 4.9 Hz. Our own sun vibrates at a rate of once every 2 hours and 40 minutes. The Earth's Fundamental Resonant Frequency (Schumann Resonance) is approximately 7.8 Hertz. Is it possible, that our universe collectively resonates at a specific frequency? Based on current astronomical research I believe it does. And the beauty of this is, for our purposes of course, that another universe can occupy essentially the same space as us, and yet vibrate at a different resonant frequency, and we would almost never know it was there, unless of course there was interference between the two universes. Here are some additional interesting frequencies to add to the mixture.

Biorhythms

Physical cycle (23 days; Circavigintan), Emotional cycle (28 days; Circatrigintan), Intellectual cycle (33 days; Circatrigintan).

The Brain

Science knows that the brain is an electrochemical organ. Some have suggested that the brain is capable of generating as much as 10 watts of electrical power. I'm not quite sure how they arrived at this figure, but we do know about brainwaves, which are of course, electrical energy. Alpha brainwaves range from 7 to 14 cycles per second. Beta waves range from 13 to 60 cycles a second. Theta brainwaves range from 4 and 7 cycles a second. Delta brainwaves range from .1 to 4 cycles per second.

So the brain has frequency, light has frequency, sound has frequency and even Electromagnetic Fields have frequency. Every dynamic entity in the universe has an identifying frequency associated with it!

Is matter just a resonant pattern of spatial energy? Nothing in physics prevents this from being the case. Matter may just be the organized nothingness of space arranged in specific patterns, at specific frequencies. Our perception of a three dimensional universe may be the result of the human nervous system interacting with this energy field. The Zero Point Energy Field is indeed the Genesis Energy of the Universe. Our brain is put together in such a way that everything appears to us as three dimensional. But we know that the reality of this is an illusion created by our nervous system, because M-Theory tells us there are many more dimensions that we can't perceive. I believe that Matter and Energy are hyper-dimensional. All matter in the universe has a hyper dimensional projection associated with it which is beyond our perception. This "holographical" matter that we only see as three dimensional *could be* just resonance's in space. Elementary particles *might just be* node points of this energy which interacts with the fabric of space-time to form stable configuration patterns of energy that are mutually intertwined to the fabric of space-time and create our physical reality. The bottom line here is that our limited perception of the universe may only be a fraction of a greater reality that is beyond our ability to recognize. Resonant frequencies and double helixes of electrical fields consisting of positive and negative polarities of energy merging together into vortexual shaped flux loops that form stable foundations of energy in phase with each other around a closed circular orbit may be what the paranormal is all about. Whew, was that a mouthful or what?

Physicist Jon Wheeler has speculated that all matter may have been conceived out of the fabric of space. Simply put, subatomic particles could be made up of curved empty space. Perhaps this energy flow creates eddy currents that form stable vortex patterns or the ring like structures of subatomic particles. These flux loop particles could be fueled by the infinite flow of hyperspatial energy, the "zero point energy" field. And if the zero point energy field is higher or multi-dimensional in nature, and if it flows undulating through many different three dimensional universes recycling energy through them, then all subatomic particles may indeed be connected to this infinite energy flux or hyperspatial energy grid. Is this what causes entanglement? Space could be filled with a virtually infinite number of mini-white holes and mini-blackholes that act as hyperspatial energy channels gating in and out currents of energy through these spinning vortices with mini-whiteholes having rotation in one direction and mini-blackholes having rotation in the opposite direction. This double helix model could be a loop of flux from the very microcosm, to the macrocosm connected by a mini-white hole and miniblackhole. It could be this constant energy flux through these mini-wormholes that inhales and exhales all of the manifestations of matter and energy that is experienced in our reality. While this has potential to explain many mysteries of the universe, what does it tell us about the paranormal?

Let's assume for a minute that all matter is formed by manipulations of frequencies and in this ZPE field. This would mean that everything in the universe is connected via this grid of energy. All the information that was, or ever will be, travels through this grid, and like a gigantic matter replicator, spits out reality across time and space. Mediums may tap into this field to get their information. Psychics may also get their information from this grid. And all of what we call paranormal, may emanate from vortexual energy transmitted from the power grid. Infinite dimensions or collectives of dimensions may exist in layers that each have a reality of their own. Or many possible realities.

I have also been thinking recently about the possibility that within each of these higher frequency dimensions, still other dimensions may exist even within the same frequency band and space as other dimensions but are out of phase with each other to varying degrees. It could also be possible that this universe is based upon a specific energy/frequency pattern and that the modulation and propagation (frequencies and transmission) of this energy determines the parameters through which matter can form. In other words there may be a set of operating parameters (spatial, frequency) in each domain that provide boundaries for the creation of matter (structure) allowing only certain field configurations of energy to exist. I admit this may sound like gobledegoop, but the point is that the probabilities can be endless. In that aspect, to not have pockets of perceived paranormal activity on earth would be abnormal. Our task is to explain what happens in these pockets, and why they form.

If some of my diatribe were true, or even just in part, the implications would be phenomenal. At this very moment there could be universes very different from this one coming into and out of existence. There could be much different intelligence with some being more advanced than others by many, many degrees of intellect and logic. The entire UFO phenomenon may be a reflection of this notion. There could be different forms of matter within this same spatial dimension that have different physics but are still operating within the parameters of the energy patterns that exist within or makeup the framework of this universe. This might go far to explain aspects in Cryptozoology! If these different forms of matter do not interact except under strange or unusual circumstances that do not usually occur naturally or if so very rarely, then we may in fact have an explanation for paranormal phenomena.

Ghosts, and places for them to live CAN exist. What if our reality was a set of frequencies riding within a fundamental resonant carrier frequency, much like radio carries audio information, and TV carries sound and video? What if all the frequencies of our reality were at a certain phase? We would not be able to see or interact with other carrier frequencies, and there may be millions of them. And what about Ghosts? How is it that at times they can be seen, or felt? Well, what if when we die, our awareness shifts frequency to a separate reality? And what if, due to some issue, we only shift halfway? We would walk both realms, being a part of neither, but having an affect (interference) on both, because we are vibrating at the wrong frequency.

Think of it like this; two sheets are hanging parallel to each other on a clothes line rig with multiple parallel lines to hang cloths on. As the wind blows, the two sheets blow and flap with the wind force, often touching in different spots along the fabric. Where this touch occurs, matter from one sheet transfers to the other, and vice versa. Something is creating vortexes, or wormholes between these two realities, and stuff (matter and energy) is traveling back and forth. While it may be possible with the introduction of exotic matter to stabilize one of these wormholes for human passage, to date this has not been the case. However, energy seems to be able to penetrate the "veil" such as with the appearance of spontaneous electromagnetic fields appearing in the center of a room with no apparent source. And this concept led me to my current research on wormholes, or at least some type of portal that provides a conduit for paranormal activity to manifest in our reality.

The portal theory

For a long time now I have believed that there are fixed doorways or "portals" in certain areas of the world that may allow entities to travel from their domain into our universe. These entities may be spirits, demons, strange animals, extraterrestrials, or something we can never even imagined. I reached this conclusion based on reports of repetitive phenomena that has persisted over long spans of time linked to a specific location or region. Those of you who are old enough to remember the works of Ivan Sanderson will know what I mean, as he came up with the "Vile Vortices" theory after reviewing the data of ship sinking's and aircraft disappearances from around the world.

Evidence seems to indicate that many portals are at fixed places all over the world, and that they remain constant. Controlled experiments performed around some of these suspected portals have shown that there are definite unexplained temperature fluctuations, increased low frequency spontaneous EMF readings, increases in negative and or positive ion counts (in some cases like pulses or waves), transient spikes in alpha, beta and gamma radiation with no apparent source, increased background static electricity, and increased electrical as well as magnetic fields.

A case in point, I recently ran a time shift detector at a Leni Lenape burial mound located near my home that has been associated with paranormal activity and believed by many local residents to be a portal or "gateway of the damned". I recorded 14 time shifts over a ten minute period.

Photographs taken at many of these alleged portals have on occasion revealed mists, orbs, light streaks, figures, and even UFO activity. Many of these fixed portals are associated with the vile vortices areas of the world, as well as some Native American burial grounds, and other indigenous burial grounds around the world. Apparently, the tribal cultures had a way of identifying portal areas, allowing them to locate their sacred sites in a place where they would have the highest level of success in communicating beyond the veil.

While there may be several different types of portal phenomena, instead of going into the stable portals I want to concentrate on what I will call the dynamic portal; the opening that appears for a specific time then disappears. This blinking in and out indicates that the portal is in a state of flux, most likely due to dimension shifting or adjacent universe overlap. These portals can appear in many forms, the most common being a distortion of the area much like heat rising off the pavement on a hot summer day. Other portals may resemble a spinning cloud of mist, a shimmering curtain-like phenomenon, a near transparent sheet fluttering in the wind, or even a dark area.

Activity around the portal is abnormally high in retrospect to the surrounding areas, due possibly to the higher level of environmental anomalies or perhaps even the cause of those anomalies. Many of these portals are incomplete, meaning they do not fully open between two dimensions or universes, but rather partially open, allowing information to flow back and forth, but limiting the type of information that can pass, much like a filter. For example, electrical or magnetic waves may pass, but physical matter may not. More commonly, only what I call metaphysical matter may cross over. Metaphysical matter is a term I use to describe partial manifestations that may be the result of pure energy interacting with our reality. Plasma, mist, fog, shadows, shimmering apparitions, all I consider to be metaphysical matter. While the phenomena observed is certainly not fully physical, it has enough substance to be visible, to move objects, and possibly make noise or have an audible voice.

I postulate that a portal occurs when two or more dimensions or universes begin to overlap and interact physically upon one another. What this means is, in the case for a dimensional overlap, two branes begin to merge, and instead of creating a big bang when they touch, they superimpose, at least in a limited spatial position. This is possible due to both brane frequencies being compatible, or sharing a harmonic frequency with each other, allowing them to partially resonate without a phase differential. When the resonance occurs, we may have a partial or in some rare occasions, a full opening between the worlds. While it may be rare for physical matter to pass through a partial opening, it may be possible for a human or animal to pass through a complete opening unscathed. As I hinted to earlier, this may explain cryptozoological creatures that appear and disappear seemingly at will, or UFOs for that matter. M-Theory and Superstring Theory both support the existence of other dimensions, as does Holographic theory and my own Frequency Theory. Multiple universes have been proven mathematically in accordance with the Many World's Theory, or Multiverse Theory by Dr. David Deutsch of Oxford University. It is not a question of if they exist, but where and when. Activity around such portals tends to be dynamic and unique to the portal. When the portal involves parallel universes and not dimensions, it is called a worm hole. Paranormal interactions may be the normal result of two universes rubbing together. Instead of getting a fire, we get ghostly phenomena.

While it may be that there really is such a thing as ghosts, they may not be what we have led to believe from folklore. It may be that it is an inter-dimensional entity, a resident of a parallel universe, or even a version of us, from another reality parallel to our own. Imagine standing before a portal and having the fog clear enough for you to catch a glimpse of the other side, with your instruments at the ready, only to see yourself as if in a mirror, holding those same instruments and looking at you from beyond the veil. Keeping this in mind, I set out to see if I could find some answers.

The hardest part of the project is to remain objective. Let's take the initial trip to Williamsburg I reported in Chapter 6. The first inkling that I was on to something was the discovery of time anomalies surrounding paranormal places and events. The second clue was a burst of gamma radiation associated with recorded paranormal events. The Gamma radiation could have only been caused by particle annihilation. Something has to cause particle annihilation, and since no man made atom-smasher or nuclear war head detonation was present, there had to be another answer. A portal opening between two universes that allows matter from one to mix with matter from the other may be the answer to the mystery, and if it is, the implications are huge.

When we die, our consciousness may maintain its integrity as pure energy, and vibrate at a higher frequency, shifting it via a wormhole as pure energy, to a parallel universe. As I have previously mentioned, this coincides rather nicely to descriptions of people who have had near death experiences who report traveling along a dark tunnel with a light at the end. It is certainly food for thought, and experiment! So I built a wormhole detector of sorts.

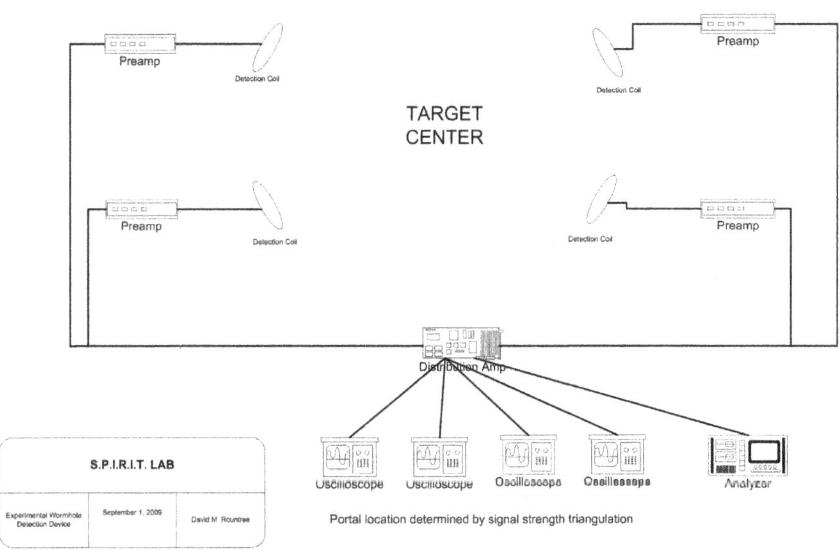

Wormhole Detector

After assembling the above device, I had a very unusual thing occur while I was in Williamsburg, Va. Labor Day weekend. I won't go into the details of that event since I covered them in Chapter 6, but I will go into the follow up experiment. I had to know if this was an isolated singularity or a common paranormal event. One case does not fundamentally prove anything, other than to increase certain probabilities. But I was quite excited over the fact that the answer to the source of paranormal phenomena may literally be at my fingertips! Consequently, a repeat experiment had to be arranged. So over the Christmas holiday, I returned to Virginia, and with some modification of the equipment and the addition of other devices, some borrowed as I had lent some equipment to a team member for use on an investigation, and I attempted to set up similar conditions in hopes of getting a repeat performance. I was not disappointed.

This time, there was not a telekinetic event such as the pewter salt shaker. This time a cold spot appeared and moved about the room, in conjunction with several EVPs. However, new phenomena and associated data was recorded. The event began with the appearance of a low frequency standing wave of brief duration. An EMF wave of 7.4 Hz appeared for approximately 1 second at an amplitude of 120 dB. The standing wave then began to vary from 7.4 to 2.5 Hz, but the amplitude remained constant. Additionally, Beta radiation was observed from four radiation detectors placed around the room (232 mRAD/hr, 328 mRAD/hr, 292 mRAD/hr and 392 mRAD/hr respectively) and low level Gamma radiation was present (310 mRAD/hr), and there was a time shift observed, causing the beat frequency of the Time Shift detector to decrease from 700 Hertz to 492 Hertz and hold there. Boom, the cold spot entered the room. The blob of cold was measured at 41 degrees F., while the ambient temperature readings were consistently 74 degrees F. The Blob of Cold was not stationary, but rather moved about, changing direction several times (five in all).

No air currents were measured in the room, and while cold air was seeping in from outside, the temperature differentials were confined to near the windows and doors. Some convection currents were present, but again these were caused by the heating system, which was on. Ion counts dramatically increased at the beginning of the event, using the Alpha Lab Air Ion Counter, from 345 positive ions/cm^3 to 4100 ions/cm^3, and Negative Ions increased from 635 ions/cm^3 to off scale. The air actually felt charged. Static energy increased from -635 volts to +800 volts, and the ion counter fluctuated for the duration of the event, but always higher than the original base readings. There was no significant RF present, and EMF present was ranging in Alpha Wave Territory through the audio spectrum. Two video cameras were used, and they went dark at the onset of the phenomena, and recorded darkness for the duration of the event, which lasted 4 minutes and 33 seconds. Post event analysis showed both cameras to be fully functional. The standing wave may have knocked them out. Barometric pressure dropped from 29.8 inches of Mercury to 29.1 Inches of Mercury, Relative Humidity remained constant, and a brief Ultraviolet burst was recorded.

At the conclusion of the event, the cold spot vanished, there was an audible pop, and the environmental readings briefly went off scale, a burst of Gamma Radiation was recorded, (390 mRADs/hr) and the readings stabilized to pre-event levels. It was over in less than five minutes! So, what did I encounter?

The Analytical responses were discussed in two different yahoo groups that deal with theoretical physics. Below are excerpts from these conversations.

From Tony Bermanseder

"What can I comment upon in your report above?"

First of all, your 7.5 Hz Standing Wave is the basic Schumann resonance is the 'auric' envelope of planet earth itself. It takes a lightpulse 2/15=1/7.5 seconds to travel the perimeter of 40,000 km of the earth as a 'great geodesic circle'.

The amplitude of 120 dB remained constant; meaning your power input and output remained constant in the frequency modulation from 7.4 Hz to 2.5 Hz in 7.4/2.5=2.96.

This factor of 3 so shows you that the Earth frequency modulated in allowing the ZPE to manifest this factor from the 'earth higherD field' as the 'cold blob'. Your 700Hz/492Hz ratio then is about half this factor in 1.4, which perhaps (I am by no means very familiar with electronic engineering) implies a rms Srt(2) averaging of the Schumann resonance coupled to the ZPE at say 5.3 Hz (7.5/Sqrt2) and as the arithmetic mean is 9.9/2=4.95 and the geometric mean is 4.3 between your two frequency bounds.

Secondly, the T-drop was 74-41=33 degree F or 23.33-5=18.33 degree C

18.33 Kelvin imply a boson eigenstate of so 1/622 eV or 1/32 of the neutrino background ZPE induction of 0.052 eV {A thermal neutron has half this energy moving at standard speed of 2200 m/s=Sqrt(2kT/m) at 20 degrees C (293K) in equilibrium}.

This so (and I am speculating here) then allows an intrinsic neutrino background (0.052 eV) of the universe (proven at Super-Kamiokande in June 1998) to allow a quasi-MASSINDUCTION in energy to 'energize ' this 'cold spot'.

To be more precise; the 0.052 eV becomes the mesonic ring quark-gluon coupling as the difference in energy level at the 3 eV energy self state, say 3+0.026=3.026 and 3-0.026=2.974 (eV). In elementary physics then, your cold spot becomes a ZPE energization from the cosmic intrinsic neutrino background as has as such little to do with wormholes.

The gamma emission is, as it must be, the pair-annihilation energy of a then say neutrino-antineutrino VPE as the experimentally confirmed muon-tau neutrino oscillation of 2xneutron equilibrium energy=neutrino energy. 0.052 eV/0.0016 eV~32.5 and this should mirror the change in your measurement parameters.

Your positive ion ratio was about 12 overpowered by the negative ion ratio and your voltages changed in |-635|+800=1435 magnitude for the 'charging'. If you identify say a standard neutron beta minus decay as a this 'change in ion counts', then the charge neutral antineutrino could account for the KE asa the manifested ZPE and the accompanying parameter changes.

So if one beta minus decay allows 0.052 eV to manifest as a 'pure ZPE'; then a thermal neutron diffusing in equilibrium as average KE (3/2) kT~2.8x10^-21 J or 0.017eV and most probable KE of 0.006 eV for 300K at so 2,200 m/s.; then the E=kT is about 4x10^-21 J or about 0.026 eV.

In first principles then it is a DOUBLE- or DINEUTRON beta-minus decay (supersymmetrically bosonic in higherD say), which 'taps' the ZPE to allow the quasi-pair production NOT as matter-antimatter manifesto, but as neutrino-antineutrino manifesto based on the Higgs-Neutroni energy induction as a gauge.

-Tony-

This is somewhat what I concluded as well, but the question remains, what triggered the event…
-David-

Your consciousness and efforts coupled to the physicality of 'volume' in which the experiment took place. Intent CAN influence experiment - as you surely know from half a century of paranormal research.
-Tony-

Wonderful. So I compromised my own experiment?
-David-

No, because the 'energy of intent', whilst ZPE only triggers the energy exchange, it does not add to it - in the standard lowerD physics of the conservation laws. The energy transformations, say in thermal neutrons interacting with the 'air' can be described conventionally, but the trigger is higherD in yet another energy exchange between the higher Ds.
-Tony-

This may be a parallel to the observer effect in QM in which field collapse is caused by the observer, but in this case, the power of intention, first pioneered at Princeton in the department of Physics (Princeton Engineering Anomalies Research LAB) by Dr. Robert Jahn, and further experimented with by Lynne McTaggart, may be a factor in the findings? This rather complicates objective experimentation then doesn't it?
-David-

Another offering from another group was thus:

"Presuming that no part of any exotic 'dark matter' has anything to do with the bio-realm seems unwarranted, in view of so many theoretical and experimental work including a recent claim that certain type of axions has been detected. A class of Bio-axions may yield axion chemistry akin to SUSY chemistry. This will involve ordinary chemical principles as duet, octet configurations, force carrier particles, spin and Pauli Exclusion Principle. The brain is then a many-particle system of neurons permeated by their bio-axion counterparts at an energy level relevant to mental activity which is co-produced by the visible brain and its invisible axion counterpart. It is likely that the entire visible body of an organism and its constituent's parts down to cellular levels may be coupled to and supervened by corresponding dark matter components. A differential distribution of the dark particles in plants, animals and humans, and their weak interactions with ordinary matter seems to have experimental support in the differential biophoton emission rates across the taxa. The predicted ratio of these rates between plants and humans agrees with the reported experimental value. Decoupling of the dark body from the visible body may leave it at a very low energy state, perhaps negative (- E = mC2). Though 'ghost' phenomena may therefore be unlikely unless this energy is acquired, paranormal phenomena such as 'channeling' in living humans may be possible by alien 'dark matter beings' who are already at a higher energy state.

-P.B.-

And a reply:

The axion is the RMP David. It supersymmetrises the strong interaction as the fifth gauge interaction and solves the CP-symmetry 'violation' in QCD. The RestMassPhoton (my label) is the vector Goldstone Boson as the precursor for the scalar (spinless) Higgs Boson template.

It is always left-handed and so couples to right-handed gluons and the suppressed antiphoton (see the gauge post you liked). The axion is massless, the inertia effect being the 'consciousness photonic quasimass' say as a neutrino energy. It so links to your EMF produced NOT from prior mass coupling (such as fusion protons accelerating producing EMR), but from the ZPE field without medium (space itself in free space impedance is superconductive 2ef=dq/dt with electron inertia flow in normal current dq/dt=i replaced by 2ef with chargequantum now a coefficient for frequency function f(t=N.2ef).

-Tony-

So in the end, there is not enough data to reach a conclusion. Additional controls will need to be developed to determine if there is indeed an observer effect, or if we are actually encountering evidence of a real and valid wormhole phenomena. The work continues.

If you suspect that you are dealing with a portal, use instrumentation to attempt to map out the size and shape of the opening. It may be possible to track it if it moves along at a level that is within reach so that you can measure any environmental fluctuations associated with it. While the results I have are so far inconclusive, they offer promise to a solution down the road.

And as always, like any researcher, I reserve the right to completely change my mind at a moment's notice.

Now that I have had my fun and turned everyone's brain including my own into Jello, let's move on to some interesting experiments you can try at home...or in the field.

Chapter 23
The Biofield Experiment

"One thing they don't tell you about doing experimental physics is that sometimes you must work under adverse conditions ... like a state of sheer terror."
-W. K. Hartmann-

Alpha brainwave detection may hold the key to identifying the nature of some paranormal activity. I base this statement on the fact that in many reported out of body (OBE) experiences, alpha waves flat line in the subjects. This would seem to imply that Alpha waves and consciousness are interrelated, but it also implies that Alpha waves may be the secret of our soul, so to speak. The problem is, how to measure free air alpha waves, and how to connect these emanations to a paranormal event? We are exploring the possibilities now with a modified EEG (Electro-Encephalo-Gram) device with a special sensor array in order to attempt to detect Alpha-like waves in the environment.

Electroencephalography monitors the activity of brain waves in an effort to correlate brainwave activity to various mental states, such as wakefulness, relaxation, calmness, light sleep and deep sleep. EEG is also used as a diagnostic tool to identify problems or potential problems in the brain.

We are also looking into another potential clue concerning reported phenomena known as biophotons. Biophotons were first discovered in 1923 by Russian medical scientist Alexander G. Gurvich. During the 1930s biophoton research was explored in Europe and the United States. Research however, was limited as the work essentially hit a roadblock with the limitations level of technology available to researchers of the day, and the concept was largely forgotten. It wasn't until the 1970s that biophotons were "rediscovered" in many experimental and theoretical investigations by European scientists.

In 1974 for example, German biophysicist Fritz-Albert Popp proved their existence, linking their origin to DNA, and later their coherence. These findings led his development of "The Biophoton Theory" in an effort to explain their possible biological role.

According to his theory, biophoton light is stored in the cells of the organism, specifically in the DNA molecules of the cell's nuclei. A dynamic flashing of light is then constantly transmitted and received by the DNA. It is believed by some contemporary researchers that there is a very real possibility that the biophontonic process may connect cell organelles, cells, tissues, and organs within the body and make up the organism's primary neuro-communication network and act as the principal regulating protocol for all life processes. Morphogenesis, growth, differentiation and regeneration seem to be defined by the structuring and activity of the coherent biophoton field. Additionally, according to neurophysiologist Karl Pribram an others, the "holographic" biophoton field of the brain and the central nervous system, may be the very substance of memory and other phenomena of consciousness. It has been theorized that the consciousness-like coherence properties of the biophoton field give may have a possible role as an interface to the non-physical realms of mind.

The bioenergetic field, in my opinion, is some special form of electromagnetism I'll call Bioelectromagnetism. I am in good company with this belief, since there are quite a number of advocates who claim that measurable electromagnetic waves are emitted by humans. I happen to be one of those folks who have wired people up and measured their radiation. And why would this seem fantastic to some scientists? We know and it is generally accepted by all scientists that black-body laws can be applied to human beings. We radiate energy in the form of electromagnetic radiation, as infrared heat dissipation. If our very essence, DNA, emits EMF in the realm of light, the whole concept of humans being luminous beings takes on a whole new meaning. This of course brings up the subject of "spiritual healing".

Elissa Patterson published a rather lengthy article called "The philosophy and physics of holistic health care: Spiritual healing as a workable interpretation" in the British Journal of Advanced Nursing (1998, 27, 287-293). In it, she associates "spiritual healing" to the notion that "we are all part of the natural harmonious energy of the universe." She goes on to point out that is a universal human energy field "that is intimately involved with human life, often called the 'aura'."

The aura…hmmmmmmm…

Paterson's evidence is subjective and anecdotal. She may be close, but she missed the boat a tad bit.

Some self-described psychics claim that they can "see" the human aura. In spite of what you may have been told, the claim has not been scientifically substantiated (Loftin 1990). Indeed, humans have an aura of sorts that can be photographed with infrared-sensitive film. But as I mentioned previously this is due to simple "black body" electromagnetic radiation in the form of heat dissipation. In fact, we "radiate" mostly in the infrared region of the light spectrum that is invisible to the naked human eye but easily seen with infrared detection equipment, or by your dog or any other animal with night vision capability.

An interesting footnote here is that due to the inability of the wave theory of light to explain the black body spectrum, Planck's conjecture that light comes in bundles of energy called "quanta" (thus triggering the quantum revolution) was born in 1900. These quanta are now recognized as material photons. I find it somewhat ironic that holistic healers find such comfort in quantum mechanics, which replaced ethereal waves with material particles. It is also painfully obvious that they have little in the way of any education in physics.

In spite of the spin these new age healers put on black body radiation, it is not a candidate for the theoretical bioenergetic field, for if it were, then even the cosmic microwave background, 2.7K radiation left over from the big bang, would be considered "alive" (but then again, maybe it is by some definition). The reality is that black body radiation lacks any of the complexity we associate with life. It is as featureless as it can be and still be consistent with the laws of physics. Any fanciful shapes seen in photographed human "auras" can be written off to optical and photographic artifacts and effects, uncorrelated with any property of the body that one might identify as "live" rather than "dead," with a healthy dose of the tendency for people to see patterns where none exist (Pareidolia).

Stefanatos (1997) wrote that the "electromagnetic fields (EMF) emanating from bacteria, viruses, and toxic substances affect the cells of the body and weaken its constitution. So the vital force is identified quite explicitly with electromagnetic fields and said to be the cause of disease. But somehow the life energies of the body are balanced by bioenergetic therapies. "No antibiotic or drug, no matter how powerful, will save an animal if the vital force of healing is suppressed or lacking" (Stefanatos 1997). So health or sickness is determined by who wins the battle between good and bad electromagnetic waves in the body. How dramatic! I also think Stefanatos was entirely too subjective in his research and relies on anecdotal evidence, as NONE of this has been proven. Not only is this vital force associated with common electromagnetic fields, it is also confused with quantum fields or wave functions. This is psuedophysics at its finest!

It would seem that all these effects of electromagnetic fields in living things would be easily detectable, given the great precision with which electromagnetic phenomena can be measured in the laboratory. Physicists have measured the magnetic dipole moment of the electron (a measure of the strength of the electron's magnetic field) to one part in ten billion, and calculate it with the same accuracy. They certainly should be able to detect any electromagnetic effects in the body powerful enough to move atoms around or do whatever happens in causing or curing disease.

Sadly, neither physics nor any other science has witnessed anything that justifies going beyond well established physical theories. No elementary particle or field has ever been found that is uniquely biological. None is even hinted at in our most powerful detectors. The search is still on.

Aside from the infrared black body radiation already mentioned, electromagnetic waves at other frequencies are detected from the brain, central nervous system and other organs in the body. As mentioned, these are often claimed as "evidence" for the bioenergetic field. In conventional medicine, they can provide powerful diagnostic information. But these electromagnetic waves show no special characteristics that differentiate them from the electromagnetic waves produced by moving charges in any electronic system. Indeed, they can be simulated with a computer. No marker has been found that uniquely labels the waves from organisms "live" rather than "dead." Then there is the whole Kirlian photography hoax.

Kirlian Photography is often cited as evidence for the existence of fields unique to living things. For example, Patterson (1998) also claimed that the "seven or more layers within an aura, each with its own color," have been recorded using Kirlian photography. This begs the question, "Who the heck was Kirlian and just what is his photography all about"???

Semyon Davidovich Kirlian was an Armenian electrician (not scientist, not engineer). In 1937 he was playing around with photography and discovered that if he placed live objects in a pulsed high electromagnetic field and photographed them, a remarkable colorful "aura" seemed to surround them. In a typical Kirlian experiment, an object, such as a freshly-cut leaf, is placed on a piece of photographic film that is electrically isolated from a flat aluminum electrode with a piece of dielectric material. A pulsed high voltage is then applied between another electrode placed in contact with the object and the aluminum electrode. The film is then developed.

The resulting photographs indicated dynamic, changing patterns, with multicolored sparks, twinkles, and flares (Ostrander 1970, Moss 1974). It was also discovered that dead objects do not have such lively patterns! Was this a EUREKA moment? In the case of a leaf, the pattern is seen to gradually go away as the leaf dies, emitting cries of agony during its death throes. Ostrander and Schroeder described what Kirlian and his wife observed: "As they watched, the leaf seemed to be dying before their very eyes, and the death was reflected in the picture of the energy impulses." The Kirlians reported that "We appeared to be seeing the very life activity of the leaf itself" (Ostrander 1970). Naivety is a wondrous thing. EUREKA! EUREKA! Well, not really.

As has been amply demonstrated by serious scientists studying the phenomena, the Kirlian aura is nothing more than a corona discharge, known about from as far back as 1777 and completely understood in terms of well-known basic physics. Controlled experiments have demonstrated that claimed effects, such as the cries of agony of a dying leaf, are sensitively dependent on the amount of moisture present. As the leaf dies, it dries out, lowering its electrical conductivity. The same effect can be seen with a long dead but initially wet piece of wood (Pehek 1976; Singer 1981; Watkins 1988, 1989).

Once again, like the infrared aura, we have a well known electromagnetic phenomenon being paraded in front of innocent lay people, unfamiliar with basic physics, as "evidence" for a living force. Unfortunately, it is nothing of the sort.

Proponents of alternative medicine would have far fewer critics among conventional scientists if they did not resort to this kind of dishonesty, trickery, quackery and foolishness. But then having talked to several of the pundits personally, some sincerely believe their propaganda.

All things considered, however, Biophotons hold promise for other reasons. Biophotons are ultra weak nearly undetectable photon emissions from biological systems. They are comprised of EM waves in the light range of the electromagnetic spectrum. All living cells emit biophotons that cannot be seen but can be measured by very specialized equipment. This light emission is a reflection of the state of the living organism being measured, and it can be used to assess and diagnose the cell's functional state.

There is a condition in the field of quantum mechanics in which the energy of quantum fluctuations can result in virtual particles spontaneously "flashing" into existence. These beacon particles (essentially matter-antimatter twins) interact, but due to Heisenberg's uncertainty principle they disappear according to parameters defined by Planck's constant. The theory has actually been proved by the Casimir Effect, which says, "*Two uncharged, perfectly parallel, conducting metal surfaces automatically attract one another if they get close enough.*" Having performed this experiment and detecting energy between the two metallic plates, I can say this is true. I use a modified version of the experiment in order to measure the air's conductance ability. Instead of reading current, I measure the air gap capacitance.

There are also biological waves (Bioradiation) emitted and resonated by all living organisms. The human body itself has a wealth of frequencies associated with it. If we are ever going to connect paranormal phenomena with the dead, we will have to utilize methods that can also acknowledge the living. Of course rigorous controls must be employed to isolate readings from the researchers from the readings of the researched. For reference purposes, I have listed a couple of key human generated frequencies.

The human body cell vibrates in the range of 1,520,000 Hz (1.52 GHz) to 9,460,000 Hz (9.46 GHz). Electromagnetic brain waves vibrate from 0.1 to 30hz.

The brainwave range brings me back to Infrasound, which I can't seem to shake free of. Key frequencies of consciousness fall into the realm of infrasound, therefore it is imperative to measure and detect its presence during a paranormal event. What we may think is infrasound may instead be a manifestation of a biological life force.

While it is true that energy can be transformed from one form to another, such as thermal energy becoming electrical energy, or mechanical energy becoming thermal energy etc., it cannot be created or destroyed. This conservation of energy along with the parallel conservation of matter are basic principles of traditional mechanics, thanks to Maxwell. But these two principles are gospel only with velocities (speeds) that are small compared with the speed of light. Once velocities approach the speed of light, energy and matter become interchangeable. Quantum physics demonstrates that light exists as two interchangeable forms: a particle (form and structure) and a wave (movement and vibration) also known as "wave particle duality". This holds true for the rest of nature as well. Everything can be experienced in the form of a particle and a wave. A simple example of this is to observe water in the ocean. It is both particles of water and movement of coastal currents, thermal layers and tides. As is true in the ocean, the human body contains and is affected by energy that can be blocked, flow freely or vary in frequency. Various forms of energy to explain this theory have been postulated:

1. An all-pervasive background frequency without form that extends beyond the limits of the body's boundaries
2. Vertical energy streams that act as conduits to external energy
3. Additional currents of energy with identifiable paths and patterns

The range of effect of these proposed background fields extends beyond a person at a distance unique to the person. Some people claim that they are sensitive to these fields and are able to see, hear or otherwise sense them. As I previously mentioned, heat emanating from the body is another form of energy and an expression of that person's energy field. Simple logic dictates that if we are made up of energy, or we radiate energy, that energy may still be present at the scene of a haunting involving a human who has "passed on".

Identifying and evaluating biofields presents particularly difficult challenges. Many components of energy such as temperature, sound, electrical charge, magnetism as well as visual effects have been measured in the laboratory. In addition to these easily measured energy mediums, other components may exist that are not measurable with our current technologies, or are possibly detectable or measurable but we are not quite sure of what and how to measure them. Quantum physics and associated technologies are changing this area of study rapidly as evidenced by the proliferating practice of using complex superconductors as sensors to measure concentrated energy bio-generators in preventative medicine such as the heart and brain.

All things equal, using superconductor sensors is a relatively new concept in medical science. As such, doctors and researchers are being challenged to find effective ways of measuring and quantifying their effects as well as the accuracy of their data via analysis. Additionally, standards for conducting biofield energy research have not yet been fully defined and are a work in progress, primarily because we have not properly defined the field that we are trying to quantify. Up until recently, research into biofields has been the domain of practitioners of alternative medicine, a field that has a tendency to contain a high degree of fraud.

There is a bright light in the darkness, and it comes to no surprise to the serious researchers at work in the paranormal field. The Center for Frontier Medicine in Biofield Science at the University of Arizona, with Gary E. Schwartz, PHD as Director, is blazing trails in cutting edge biofield research. We are discovering parallels within our own research to areas Dr. Schwartz is exploring from a much different perspective, (in his case, healing, in our case, discovering the nature of a haunting) although we think our work is closely related. Dr. Schwartz is well known for his work on the After Life Experiments, in which he performed a series of double blind and triple blind experiments with some well known mediums and discovered some very compelling evidence that supports the survival of consciousness after death. In the same vein, biofields may hold the key in linking certain types of haunting manifestations with a formerly alive person, which would finally help define the word "ghost". The trick is in measuring them, and then knowing that what you measure is indeed what you are trying to measure. Sorry for the play on words, but it's the truth. The frequencies so far associated with biofields fall in the range of Infrasound. Coincidence?

I think not.

So the experiment I designed involves using sensors designed to detect and measure low frequencies of electromagnetic energy. Instead of using traditional electrodes designed to detect and measure energy through the human skin, we will be using an array of coil antennae. The measuring devices will include a modified EKG machine and an oscilloscope. The EKG machine works on the principle of *triangulation*. Essentially, there are twelve leads, divided into four sets of three. Each lead will get a coil antenna. Each triad will be arranged in a triangle. Each triangle will be arranged to form a rectangular sensor area.

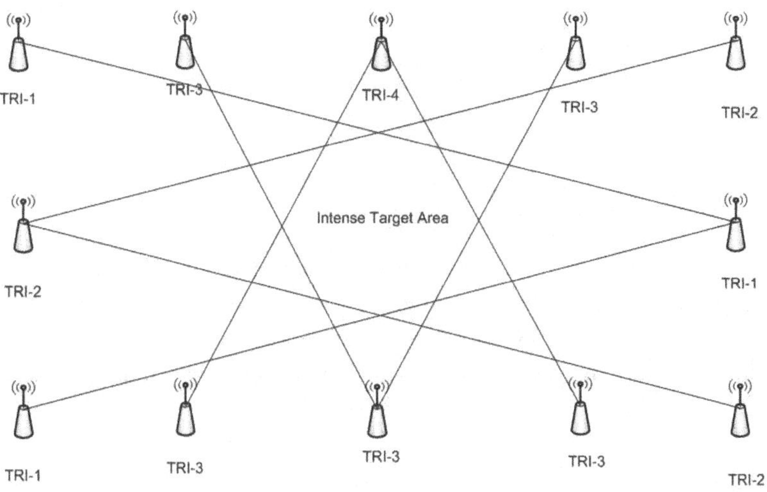

Biofield detection array

This will form an intense area of scrutiny as well as fringe areas of scrutiny. We will record any waveforms captured, identify the frequency or frequencies present, and correlate them with other data collect at the scene. We will then compare these waveforms with those on file of known biofield measurements. The end result may reveal information concerning the nature of a haunting. Our work to date has demonstrated a need for pre-amplification, so suitable pre-amplifiers are being studied for compatibility. This particular series of experiments is in its infancy and as such is still under development. We will update the website, www.spinvestigations.org when information becomes available.

Chapter 24
The Ion Bombardment Experiment

"The most exciting phrase to hear in science, the one that heralds the most discoveries, is not "Eureka!" (I found it!) but "That's funny"... "
-Isaac Asimov-

The ION Bombardment Experiment

Ions, simply put, are molecules that have "acquired" or "shed" an electrical charge. They are created naturally as air molecules that break apart due to sunlight, radiation, or moving air or water. Some researchers claim that it is possible to "feel" the power of negative ions by walking on a surf pounded beach or standing beneath a waterfall. The air circulating in the mountains and the beach is said to contain tens of thousands of negative ions, way more than the average home or office building, which contain dozens or hundreds, or perhaps none. But the real question is, since we believe that ion count is affected by paranormal activity, we then need to determine if it is a contributing source of the activity, or caused by the activity. Again, we need to monitor the injection of negative ions into the air at a reported active location. While our initial experiments seem to indicate that elevated ion count may be the result of paranormal activity and not the cause, much more data is needed before a conclusion can be reached. On the other hand, if there is some type of portal opening that facilitates the migration of matter from one universe to another, then it would be no surprise that ion counts under these conditions would elevate significantly near the opening of the portal. But what is an ion? Essentially there are two kinds.

Positive Ions

A positive ion is formed from the shedding of negatively charged electrons. While the total number of protons does not change in the ion, there is an excess number of protons over electrons which produces the positive charge. All electrons in the outer energy level are lost. Positive ions have been linked by some studies to health issues in animals, plants and humans.

Negative Ions

A negative ion is formed by shedding protons. It is the reverse or mirror of a positive ion in every respect. I have gone into the aspects of ions previously in Chapter 8, so a review of that chapter may help in understanding this as we move forward. The key take-away to keep in mind is that there seems to be a significant number of studies that have associated negative ions as being good for us and positive ions bad for us. The question is which are best for paranormal phenomena? Is the ion count a precursor to the manifestation of paranormal activity, or is it a product of it? What is the source of these ions, and how does the ratio of positive and negative change and affect the phenomena? We have designed an experiment to attempt to find out.

Prior to an investigation, when the site is inactive, the area to be investigated should have several air ionization units running at full power. Negative ionization of the air removes most of the particulate matter that floats in the air. Under normal conditions, dust and other particles are suspended in the air by the normal convective air currents present in the room. By running the ionizers and keeping the windows closed, you will effectively remove any dust from the air.

This will help eliminate the photographing of false orbs. This also dramatically increases the negative ion count in the room, and alters the ratio of negative and positive ions present. This should be standard operating procedure before any investigation.

Because we want to determine the effects of negative and positive ions, generators for both are required for the experiment. The path we have chosen is to purchase two ion generating kits from Hobbytron Inc.

http://www.hobbytron.com/product1432.html

The cost at this writing is 14.95 each. As a kit, they have to be built, and placed in an enclosure (not included with the kit). However, the device can be built to produce positive or negative ions, depending on the configuration of the diodes. For control purposes, we want to produce similar quantities of each type of ion for the experiment, so using similar ion generators is vital. Dissimilar generators may produce drastically different ion concentrations.

Once the room has been swept of dust by the purifiers, air sampling should be taken. Note the ion counts, both positive and negative. Energize the positive ion generator and begin taking your readings, and note any unusual phenomena that take place. After an hour, switch to the negative ion generator and note any unusual activity. By repeating the procedure over a period of time, you should be able to determine the influence, if any that artificially generated ion counts have on paranormal activity.

The goal of the experiment is to find out if there is a correlation between ion count and paranormal activity, and to find out what that correlation is with quantifiable data. It may be that in the future we will be able to enhance or possibly create activity by adjusting the environment to create a more conducive atmosphere to manifestations. It may also prove that we can lessen the effects, and possibly even rid the area of activity. It will be an interesting experiment to say the least. The other aspect to think about is, if my theory on portals is correct, then it may be possible to trigger a portal opening artificially by altering the atmospheric conditions in an area where paranormal activity has been noted in the past. To date, our own research indicates that elevated ion counts may be indicative of the fascilitation of a paranormal event, but not the cause. In other words, ion increases seem to be a by-product of whatever conduit is allow the phenomena to materialize. But this will have to be verified by many more researchers to be a valid conclusion.

Reportedly, research of ionic influence has been undertaken by many organizations with varying degrees of claimed success. The key issue I have with the reported conclusions from this research is that vital elements of the experiments have been omitted. Hence, replicability is not possible to support their claims. Hence the inclusion here of the simple generation experiment I have outlined above.

If, a portal does open between two "existences", be it a dimension, group of dimensions, or a parallel universe, then the point at which the interface or "throat" occurs between those two existences will most likely display some severe aberrations from the norm in the effects on the localized environment. My own experiments have shown that numerous alterations occur at this "paranormal" event horizon. Ion levels increase dramatically. Barometric pressure drops', indicating a change in air pressure is occurring at the interface, indicating a portal may be opening up and displaying these differentials. Additionally, I have recorded time abnormalities, elevated EMF in low frequency ranges, increased EVP capture, increase of air conductivity, increases in background static electricity, and bursts of Gamma radiation that would indicate that there are particle annihilations occurring at the interface, which could be due to differences in the matter flowing into our existence from the other. I can't help but wonder if the same thing occurs at the other end of the tube.

Recent discoveries in biophoton research have added a new dimension to our field. It has been discovered that our DNA emits photons at a very low level. One way to link paranormal activity to those who have passed beyond the veil would be to detect any photo activity similar to biophotons associated with this theoretical opening between the worlds. Since we have noted elevated ultraviolet radiation associated with paranormal phenomena, tracing this with a spectrograph would be very revealing in my opinion. Unfortunately, at this writing, the equipment is beyond my budget, and most other research groups currently in the field. But with this experiment, we can isolate one aspect of the preponderance of evidence mounting that may prove once and for all that at least some paranormal activity may indeed be related to the interaction of the dead, with the living.

Chapter 25
The Energy Injection Experiment

"There ain't no rules around here! We're trying to accomplish something!"
-Thomas Alva Edison-

It is generally accepted as fact that paranormal activity and its intensity are directly related to the amount of radiated energy in the environment. This is reflected by the statistical effects of Space Weather (Solar Flares, Geomagnetic Storms, Solar Wind, etc.), the draining of batteries during a paranormal event, and the momentary interruptions of power (such as flickering lights). Since there is precious little written concerning formal experiments proving the case for energy influence, and the only evidence we have is statistical, I decided to design an experiment in order to discover a demonstrable correlation. To do this, we chose to use a Tesla Coil to inject massive amounts of energy into the air at a reportedly active site. However, I believe experiments should also be performed with other devices, such as a Van de Graff Generator and even a Jacob's ladder. But it is important to understand how a Tesla Coil works, as this may be a formula for inducing paranormal activity.

Aside from alternating current as a commercial power source, the Tesla Coil is most likely Nikola Tesla's most famous invention. There are numerous groups around the world dedicated to building and experimenting with Tesla Coils. Stripped away from all the magical mumbo-jumbo hype, the Tesla Coil is basically a high-frequency air-core transformer. Using standard house voltage as a supply (120 Volts AC) it is designed to step the voltage up to extremely high levels. Voltages can and do get to be well above 1,000,000 volts and are discharged in the form of electrical arcs, much like lightning. Tesla Coils are unique devices in the fact that they create extremely powerful electrical fields simply by operating. How it works is simple; electrical energy from the secondary and toroid is transmitted to the surrounding air as electrical discharge or arc, creating heat, light, and sound. The electromotive force that flows through these discharges is created by the rapid shifting of quantities of charge from the top terminal to the nearby air, called "space charge regions". While the space charge regions around the toroid are invisible, they play a vital role in the appearance and location of Tesla Coil discharges.

As the spark gap fires, the charged capacitor discharges into the primary winding, causing oscillations in the primary circuit. This oscillating primary current creates an electromagnetic field that transfers to the secondary winding, causing it to oscillate in conjunction with the toroid capacitance. The energy transfer occurs over an adjustible number of cycles per second, and most of the energy originating in the primary side passes into the secondary side. The variable is the greater the electromagnetic coupling between windings, the shorter the time required to complete the energy transfer. As the energy intensifies within the oscillating secondary circuit, the level of the toroid's RF frequency range voltage dramatically increases, causing the air surrounding toroid to undergo "dielectric breakdown", and this is what creates the "lightning". The breakdown strength of air is approximately 30 kV/cm or 3 MV/m in standard conditions. The factors that affect the actual breakdown strength are air pressure, gas composition, and humidity.

To continue, as the secondary coil's energy increases, larger pulses of displacement current ionize and heat the air at the point of initial breakdown or the Tesla Horizon as I call it. This forms a very conductive mass of hotter plasma, called a leader that blasts outward from the toroid. The plasma of the leader is considerably hotter than the "lightning", and is significantly more conductive. The leader scatters out into thousands of thinner, cooler, spider web-like discharges called streamers. The streamers appear to be a bluish fog at the termination point of the more luminous leaders, and it is these streamers that actually transfer the charge between the leaders and toroid into the nearby space charge regions. The displacement currents from the streamers feed into the leader, keeping it hot and highly conductive. At this point you approach maximum resonance.

In a spark gap Tesla Coil like the one we use, the primary-to-secondary energy transfer process happens at typical pulsing rates of 50–500 times/second. This rate can be manually adjusted by "tuning" the gap. In our case, the gap is formed by two threaded bars that can be screwed in either direction to increase or decrease the gap. An increase of the gap reflects in a lower oscillation, and decrease in the gap causes a higher oscillation. The interesting part of the process is the fact that the previously formed leader "spider webs" never get a chance to fully cool down between pulses due to the frequency of the pulse. Subsequently, the newer discharges on the successive pulses build upon and follow the hot pathways left by the preceding discharges. I like to call this "Blazing a Quantum Trail". The net results are incremental increases of the leader intensity from one pulse to the next, lengthening the entire discharge on each successive pulse, creating a growing field of energy. By repeating the pulsing, the discharges grow until the average energy that's available from the Tesla Coil during each pulse balances the average energy being lost in the discharges as heat, light and sound. At this point, dynamic equilibrium is achieved, or what I call maximum resonance and the discharges have reached their maximum output power level. This creates long, wiry discharges that are spectacular to witness in the dark. They appear as multi-branched arcs which have a purplish blue color. An indication of operation is the strong smell of ozone and nitrogen oxides around the device while operating, as a result of the enormous amount of ionization the device creates. The important factors for maximum discharge length are identified as voltage, energy, and still air of low to moderate humidity (below 65% for our purposes).

The experiment also has some interesting spin offs; as mentioned it also increases ion counts and ozone levels in the air. We must search for the correlation, if any, this plays on paranormal activity.

Keeping all this in mind, I set out to determine if increasing the energy in the air would have any effect on paranormal activity. The site chosen for the initial testing had a rich history of moderate paranormal activity and is a private residence. The house is over 150 years old.

The equipment was set up and initial readings were taken in the area that was to be tested. Some stray EMF patterns emerged, but there were no significant spikes to indicate any activity was occurring. The frequency of the EMF was identified to be 60 Hz, indicating it was man made by nature and was traced to obvious electrical sources in the room. A cold spot was noted about two feet off the floor near the set up area. Mapping of the cold spot showed it to be drifting about, changing direction frequently and having a blob-like shape. The site showed elevated environmental levels for ion counts and some Alpha and Beta radiation. After a few minutes the cold spot moved off or dissipated and the experiment began.

I energized the coil and ran it at full power for three minutes. The resulting energy surge was pegging all of the sensors and meters being used to monitor the event. We temporarily shut down all sensing equipment until the coil was de-energized to avoid equipment damage. The result on the environment of course, was immediate (Note to all, when using a Tesla Coil, turn off all of your sensitive electronics! Cell phones included!).

There were several loud thumping noises, several migratory cold spots, numerous EMF spikes in the 8-10 Hz range, and an increase in photographed Unified Field Plasmoids (Orbs). None were present prior to energizing the coil. I did not capture any intelligible EVPs, but the frequency and intensity of recorded phenomena verses what was heard by the ear increased dramatically. It appeared that energizing the air in the room where the activity reportedly occurred contributed to an increase in paranormal-like activity. This is by no means proof positive of a definite correlation, but it is promising, none the less. Of course, we will have to repeat this experiment many times to determine if the data is real or artifactual, and others must duplicate the experiment and arrive a similar results. It will also be important to note any differences that other devices that increase the energy level in the environment cause to the perceived activity. It is also possible that by bombarding the environment with high energy and plasma may have resulted in opening a portal.

Chapter 26
The Voice Identification Experiment

"The task of asking nonliving matter to speak and the responsibility for interpreting its reply is that of physics".
-J.T. Fraser-

Recently, a friend of mine and I had a discussion concerning the use of voice identification technology to identify a ghost, specifically if you had a recording of the person alive, as well as an EVP that you suspected was from the same person. A correlation of the two files would be a significant piece of evidence that would prove that at least some instances of EVP is indeed from the dearly departed. It would also do much to prove the reality of survival of consciousness after death. First though, in order to perform a successful match, we would need certain reference files to work from, created by the dearly departed, before they departed.

The fundamental theory for voice identification is based on the concept that much like a fingerprint, every voice is individually characteristic enough to distinguish it from others through voiceprint analysis. There are two basic factors involved in the uniqueness of human speech. The first factor in determining voice uniqueness is the size of the vocal cavities. This means the throat, nasal and oral cavities, and the shape, length and tension of the individual's vocal cords located in the larynx all have contributions to make to our voice identification. The vocal cavities are resonators, sort of like the box you mount a loud speaker in. This "box" reinforces some of the overtones produced by the vocal cords, which produce unique identifiers. The odds that two people would have all their vocal cavities the same size, configuration, resonance and integrated identically is rather astronomical.

The second factor in determining voice uniqueness, and probably the most significant source of personal "identifiers", is the manner in which the muscles that we use for speech are manipulated during speech. The muscles encompass the lips, teeth, tongue, soft palate and jaw muscles whose controlled interaction produces intelligibility. Intelligible speech is developed by the rather random learning process of imitating those around us who are communicating. The probabilities that two people could develop identical use patterns of their articulators are astronomical.

Conclusively, the possibility that two speakers would have identical vocal cavity dimensions and configurations ion addition to identical muscular use patterns is extremely remote. Additionally, while there have been claims made that several voices have been found to be indistinguishable, no evidence to support such allegations has ever been published, offered for examination or demonstrated to the public.

On the other hand, several studies have been published confirming the ability to reliably identify voices under certain conditions. In fact, B.E. Koenig published an article in the Journal of the Acoustical Society of America in 1986 titled "Spectrographic Voice Identification: a forensic survey", in which he cites a Federal Bureau of Investigation survey on its examination of 2,000 forensic cases in which positive voice identification was employed resulting in an error rate of 0.31 percent for false identifications, and 0.53 per cent for false eliminations. I don't care what camp you are in, those are good odds.

There continues to be argument and disagreement in the scientific community on the degree of accuracy that can be achieved under all conditions, but there is agreement that voices can, in fact, be identified.

In order to make the visual comparisons of voices, a sound spectrograph must be used to analyze the complex speech wave form into a graphic display on what is called a spectrogram. The spectrogram displays the speech signal with the time along the horizontal axis, frequency on the vertical axis, and amplitude indicated by the amount of shading on the display. The resonance of the voice is displayed in the form of vertical signal markings for consonant sounds, and horizontal bars for vowel sounds. The graphic representation displayed is characteristic of the articulation involved for the speaker producing the words and phrases. The spectrograms serve as a permanent record of the words spoken and facilitate the visual comparison of similar words spoken between and unknown and known speaker's voice. There are other ways of identifying potential voice prints, and we will touch on those in a moment.

Now in order for this experiment to work, we will have to have a voice sample of the subject prior to their death. Consequently, this experiment requires quite a bit of preplanning. A predetermined set of questions should be formulated to ask prior to the subjects death, and afterwards. The questions should be the same in both cases. The idea is that speech samples obtained should contain exactly the same words and phrases as those you hope to get on an EVP after the fact as only like speech sounds can be used for an accurate comparison. Due to the nature of the voice, the results on any given day will be dynamic and contain nuanced variations, so it is important to get several samples of each spoken phrase that will be used for analysis.

Just like fingerprints, there is no universal standard for the number of words required for a positive identification. In Law Enforcement and intelligence services, the number varies from a minimum of 10 words for some agencies and 20 for others. An interesting anecdote here is that The Internal Revenue Service (yes, the IRS) has chose to use 20 or more like speech sounds to conclude a positive match.

Visual analysis of spectrograms requires the examination of spectrographic features of like sounds on the basis of time, frequency and amplitude. Specific sounds like consonants, vowels and semi-vowels in isolation or in combination, include the pitch, bandwidth, mean frequency, trajectory of vowel formants, distribution of formant energy, nasal resonance, stops, plosives, fricatives, pauses, as well as other idiosyncratic and pathological inferences. A veritable plethora data can be gleaned from the sound file comparison process.

Since this experiment hasn't been performed yet and is at this point a mental exercise, let's explore the possibilities.

First, we will have to devise a phrase or series of questions that would contain as many identifying features of the person's voice as possible, enough to grant a positive identification to the person. Then we would have to make an agreement with a test subject who was going to die, and then record a control message from the subject for correlation after the death. An agreement would be made that the subject would attempt to purvey this message during an experiment after his death.

Then there is the small matter of equipment. I personally have some very expensive audio analysis software, SmaartLive 5.0 ($695.00) and AcousticTools 4.0 ($600.00) that could do a general match up, but for an exact match, you would need some additional highly specialized equipment.

Equipment:

Present laboratory spectrographic and/or computer voice comparison systems do not produce conclusive results, but meaningful findings are possible with careful analysis of speech samples collected under forensic conditions. The minimum requirements include the following equipment (IAI Voice Identification and Acoustic Analysis Subcommittee 1991; Committee on Evaluation of Sound Spectrograms, National Research Council, National Academy of Sciences 1979; Tosi 1979; Koenig 1993; Koenig 1986):

1. An analog sound spectrograph that produces excellent voice spectrograms, especially under noisy recording conditions. It is being quickly replaced with specialized spectrographic software.
2. Specialized spectrogram software that produces digitally calculated spectrograms that have been optimized for the speech and forensic communities. This software should be user-friendly and allow the operator to control all the important time and frequency characteristics of the graphic representation.
3. Specialized forensic voice identification algorithms that are presently being developed (Nakasone and Beck 2001; Reynolds et al. 2000). When fully developed, this specialized, computer-based software will allow automated and/or operator-assisted voice comparisons between different voice samples.
4. Editing software that allows two or more recorded voice samples to be selectively isolated and combined into a new recording.
5. A headphone-switching box that allows the rapid toggling between two input signals containing separate voice samples for aural comparison.

Cost

Adding spectrographic and computer-based voice identification capability to Phases I and II would cost between $12,000 and $25,000 and would allow comparisons between unknown recorded voices and known voice exemplars.

While this is possible it is way too costly for most paranormal research groups. But could you imagine the impact a successful identification would have? There would be proof positive that we have consciousness after death, and maintain awareness, as well as have the ability to communicate. It would be huge!

A different friend was asking me about Facial recognition software to compare images of the dead to the living. This technology also exists. For example, there are some CCTV enterprise management systems that have the capability to detect several points of identification of a face, and compare it to a known database. The cost of this technology is upwards of $50,000.00. Now all we need are qualified subjects and a ton of money! If you meet the criteria and want to advance science, please, apply within...and send a check!

Chapter 27
The EMF – Digital Camera Correlation Experiment

"The most important fundamental laws and facts of physical science have all been discovered, and these are now so firmly established that the possibility of their ever being supplemented in consequence of new discoveries is exceedingly remote."
-Abraham Michelson Albert-

Often times the mere act of investigating a reported paranormal event inspires research into aspects of the actual equipment. Such is the case with this experiment. Is there a correlation between high levels of electromagnetic energy and anomalous photos taken with a digital camera? Over the years since the introduction of digital technology in photography I have collected evidence that would indicate that this may indeed be the case. While the evidence is not definitive, it is somewhat compelling.

Back in the fall of 2006 we visited a location in Flemington, New Jersey where we documented significant photographic anomalies. About a year later the team returned to the scene in an attempt to gather additional evidence to support some of those photographs. While we didn't get the evidence we were seeking, we actually got something completely different and interesting.

Upon the preliminary investigation of the house originally, we discovered a very high level electromagnetic field centered on the electrical service box in the basement. The initial EMF readings were over 200mG all around the panel.

As I mentioned above, we discounted these photos as anomalies based on the high EMF and the unnatural appearance of the photos (they revealed a somewhat fluorescent yellow-greenish fog and in some cases orb-like shapes, also of this odd green color).

During the actual investigation, EMF readings peaked above 250mG and the anomalies took on more of an orb like appearance and turning an almost "glowing" florescent green in hue. In our follow up investigation, similar photos were obtained using a different digital camera and different photographer. While the effect was less intense, it appeared non-the-less. A re-testing of the EMF revealed the field to be significantly less than the original measurements (70mG), but still way above base readings.

This would lead one to the possible conclusion that intense EMF may cause a digital camera to print anomalous imaging due to electromagnetic interference with the video processor. I may also suggest that certain orb-like imagery and perceived ecto-plasmic imagery may be related to above normal EMF. My team continues to repeat this procedure in the field, of photographing objects or areas of intense EMF strength. The procedure is simple;

First, check the area around the electrical panel or object emitting high EMF (over 50 mG) for high EMF, ion count, static electricity, radiation, and RF levels if possible. For sure, check and monitor EMF closely. Photograph the electrical panel or object from different angles with different cameras (at least two) and include the EMF meter in the shot. Continue with other aspects of the investigation. You should document the team's activities with video and audio for record keeping and verification of evidence, as well as to place a time frame on everything in the investigations. If you employ a roving video camera as part pf your investigative protocol, film the area in question as well. Record findings and compare photographs later to see if any anomalies are present and discuss findings.

The ramifications of this are enormous. A correlation between EMF and photographic anomalies may indicate that much of the phenomena we encounter in this field have a natural explanation. It also may indicate that there is an unknown source of EMF that may be the effect, cause, enabling factor or by-product of a paranormal effect. It may also indicate that EMF feeds or intensifies paranormal phenomena, which would explain why some places are "haunted" and some are not. It will also require mapping EMF during an event, and trying to pinpoint its source. The data may indicate that a resonance is occurring between two or more dimensions or parallel universes, and the EMF burst is a reaction of that interface. The possibilities are fascinating! It is also possible that we may have accidentally stumbled upon an example of the Zero Point Energy Field, or any number of a thousand other possible explanations.

It is imperative that we gather as much data as possible. Measure everything, correlate it on a timeline and document it. But this type of research is not limited to areas where activity is reported. It is also important to perform the experiment in areas where activity is known to NEVER occur. Measure your own homes, as it will establish viable control readings as well as possibly identifying wiring issues in your home that may be a fire hazard. What I do know, is if this is a real and not artifactual occurrence, then it only strengthens the need to identify the sources of EMF in the field. While the team I work with is already working on this phenomenon, the possibilities that the reality of this imposes are numerous, requiring measurement of every segment of the radiation spectrum, which will require new equipment configurations as well as protocols for detecting and measuring the possible sources.

This leads me to believe that something is creating a resonance that allows two fields that don't normally react to each other, interfere with each other. This resonance is creating an environment conducive to paranormal activity or paranormal appearing phenomena, by creating either a portal for it to enter from parts unknown, or feeding a naturally occurring condition to intensify the effects. Or it could simply be normal laws of physics from an unknown as of yet source.

This is an example, along with the possible correlation of EMF and EVP that makes the field exciting. It is conceivable that the answer to the paranormal question may open up a realm of Quantum Mechanics that has here-to-fore been relegated to pure theory. It may unlock the secrets to time, dimensional and inter-universe travel. If we can identify and measure the effects, then we can attempt to artificially recreate them. If we can recreate them, then it is possible to open the threshold, at will, to the cause and source of what we term paranormal phenomena.

Chapter 28
The Enigma of Water Pipes

"It is a capital mistake to theorize before one has data. Insensibly one begins to twist facts to suit theories instead of theories to suit facts."
-Sherlock Holmes, the fictional creation of Arthur Conan Doyle-

Every paranormal investigation is a new adventure. Generally, a good investigator measures the EMF fields in every room, at selected appliances, and around the outside property. But only a few folks measure magnetic fields. Whether one performs a comprehensive contour or spot measurement survey, the process is rather straightforward: measure and record the magnetic field levels, note significant levels, identify sources, establish base readings for each room. The electromagnetic fields from nearby electrical power line sources (transmission, distribution, and service) are easy to measure and identify. Appliance sources usually jump right out of the display as you walk by. But few investigative groups measure magnetic fields as they either don't have the equipment, or they rarely have any readings to compare the data to.

The reality is everything we can think of needs to be measured and monitored. A case in point, high levels of magnetic as well as electromagnetic fields in a home environment can have effect on the long term occupants who are exposed to these levels. Both EMF and MF have been associated with visual hallucinations as well as mental hallucinatory effects. While it is obvious that appliances and other power using machinery emit EMF, what is not so obvious is plumbing can as well. In fact, magnetic fields from plumbing and ground currents can mystify and perplex the most experienced investigator, particularly if they are not even aware of their existence.

If there is an elevated magnetic field near a metal water pipe, especially next to the shut-off valve at the point of entry, then plumbing currents are probably the source. Any horizontally polarized magnetic fields perpendicular to the water pipe axis radiate out from the pipe diminishing in magnitude at a linear 1/r rate. The current on the pipe can be calculated as follows:

Iamps = .15(BmG)(Rfeet) where BmG is magnetic flux density in milligauss.

However, if you aren't a math wiz, it is much easier to use a clamp-on amp meter around the water pipe, preferably near the entry point. In a residence the typical plumbing current measures between .25-2.5 amps, depending on the local neighborhood electrical conditions. Place the clamp-on meter around the water pipe and monitor the current which normally fluctuates (sometimes dramatically) over several minutes. Be sure to note this in your base readings and brief your team. This is a dramatic source of magnetic and EMF that are not only false readings, but may be the actual cause of the perceived paranormal activity! Additionally, notify the client and the local power company should be notified if the external plumbing current exceeds 3-4 amps.

Plumbing currents can migrate from the water pipes into HVAC ductwork, metal conduits, BX metal sheaths, and grounded equipment housings (sink disposal, coffee machine, etc) emanating magnetic fields everywhere. To eliminate an external plumbing current source, a licensed plumber must install a high-quality dielectric coupler a few inches from the water meter near the street. This will not only eliminate the high magnetic/EMF, it may also eliminate the ghost.

The experiment is this; using a clamp on amp meter, check the water pipes of the home at the source and determine if there is a high magnetic field present. Chances are the data will reveal that all homes who report paranormal-like occurrences will also have a high magnetic field associated with the water supply. If this is so, reducing that field may also reduce the effects.

Chapter 29
Dowsing

"I do not know what I may appear to the world; but to myself I seem to have been only like a boy playing on the seashore, and diverting myself in now and then finding of a smoother pebble or a prettier shell than ordinary, whilst the great ocean of truth lay all undiscovered before me."
-Sir Isaac Newton-

Dowsing has long been viewed as magic in folklore, and a hoax by science. But now, a popular trend in paranormal circles is to use dowsing as part of the investigative process. A lot of people have asked me about the validity of this practice, and my initial response has been to say that there is no validity to the use of dowsing in performing research into the paranormal.

There is however, evidence that Dowsing may be indicating something rather mysterious. The whole effect of dowsing in general was studied scientifically at a barn in Germany a few years back in what has come to be known as the "Munich Experiment".

In this experiment, researchers came to the conclusion that the dowsing phenomenon is in fact real. The realness of it is not based on subconscious or collective hallucination, but in the response of dowsing rods without human interaction to what appears to be a form of unknown energy flow.

It has been proven time and time again that dowsing requires no special talent or personal power. You can try this yourself. Take two wire coat hangers and untwist them. Cut away the areas you cannot straighten with pliers, and cut them to the exact same length. Take the two straight pieces of wire and bend one end of each with a 90° bend, creating a "handle about 8" long. Next take a soda straw and cut it in half. Insert the handles through the straws and hold them about 6 inches apart, with the rods pointing out in front of you. Walk around in your yard. You will find an area where the rods converge, or where they move apart, almost magically, regardless of what your hands are doing.

I took the exercise a bit further; I searched around in my shed and grabbed my fertilizer broadcaster. I then fixed the two rods to either side of the handles using tie-raps, and pushed it around the yard to find an area that affects the rods. The idea is to remove hand movement from the mix entirely. It's a lead pipe cinch at some point, the rods will move as if by themselves. Magic? Hardly.

Paranormal? No way!

Or is it?

Additional scientific based research has been performed, but it seems to center around the person as the enabler, not the device. While the Munich Experiment has been refuted by many scientific organizations, the enigma of dowsing remains; the basic truth is it works for me and I have no special abilities to my knowledge. I use it around the house to locate buried water pipes and electric lines, and recently used it to locate a buried phone line. I got the practice from my Uncle Raymond, who still uses two bent coat hangers around his yard to this day. It works.

But how?

I have always thought that the rods were responding to a directional magnetic field. However, I was recently watching a show that covered the case of UFO's reported around prehistoric sites, and of course it included trying to track "ley" lines with dowsing. Bearing in mind it WAS a TV show, hence any semblance of reality was for the most part buried in drama, but it made me think. The researchers used a magnetometer to measure the field present when the rods reacted. According to them, there was no magnetic field present. This seemed to shoot my theory in the foot. Now my curiosity was peaked. What DOES cause the reaction in dowsing rods?

It has been proven by many researchers including James Randi that dowsing is unreliable in finding wire, metal objects and water. On this note I would tend to agree, except now there seems to be new research to the contrary, as reported in this article in Popular Mechanics:

http://www.popularmechanics.com/science/research/1281661.html

Some proposed explanations

Most serious scientists scoff at the idea of dowsing being anything other than fantasy (as would I, had it not worked for me and continues to do so).

But some researchers have weighed in on the subject offering possible causes for the dowsing phenomenon. Recent experiments have been conducted into a phenomenon called electroreception. Electroreception is the biological ability some animals possess that allows them to receive and make use of electrical impulses. It is much more common among aquatic creatures, as water is a far superior propagation medium than air. Electroreception in nature is primarily used for electro-location, or the ability to use electric fields to locate objects, such as food.

I have discussed this concept with a friend who is a marine biologist. He enlightened me on the subject by explaining to me that primitive fish such as sharks, rays, lampreys, lungfish, coelacanths, and sturgeons have electroreceptive senses. Strangely, electroreception appears to be absent in most relatively modern fish except for the catfish, and the electric eel. There are two main modes of electroreception, active and passive. Active electroreception creatures are sensitive to high frequencies (20-20,000 Hz). Passive electroreception creatures utilize receptors which are sensitive to low frequencies (below 50 Hz). To me, this stuff is absolutely fascinating!

Active electroreception

An animal that uses "active" electroreception senses its surroundings by generating electric fields and detecting anomalies in these fields using their electroreceptor organs. Much like a bio-radar, this ability is important in cloudy water, where visibility is low. An example of this would be the weakly electric fish which generates very small electrical bio-pulses via an organ in the tail made up of two to five rows of modified muscle cells called electrocytes. They can actually discriminate between objects of differing resistance and capacitance values, which many marine biologist believe may help them in identifying an object. The weakly electric fish kicks it up a notch however, in that they can also communicate with each other via modulating the electrical waveform they generate; this is called "electrocommunication". Active electroreception generally is short ranged, only about one body length. An interesting anecdote is that objects with an electrical resistance similar to that of water are nearly undetectable by these animals.

Passive electroreception

An animal that is able to employ "passive" electroreception senses the weak bioelectric fields generated by other animals, much like passive sonar detects shipping. Sharks and rays are typical examples of creatures that use passive electroreception. Since there isn't a shred of evidence to indicate humans have this ability, and unless your dowsing is being performed by a lungfish, I think it is safe to say that this is most likely NOT a contributing factor to human dowsing.

Another proposed possibility which may have some merit is Magnetoception. Magnetoception is the ability to detect changes in a magnetic field to perceive direction or altitude and has even been postulated as a method for animals to develop regional maps and assist with migration. This is pretty amazing stuff when you think about it. It is most commonly observed in birds, though it has also been noted in many other animals including insects such as honeybees and amphibians, specifically turtles.

Researchers have identified a probable sensor in pigeons as a small, region of the skull which contains biological magnetite. Interestingly I found out that Humans have a similar magnetite deposit in the ethmoid bone of the nose, and there is some evidence this gives humans some magnetoception. This would explain a lot of things in my humble opinion, as it offers a scientific explanation for human conditions such as Electromagnetic Hyperactivity Sensitivity and Disorder, something many scientist dismiss. It also brings up the question, is an elevated sensitivity to magnetic or EMF energy a factor in Medium and psychic performance?

Although there is little dispute that a magnetic sense exists in most birds since it is essential to the navigation of migratory birds, it is a controversial and not well-understood phenomenon. To compound the issue, certain types of bacteria called magnetotactic bacteria, and some fungi are also known to sense flux direction, through organelles known as magnetosomes. In bees for example, magnetite is embedded across the cellular membrane of a small group of neurons. The theory is that when the magnetite aligns with the Earth's magnetic field, induction causes a current to cross the membrane which depolarizes the cell. Now this has some real possibilities in the field of paranormal research AND dowsing.

A telluric current (from Latin tellus, "earth") is a special kind of electrical current that can move through the ground or through the sea. Telluric currents result from both natural causes and human generated activity, and these simple currents interact in a highly complex manner. The currents are extremely low frequency and travel over large areas at or near the surface of the Earth. Telluric currents are phenomena observed primarily in the Earth's crust and mantle. In September of 1862, an experiment to specifically address Earth currents was carried out in the Munich Alps (Lamont, 1862). The currents are primarily induced by changes in the outer part of the Earth's magnetic field, which are usually caused by interactions between the solar wind and the magnetosphere or solar radiation effects on the ionosphere. Space weather! Tellurics also result from thunderstorms. Both of these areas are believed to be related to the frequency and intensity of paranormal activity, at least statistically.

The electric potential on the Earth's surface can be measured at different points, enabling us to calculate the magnitudes and directions of the telluric currents and subsequently from these equations we can also calculate the Earth's conductance. Telluric currents move between each half of the terrestrial globe endlessly. Telluric currents move toward the equator in the daytime and towards the poles at night. The field varies in time and over the frequency range 0.001 to 5 Hz (Krasnogorskaja & Remizov, 1975). Electrical potential caused by telluric currents range from 0.2 to 1000 volts per meter. (Krasnogorskaja and Remizov, 1975; Vanjan, 1975). At any location, the current density is a direct function of the inter-hemispheric currents and their potential gradients (In vector calculus, the gradient of a scalar field is a vector field which points in the direction of the greatest rate of increase of the scalar field, and whose magnitude is the greatest rate of change). Telluric currents are scalar fields.

Scientists estimate that telluric currents can generate between 100 and 1000 amperes during a twelve hour period in one hemisphere. At this level there is sufficient energy to move the air to create atmospheric electricity, from global fair weather to the most violent of thunderstorms.

Both the telluric and magnetotelluric currents are used commercially for exploring the structure beneath the Earth's surface. For mineral exploration and mining the targets are conductive ore bodies. Other commercial uses include exploration of geothermal fields, petroleum reservoirs, fault zones, ground water, magma chambers, and plate tectonic boundaries. Telluric currents can be harnessed to produce a useful low voltage current by means of earth batteries. Such devices were used for telegraph systems in the United States as far back as 1859. I know a lot of conspiracy fanatics who preach that the High Frequency Active Auroral Research Program (HAARP) in Alaska is responsible for all manner of weather controls and other nasty phenomena, but it simply isn't so. The reality is that the Ionospheric Research Instrument (IRI), which is a high power transmitter facility operating in the High Frequency (HF) range is used to temporarily excite a limited area of the ionosphere for scientific study, much like high altitude solar bombardment affects the ionosphere. It artificially stimulates the Aurora Borealis, but has no influence on the weather. It operates at too high a frequency. This brings us to quantum biology.

Quantum Biology (QB) is a highly speculative and interdisciplinary field that seeks to link quantum physics and the life sciences. A branch that is becoming really popular these days is Quantum Neurology (QN). QB is an attempt to study biological processes in terms of quantum mechanics

(QM), using quantum theory to study the structure, energy transfer and chemical reactions of biological molecules in an effort to apply quantum principles to macroscopic systems as opposed to the atomic or subatomic realms generally described by quantum theory. Quantum biology uses mathematical computation to model biological interactions in light of QM effects. The current study of biophotons and biofields fall into this realm of science. While QB deals with the entire biosystem, QN deals with the mind-brain connection.

Some of the biological phenomena that have been studied in terms of quantum processes are the absorption of frequency-specific radiation such as photosynthesis and vision; the conversion of chemical energy into motion; magnetoreception in animals and Brownian motors (nano-scale or molecular devices by which thermally activated processes are controlled and used to generate directed motion in space and to do mechanical or electrical work) in a wide variety of cellular processes. The field has also been active in researching QM analysis of magnetic fields and bird navigation, and may possibly shed light on Circadian rhythms (a circadian rhythm is a roughly 24-hour cycle in the biochemical, physiological or behavioral processes of all living entities) in many organisms.

Ok, sorry for the side trip, but it provides a little perspective as a backdrop. In the scientific study of dowsing in Munich, five hundred dowsers were initially tested for their "skill". The researchers then selected the best 43 among them. These 43 were then tested as follows; on the ground floor of a two-story barn, water was pumped through a pipe; before each test, this pipe was moved in a direction perpendicular to the water flow. On the upper floor, each dowser was asked to determine the position of the pipe. Over two years, the 43 dowsers performed 843 such tests. Of the 43 pre-selected and extensively tested candidates, at least 37 of them showed no dowsing ability. The results from the remaining 6 were said to be better than chance, resulting in the researchers conclusion that some dowsers "in particular tasks, showed an extraordinarily high rate of success, which can scarcely if at all be explained as due to chance ... a real core of dowser-phenomena can be regarded as empirically proven" But there is a big problem with this experiment. It assumes that the field the dowser is attempting to detect is not subject to a common phenomena associated with all energy fields; The Proximity Effect.

The Proximity effect has many meanings, but they refer essentially to the same things. Essentially, a field is strongest, the closer you are to the source. The further you move away from the source, the less the effect of the field. Not only did they have the dowsers a full floor away, who knows what may have been in the floor that may have shielded the effects of the field. A cement floor, for example, with steel reinforcing mesh inside it, would completely shield the effects of any naturally occurring field, much like a Faraday Cage. So to me, the experiment was poorly conducted and the findings inconclusive.

Five years after the Munich study was published, scientist Jim T. Enright contended that these results are merely consistent with statistical fluctuations and do not demonstrate any real ability. I agree. I believe that the experiment was flawed for the previously stated reasons. More recently, a study was undertaken in Kassel, Germany, under the direction of the Gesellschaft zur Wissenschaftlichen Untersuchung von Parawissenschaften (GWUP) (Society for the Scientific Investigation of the Parasciences). The three-day test of some 30 dowsers involved plastic pipes through which a large flow of water could be controlled and directed. The pipes were buried 50 centimeters under a level field. On the surface, the position of each pipe was marked with a colored stripe, so all the dowsers had to do was tell whether there was water running through the pipe. All the dowsers signed a statement agreeing this was a fair test of their abilities and that they expected a 100 percent success rate. However, the results were no better than what would have been expected by chance. But maybe they asked the wrong question.

Some researchers have investigated possible physical or geophysical explanations for dowsing abilities. For example, Soviet geologists have made claims for the abilities of dowsers, which are difficult to account for in terms of the reception of normal sensory cues. Some authors suggest that these abilities may be explained by postulating human sensitivity to small magnetic field gradient changes. One study concludes that dowsers "respond" to a 60 Hz electromagnetic field, but this response does not occur if the kidney area or head are shielded. A review of archaeological studies in Iowa suggests that dowsing is ineffective at finding unmarked human burials. But the fact remains; I have personally found unmarked graves by dowsing! As I have said, I would dismiss the whole thing as fantasy if not for the fact that it works for me.

The confounding issue that remains is that no one seems to be able to satisfactorily explain what the rods are detecting, since they can be used supposedly to detect everything from metallic ore to water to ghosts! Since I believe any phenomena can be measured, as long as we know what we are measuring, I felt the urge to find what indeed a dowsing rod detects. So... to the LAB! The basement of my house that my neighbors complain about mysterious green glows emitting from in the dark of night!

The first order for the experiment with dowsing was to attempt to find a way to artificially move the rods in a static mount, to determine what natural means could be used to trigger the movement. To do this, I used a micro vise, a device used to hold printed circuit boards in a position to allow inspection. Using the alligator clips, I was able to set up my dowsing rig in a static position that was stable, and would isolate the rods from motion thus eliminating that as a potential cause. Now the fun could begin.

Looking objectively at dowsing rods of the metallic variety, they are a simplistic example of an electroscope. Specifically, my example of the bent coat hanger dowser is in fact a variation of Gilbert's straw needle electroscope. There is a current theory that explains the divining rods are charged with static electricity from the dowser's own body. Whether this is true or not is easy enough to determine, as static electricity can be measured with a multi-meter. To measure this voltage I would prefer to use a static electricity detector, such as ones offered by Kapital instruments. Using this device, we can determine the surface static electricity of the dowser's hands. Another method prescribed by some researchers, would be to use a multi-meter to measure the potential between the hands of the dowser, utilizing a differential amplifier across the inputs to the voltmeter.

The amount of voltage measured should vary depending on the person, the temperature, the humidity and the environment. In this matter, the dowser "charges" the rods. The idea behind this theory is the higher the static potential, the greater the success rate as a dowser.

This would indicate that a rod charged positively should move in the dowser's hand to line up parallel to a negatively charged energy flow. A rod charged negatively should remain perpendicular to a negatively charged energy flow. This is attributed to like charges repel, while unlike charges attract. This would also indicate that two rods are not required for dowsing, and on the show I watched, the dowser used only one rod. Taking this a bit further, when two rods are used, and they cross, the proposed explanation is one of the rods is being moved to line up parallel with the charged energy flow. The other rod is moving to line up parallel to the first rod. A second reason offered for the two rods crossing is that of an alternating current source, such as a pipeline or buried cable. These are usually buried shallow and are conducting ground currents as the path of least resistance. Again, this is easy enough to test!

An explanation for why conventional devices cannot detect these positive and negative charges is due to the propagation pattern in which the charged object gives off its lines of force, theoretically in all directions. Most instruments being omni-directional devices would not supposedly detect the small incremental changes in voltage along the earth's surface. But the bent rods being unidirectional devices can only turn to line up parallel to the lines of force, when they are directly above the lines of force.

Really? What about other dowsing devices?

According to this theory, the willow crotch, perhaps the most common type of dowsing device from the early history of dowsing and still in use today, begins to respond to the energy field prior to reaching the object, having its greatest amount of pull directly over the object (could the willow tree house a natural energy amplifier?). The theory goes on to state that after dowsing with the willow crotch, the crotch itself can be dowsed with the bent rods, which should indicate a charge left on each arm of the crotch, one positive and one negative. Again, this is easy enough to check out.

Also according to this theory, a metallic pendulum attached by a wire or metallic chain will take on the charge of the user's hand. A pendulum held by a nonconductive string will take on the charge of the last hand that touched it. The pendulum when rotating above an object of a similar charge or field of force, will continue to rotate and eventually swing back and forth perpendicular to the object. When the pendulum rotates above an object of the opposite charge it will eventually start to swing back and forth parallel to the object or field being dowsed.

Fascinating! However, when facing the prospects of this theory, I am from Missouri. I have to see it to believe it. While items in motion in air will accumulate a static charge based on friction derived from the movement of air molecules across its surface, i.e. a human's skin as well as the dowsing device, I am not sold on the idea that static electricity is the key to this phenomenon, but I do hold out that it can certainly be a contributing factor.

Ok, back to my experiment. First I set up my rods inside small plastic tubes and clamp them about 4 inches apart in the PC board vise. I then mounted the device on a mobile object, in my case, the fertilizer broadcaster I use in my yard. This is accomplished by the use of a very complex mounting system; duct tape. After some intricate rolling patterns the vice was secure and I was ready for a backyard dowsing safari! I can't begin to tell you about the amusement my neighbors seem to be getting out of my exploits!

I first moved around the yard and focused on areas I knew should be detectable, such as the buried gas main, water pipe, sewer etc. Incredibly, the dowsing rods responded when the path of travel carried them over these items. So unless the energy in my hands was subconsciously manipulating the rods via osmosis, the rods were responding to something relative to the buried pipes. This seems to eliminate the operator from having any contribution what-so-ever in the equation, which is what I suspected all along. Now, time to expand the scope. I carefully set up a grid search pattern and covered my entire back yard. My neighbors thought I was on drugs by this time, most likely. But this isn't unusual behavior from a fellow whose basement glows a pale green in the dark…

Consequently I was rewarded with several "hits" where there were no immediately apparent items visible to react to. That is until I dug down a few inches. I found a rusty bolt, a quarter from 1963, a piece of steel screen, a Ballantine Beer can and a rusty pair of tweezers. At this point, I was stymied. What were the dowsing rods reacting to? Metal? Magnetic variations? Static electricity? Time to return to the lab.

First let me say that my lab is a place of refuge. I go there in times of stress, discord, and on occasion, to do scientific experimentation (hence, the green glow in the dark effect). Inside the lab, I set the dowsing rods up in a controlled environment (no drafts except for those created by my movement) and one strong source of EMF, my electrical service box. The rods reacted to the electrical service. Next I took a fairly strong magnet that I use for picking up nails and screws off the floor to clean up after projects. No surprise, the rods contained at least some fragment of ferrous material and responded to the magnet. The same held true for the application of electromagnets. All of these things caused the rods to respond. An energized transformer caused the rods to respond. But I was still not firmly convinced that EMF alone or magnetic fields were the culprit to explain the dowsing operation. Time to go back outside.

By now my wife is thinking that I am insane and forget what the neighbors think. Now I turned on the garden hose. The rods detected the garden hose, which was made from a rubber type of material. The only thing that could cause this to my knowledge is a magnetic field caused by the water running in one direction inside the hose. So, are metal dowsing rods a primitive EMF and Magnetic Field detector? Does the length of the rod determine the frequency response?

Please! I have fallen into a potential quantum perplexity and I can't get up!

Chapter 30
THE ORB EXPERIMENT

"A new scientific truth does not triumph by convincing opponents and making them see the light, but rather because its opponents eventually die, and a new generation grows up that is familiar with it."
-Max Planck-

Perhaps there is no phenomenon associated with the paranormal that is more controversial than the orb. An orb is typically a circular "glowing" anomaly commonly appearing in digital flash photographs. Whether its photography or video, orbs appear to be balls of light with an apparent size in the image ranging from a pinpoint to a basketball. Orbs often appear to be in motion, leaving a "comet tail" or trail behind them.

Within the paranormal community there are two main schools of thought regarding the cause of orbs in photographs. The collection of photographic pundits sees the orb as a fairly clear-cut case of flash reflection off of dust, particles, insects, lens flare or moisture droplets in the air in front of the camera, in other words they are naturalistic. How many times have you heard one of these self assured authorities say, "all orbs are dust particles". I think it is wonderful that people can be so sure without doing any research or only limited subjective research on the matter.

The "spiritualists and novice investigators claim that orbs are all paranormal in nature, or non-naturalistic, being caused by spirits, awareness, ghosts, etc. "Orbs are the manifestation of the spirit…"

Neither side offers much in the way of proof in either direction. I will say that there is a mountain of evidence that demonstrates orbs can be dust, water droplets, etc. and for the most part, the majority of them are. On the other side, the evidence that is offered up is more on the lines of "I believe" or "I feel" or even "I sense". Neither side could be further from the truth in their position. Why?

Simply because neither side knows for sure, nor as it is becoming glaringly obvious, have test data to confirm their position. I mean I can wave around a report from a photo lab and say all orbs are dust, or I can say I feel this orb is my grandmother...but neither amounts to much unless I have additional corroborating evidence in either direction. If either side HAS this evidence, they have failed to quote and or post it. Sure, it is easy to say all orbs or dust, because so many of them are. If you are a believer in orbs as spirits it is also equally easy to claim they are all real and the sign of a ghost, or manifestations of the spirit. Instead, we should collectively work to resolve the argument once and for all.

While there are several studies out in the field that are specifically targeting orbs, so far no substantial evidence proving orbs are anything but dust has surfaced. My own journey in seeking the truth in orbs began a long time ago, in the late 1970's when I captured an orb on a 35mm SLR camera with no flash. Since then, I have followed the path that many claim to follow, but few actually do. That path is the scientific method. Here is what the scientific method is all about.

First you must have a question you desire an answer to. What is it that you are trying to find out? What is it that you are trying to achieve? Easy, I am trying to find out what an orb is. Next you must research your topic. Investigate what others have already learned about your question. Gather information that will help you perform your experiments in an effort to prove what an orb really is. Ok, done that.

Develop a Hypothesis. After thoroughly researching the topic (orbs), you should have some idea about what you think may be causing the phenomena you are studying. This should be an educated guess concerning the outcome of your search for the truth. This is called your hypothesis. Your hypothesis may change as the data becomes available to you, and you learn more about the subject you are studying. You must also state your hypothesis in a way that you can readily measure. Remember, you have to prove what you believe. Ok, my hypothesis as to what orbs are is two-fold:

1. The majority of orbs are created by dust, pollen, moisture or other particulate matter captured within four inches of a camera's lens and illuminated by the flash.
2. There are exceptions to this rule. A small percentage of these "orbs" may be a form of energy.

Test Your Hypothesis by doing an experiment. Now that you have come up with a hypothesis, you need to develop a procedure for testing whether it is true or false. This involves changing one variable and measuring the impact that this change has on other variables. When you are conducting your experiment, you need to make sure that you are only measuring the impact of a single change.

Scientists run experiments more than once to verify that results are consistent.

Each time that you perform your experiment is called a run or a trial. It is also important that others are able to replicate the experiment and discover the same outcome. This is known as replicability or the ability to duplicate, copy, reproduce, or repeat.

Analyze Your Results:. At this stage, you want to be organizing and analyzing the data that you have collected during the course of your experiment in order to summarize what your experiment has shown you.

Draw Your Conclusion. This is your opportunity to explain the meaning of your results. Did your experiment support your hypothesis? Does additional research need to be conducted? How did your experiment address your initial question and purpose?

Report Your Results and Conclusion. Write a white paper or report. Submit evidence for peer review.

Most of the "authorities" on either side of the orb controversy tend to stop and run their mouths after the "State Your Hypothesis" part of the scientific method. Others quote the fact that since dust can cause an orb, all orbs are dust. While Occam's razor states that the simplest solution is generally the correct one, this isn't always the case. Science is full of Occam's rebuttals.

The "spiritualists" on one side claim that orbs are more likely to appear in certain locales, or are attracted to human activities, especially those involving children. The images are captured in graveyards, backyards, attics, and kitchens, as well as bars, convention centers, and city streets; in fact anywhere people may be taking photos you will find an orb. Since orb photos can be taken virtually everywhere, the position of "ghost hunters" and "sensitives" who claim orb photos are more common in allegedly haunted areas is significantly weakened.

Orb photos have become so prolific in the field that some "ghost hunting" organizations are no longer accepting submissions of them, or specifying that only "exceptional" examples be presented. There is no other justification for this other than there are "Too Many" orb shots submitted. Other groups do not recognize them as evidence at all. And to be honest, an orb shot without any accompanying evidence is meaningless.

Naturalistic Orbs

Naturalistic orbs are generally the result of using digital cameras with a built-in flash. While photographers with archives of photos (including myself) have occasionally captured "orbs" with 35mm film, it is theorized that the increase in orb photos may be directly related to the common availability of digital cameras and associated rise in the number of pictures taken. There is some truth to this.

Now, there are over 2700 photographs taken every second around the world, adding up to well over 80 billion new images a year taken on over 3 billion rolls of film, according to estimates published by the United States Department of Commerce. This is film alone, not including digital photography. One can well imagine how many digital photographs were taken a second. It is estimated that fully one third of those contain anomalies that are orb like in appearance. Naturally occurring orbs can be caused by:

1. Solid orbs - Dry particulate matter such as dust, pollen, insects, etc.
2. Liquid orbs - Droplets of liquid, usually water, e.g. rain.
3. Foreign material on the camera lens
4. Foreign material within the camera lens
5. Foreign material within the camera body

Additionally there are orbs showing up without any "environmental" explanation i.e. no dust, no rain, no moisture, no snowing, no light reflections, etc. Often they appear to be partially obstructed by obstacles in the scene. While many of them can be explained, a sufficient amount cannot. These are the ones that must be investigated further.

What causes a solid orb? A solid orb, or dust orb, is created because a reflective solid airborne particle, such as a dust particle, is situated near the camera lens and outside the depth of field, in other words out of focus. The pinpoint of light reflected from the dust particle is in focus as accurately as the camera can react to it. The resulting image grows into a circle of confusion that appears like an orb. There are now certain cameras that employ "dust filters" or electronic filters that turn dust reflections into a bright diamond.

How is a liquid orb created? A liquid orb is created because a drop of liquid, most often a rain drop, is situated near the camera lens and outside the depth of field, in other words out of focus. The pinpoint of light captured by the camera behaves exactly like a dust particle. The appearance of the circle of confusion is modified by aberrations such as chromatic aberration or coma. The raindrop must have reached terminal velocity though to maintain a circular shape. I have some photos of water dripping in an old iron mine and they are tear drop shaped because of the short travel distance.

I have also photographed an orb floating along the ground at an elevation of between two and 12 inches in this mine, and because the humidity was about 96%, there is no way it could be dust or water vapor. I have never seen water droplets travel sideways in the absence of wind.

Non-naturalistic orbs

"Spirit" orbs are sometimes claimed to exist more densely around certain haunted regions, or to be the spirits of departed loved ones. These types of orbs are sometimes claimed to have faces, sometimes with discernable expressions and sometimes of recognizable persons. As far as I know, there is no evidence to directly link an orb to a dead person. There is a good body of evidence that link orbs to paranormal activity so legitimately it bears further examination.

Ions Revisited

The brain and consciousness utilizes ions and ionic energy in order to function. If a "ghost" is an extension of consciousness then it makes sense that it would respond to this kind of energy and would be able to possibly use it more effectively. In fact, it is quite possible that ions are potential power source for paranormal activity. I have outlined this in Chapter 22 "The Ion Bombardment Experiment" in order to see if there is a correlation between elevated ion levels and the intensity of paranormal activity.

While storms are a key source of approximately 40% or all natural air ions, radon in the air is also a source (radon produces about 250,000 ion pairs per atom or an additional 40%), and about 20% are the product of cosmic rays (high-energy protons from distant supernovas). Indoors, ions live an average of about 30 seconds before touching a surface and shorting to ground. Outdoor ions usually live several minutes more than indoor ions.

Negative ions sources are radioactivity, waterfalls, the pounding of surf, and evaporating water. Lightning, thunderstorms, and forest fires can contribute positive and negative ions, though these ions are not produced via common everyday conditions. Ions are also produced by high-energy events, such as an open flame or a glowing hot object. Hot objects usually emit equal numbers of positive and negative ions. High DC voltage (over 1000 Volts), especially when connected to pointed metal edges or needles, will produce ions of the same polarity as the voltage source, which is the basis of home ionizers as well as our experimental bombardment devices.

Evaporating water will produce negative ions in the air and as a consequence leave positive charges behind in the water that hasn't yet evaporated. So if you photograph an orb, and measure a dramatic increase in ionic count with no evaporating water present, you have your first piece of evidence pointing your orb to a possible paranormal connection.

Static Electricity Review

Static electricity involves objects with a net charge; typically charged objects with voltages of sufficient magnitude to produce visible attraction, repulsion, and electrical sparks (remember walking across the carpet on a dry winter's day and touching the metal door knob?). Static electricity is a serious problem in the processing of analog recording media, as it can attract dust to sensitive materials. In the case of photography, dust accumulating on lenses and photographic plates degrades the resulting picture (and can cause naturalistic orbs). It is also important to remember that the presence of an electric current does not detract from the electrostatic forces or from the sparking, the corona discharge, or other phenomena. All phenomena can exist simultaneously in the same system. Static electricity can activate dust particles into the air, stimulating movement with out air currents. On the other hand, if you photograph an orb, if you have a dramatic increase in static electricity, coupled with increased ion count, and the humidity is relatively high, you have collected your second piece of evidence pointing your orb to a possible paranormal connection. We are also gathering a preponderance of evidence by building one piece of seemingly unrelated data upon another until we reach relevance.

As we continue our investigation, let's say we notice a drop in temperature in the area near the orb manifestation. Unnatural drops or increases in temperature, without drafts or other natural causes, and specifically with a highly localized effect, such as a "blob of cold" have been linked to paranormal activity. This would be an additional indication your orb is related to paranormal activity. EMF readings increase, barometric pressure decreases, and finally you measure a burst of gamma radiation and the environment returns to base readings, then you now have a preponderance of evidence that your orb *may be* paranormal related. But remember, while you have achieved relevance, you still have not proven it is a ghost, or a dead person for that matter. You have merely quantified it as having a correlation to what may be a paranormal event. The more evidence you gather, the stronger the case becomes. So the question remains,

Are all Orbs dust or foreign particles? Certainly not! Are all orbs signs of a spirit manifestation? Certainly not! But depending on "the rest of the story" as Paul Harvey use to say, the proof is in the pudding, or in our case, additional supporting evidence.

I have been asked numerous times over the years if I believe orbs are ghosts. I have always said no, but now I can add more to the story. I think orbs are a type of cold plasma energy triggered by a sequence of events that may be an indicator or a precursor to a perceived paranormal event. Or maybe it IS Uncle Harry. So, are we any closer to the answer?

To understand the question, I have to look back at my experience with the whole orb phenomenon, and my research surrounding it. I captured my first orb in 1976 using 35mm black and white film, ASA 1000, from a Pentax Spotmatic 500 SLR camera. Since I was using manual focus (the unit didn't have an auto focus function) I assumed that I had captured a foreign particle in the near region of the lens. I accepted this explanation as the rational explanation without doing any research to validate the effect. Over the course of the next ten years, I captured many orb photos at paranormal investigation sites, and dismissed them outright. While the orbs showed up primarily in night shots where a flash was employed, I did capture several daylight orbs without using a flash. Many of these orbs were captured outside, which increases the potential for foreign particle contamination or lens flare to be the primary cause of the phenomena.

During the late 1980s I had rigged up a "portable" magnetic anomaly detector. Essentially it was a modified military surplus mine detector mated to an oscilloscope, so it wasn't "real portable". In those days, the oscilloscope I used was roughly the size of an overnight case (a Tektronix 545-B). This made for limited mobility, but it did allow for me to discover the electromagnetic nature of paranormal phenomena. I also discovered elevated readings whenever an orb was present, and generally these readings were at low frequencies, specifically between 3 and 5 Hz. This led me to reassess my concept of the nature of the photographed orbs. While most orbs I captured were in fact, dust or pollen, a small percentage defied that explanation. They seemed to affect the environment, and dust cannot do that!

Close examination of the photos revealed the appearance of a complex structure within the orb. And although an argument could be made that all orbs display this, the fact is, all orbs do not. Since I wasn't physically seeing the orbs I was photographing, I formed a hypothesis that certain orbs were essentially plasma, or plasmoidial energy possibly manifesting in the invisible realms of light. Akin to ball lightning, this seemed like a plausible explanation. This would make them photographical only if they were in the presence of an extreme photon bombardment, such is evident in the field of a photo-flash unit. This would explain how a standard film camera, which only reacts to visible light, could capture a non-naturalistic orb. Then, in 1990, I physically witnessed an orb with the naked eye. It was three dimensional, and emitted a faint fluorescence, which led me to further postulate that some orbs attract free electrons to their outer "skins" which in turn increased the fluorescence of the orb. Due to the behavior exhibited by the observable orb, it seemed that once overloaded with electrons, it headed for the closest ground to discharge itself, or it would effectively disappear in thin air from whence it came.

Of course it wasn't disappearing per se, merely returning to its non-excited quantum state. This of course led to my first orb experiment, where I used four strobe lights and a controller (I was working as a lighting designer in those days and had access to a lot of lighting equipment for the entertainment industry). I went to a home that had reported activity, set a strobe in each corner of the room, synchronized the strobes, and photographed the room with no flash. I captured a wide variety of orbs of different sizes and colors (I was using color film by now, ASA 400 Kodak and mated with a Nikon SLR Camera with auto focus), and all the orbs photographed appeared to be three-dimensional. I also captured images of what appeared to be orbs moving through walls. I now equated orbs with natural phenomena such as encountered in the Hessdalen Valley in Norway (currently a research center is located there to study the phenomena) and believed there was a correlation between orbs and EMF activity. Of course I had no practical way of proving this in 1995. Instrumentation was still not up to the current level of technology, which severely limited by data collection to support my developing hypothesis.

This would all change in 1999.

In the fall of 1999 I acquired an EMF meter, designed to monitor emissions from computer monitors in compliance with federal regulations. This became an invaluable tool for use in the field. I was able to monitor fluctuations in the background EMF and photograph the conditions of a location in conjunction with the associated spike in field strength. This led to associating certain orbs with increases in EMF at a site.

I now had evidence that suggested certain orbs were possibly plasma energy, broadcasting EMF radiation as a byproduct of their existence. This is due, I surmised to electron movement around the "skin" of the orb, creating a wide spectrum of electromagnetic radiation potentially related to an encapsulation of cold plasma the provide longevity and stability (what a mouthful). Accurate measurements of the orb itself remained elusive. It would take a few years of abstract thought and basic research (*"Basic research is what I am doing when I don't know what I am doing".* - Werner Von Braun) for me to figure out a way to measure an actual energy orb. And once it dawned on me, the solution was relatively easy.

In 2001, I moved up to my first digital camera, a Sony Mavica . This opened a huge door of perception, as digital cameras see into the extended light frequencies invisible to the human eye, such as infrared and ultraviolet. It was at about this time that orbs also became associated officially with paranormal activity, and skeptics attacked them as being simply "dust" or "lens flare". Since then, the controversy has heated up and continued.

Today, plasma orbs are referred to as Unified Field Plasmoids by many researchers, based on their quantum characteristics. A great deal of research has been done on this phenomenon, all over the world, by many levels of individuals, from scientists and lay alike. The question remains however, as to what the exact relationship between UFPs and the paranormal is. Are they a cause, an enabler, or an effect? Future research is needed to tell the rest of the story. Meanwhile, my hypothesis has refined itself more.

I now believe that an orb may be created as a byproduct of a wormhole, vortex or door opening between two parallel universes, allowing matter to exchange, creating an energy surge without having major particle annihilations. I also believe that an increase in Gamma radiation in these paranormal event horizons are the result of out of phase matter causing minor annihilations that generate the gamma bursts. I believe this may involve Quantum Loop Gravity, Zero Point Energy, and time space displacement. An orb is merely a by-product of the mixing of "incompatible" matter. Interference, in one word or less!

The Orb Question Full Circle

Let's assume for a moment that some orbs are a product of a paranormal event and not dust. Plasma Energy holds promise as being the primary source of paranormal orb activity. Plasmas are conductive assemblies of charged particles, neutrons and fields that exhibit collective effects. Further, plasmas carry electrical currents and generate magnetic fields. Plasmas are the most common form of matter, comprising more than 99% of the visible universe, and permeate the solar system, interstellar and intergalactic environments. Plasmas are essentially a collection of non-aqueous gas-like ions or a gas containing a proportion of charged particles, and are referred to as the fourth state of matter because their properties are quite different from solids, liquids, and gases. Since there is now sufficient mathematical evidence to support the existence of parallel universes, and since these could possibly interfere with one another via the brane effect, it would be possible for exotic matter to stabilize a wormhole enough to allow an energy transference between universes. To maintain balance, an equal amount of plasma must be transferred to the adjacent universe to replace that which escaped into our own. Consequently it would make a lot of sense if some of the orbs appearing in conjunction with paranormal activity were indeed plasma. Plasmas are radically multi-scale in two senses:

1. Most plasma systems involve electro-dynamic coupling across micro-, meso and macroscale.
2. Plasma systems occur over most of the physically possible ranges in space, energy and density scales.

However, the full range of possible plasma density, energy (temperature) and spatial scales go far beyond our general conception. For example, some space plasmas have been measured to be lower in density than 10 to the power of -10 per cubic meter or (10exp-10)/m3. On the other extreme, quark-gluon plasmas (although mediated via the strong force field versus the electromagnetic field) are extremely dense nuclear states of matter. For temperature (or energy), some plasma crystal states produced in the laboratory have temperatures close to absolute zero. In contrast, space plasmas have been measured with thermal temperatures above 200 million degrees Kelvin and cosmic rays (a type of plasma with very large gyroradii) are observed at energies well above those produced in any man-made accelerator laboratory. We can be sure that if UFPs are plasma, they do not have these high temperatures associated with it.

So, if an orb, or a UFP (Unified Field Plasmoid) is in fact plasma, what does that mean, exactly? Well the implications are enormous! Could it explain EMF spikes? Yes indeed! Can it explain local effect temperature fluctuations? Absolutely! In fact, many of the fluctuations that are measured during a paranormal event would be easily explained by the presence of a plasma orb.

So, have we uncovered a possible natural solution to the age old question as to what is a ghost?

Not so fast! We still have a disturbing problem that I mentioned above. Plasma is the fourth state of matter, with solids, liquids, and gases weighing in as the other three. If you heat up any gas enough (or apply a sufficient amount of any energy,) you can turn the gas into plasma. The bombardment of energy drives negatively-charged electrons off of the atoms that make up the gas, and divides the gas into positively charged ions and loose electrons. Plasma for the most part radiates a lot of visible light and heat. The electrons continue to be attracted to the ions, and tend to reattach themselves as soon as the energy or heat diminishes, so plasma is inherently unstable and doesn't last very long on Earth. And it is extraordinarily HOT.

We do, however, see examples of plasma every day. The sun itself is made out of plasma, being a giant ball of superheated glowing hydrogen. Lightning is an example of the gases in the atmosphere igniting into a streak of plasma as an electric discharge crashes from sky to Earth (however, the current flows from the earth back up to the source). Probably the most daunting challenge to the theory is that since plasma is the fourth state of matter after gas, it's extremely hot. Hydrogen plasma, one of the cooler ones, tips the mercury in at 4,000 degrees Celsius.

But wait another minute! There is an exception to the rule. A *noticeable* exception to this rule is that when certain gases are kept under low pressure, like neon tubes or fluorescent light bulbs, they turn into plasma at low voltage and give off quite a bit of light and very little apparent heat. This property disappears when the gas is exposed to atmospheric pressure. Then it is possible that the plasma could be low temperature or cold plasma, if it were encapsulated in a stabilizing magnetic field or other medium, or perhaps, was made up of exotic matter.

There is also something known as coronal discharge. This can be seen on a humid night as a slight glow around a high tension power line. It occurs when a high energy source, such as the power line, starts turning the air around it into cool plasma. The reason it takes a humid night to bring it out is that dry air itself has too much resistance to become plasma with so little voltage. The gases found in pollution will have the same effect. This too could possibly be a source for orbs. But the nagging question remains. Where does it come from?

This is where the paranormal slips conspicuously and uncomfortably back into the equation. I believe that our universe, expansive as it is, is merely a microcosm in an endless sea of ever expanding dimensions and containing similar universes and flapping branes undulating across an exosphere of unknown substance, possibly ZPE or dark matter, existing in past, present and future. I have come to this conclusion from my study of Quantum Mechanics, and recognize that this is one of many probabilities, that may come into reality by an observer collapsing the field and making it so. When any two of these universes merge at a spot and overlap, or interference occurs, an anomaly also occurs between them resulting in the interchange of matter from either side, co-mingle interact in the confines of this connection or conduit, and then exit upon opposite sides of the veil. This could create the conditions to cause a plasma orb to be created. This would further explain their behavior of blinking into existence for a brief period, then blinking out again.

Then, there is the whole Ball Lightning question. Ball lightning is an atmospheric phenomenon, the physical nature of which is still controversial. The term refers to reports of a luminous object which varies in size from an inch to several yards in diameter. It is often associated with powerful thunderstorms, but unlike lightning flashes arcing between two points, which last a small fraction of a second, ball lightning reportedly has a longer duration, in seconds to several minutes, and travels on a horizontal trajectory. There have been scattered reports of production of a similar phenomenon in the laboratory, specifically at the Max Planck Institute in Germany. There scientists created a plasma by discharging a high potential charge into a quantity of water roughly the size of a small mud puddle. Many scientists question whether it is the same phenomenon. I personally have seen ball lightning-like phenomena, which occurred when linemen working on the electrical lines were attempting to replace a blown fuse on the pole. Their first attempt missed the clips, but the grazing of the connection cause an explosion to occur creating a ball of high potential energy that floated along for several seconds before dematerializing.

While there over 10,000 reported sightings of naturally occurring ball lightning, including video and photographs, it is still regarded by some as nothing more than a myth, fantasy, or hoax (much like paranormal phenomena). Reports of the phenomenon were dismissed due to lack of physical evidence, and were often classified in much the same way as UFO sightings. A 1960 paper reported that 5% of the US population reported having witnessed ball lightning. Another study analyzed the reports of over 10,000 sightings.

Ball lightning is almost never captured on film, and details of witness accounts vary widely, but there are exceptions. Many of the differing properties observed in ball lightning reports conflict with each other, and it is very possible that several different phenomena are being incorrectly grouped together. It is also possible that the few existing photos and videos are fakes. The discharges are most commonly associated with thunderstorm activity, often the result of a lightning flash, which would lend credence to the work in Germany, but large numbers of encounters have been reported during fair weather with no storms within hundreds of miles. A report from an area of central Africa having a very high incidence of lightning indicated that ball lightning often appeared from a certain hill just before the onset of the rainy season and prior to the arrival of a severe thunder storm.

Maybe it isn't ball lightning at all, but instead, a type of high energy "hot" UFP. Ball lightning tends to rotate or spin and can possess odd trajectories such as veering off at an angle or rocking from side to side like a leaf falling. They can also move with or against the wind. Other motions include a tendency to float (or hover) in the air and take on a ball-like appearance. Its shape has been described as spherical, ovoid, tear-drop or rod-like with one dimension being much larger than the others. Many are red to yellow in color, sometimes transparent, and some contain radial filaments or sparks. Other colors, such as blue or white occur as well, much like orbs.

Sometimes the discharge is described as being attracted to a certain object, and sometimes as moving randomly. After several seconds the discharge reportedly leaves, disperses, is absorbed into something, or, rarely, vanishes in an explosion. Some accounts have the balls passing freely through wood or glass or metal, while other accounts report circular holes in the wood or glass or metal. Some report explosions when the balls contact electrical wiring or the vaporization of water when the balls enter water. Some accounts claim the balls are lethal, killing on contact, while other accounts say the opposite.

Pilots in World War II described an unusual phenomenon for which ball lightning has been suggested as an explanation. The pilots saw small balls of light "escorting" bombers, flying alongside their wingtips. Pilots of the time referred to the phenomenon as "foo fighters," initially believing that the lights were from enemy planes. Unfortunately, we know of no instance of reported ball lightning that traveled at 300 mph while performing complex maneuvers.

There are however, other theories as to the identity of the foo fighters. Submariners in WWII gave the most frequent and consistent accounts of small ball lightning in the confined submarine atmosphere. There are repeated accounts of inadvertent production of floating explosive balls when the battery banks were switched in or out, especially if incorrectly switched or when the highly inductive electrical motors were incorrectly connected or disconnected causing an arc. An attempt later to duplicate those balls with a surplus submarine battery resulted in a several failures and an explosion. Recently, this set up was employed by an amateur researcher in an effort to create ball lightning. He created an arc with the batteries in a large tub of water, and created little balls of what he thought was ball lightning. Unfortunately, what he created wasn't ball lightning at all, but a phenomenon that occurs when metal melts at high temperature in water, since his electrodes were literally vaporized by the arc. Fortunately, the failed experiment inspired Prof. Gerd Fussmann, head of the plasma physics study group at the Max Planck Institute, to successfully create plasma by reducing the volume of water!

Volcanoes and the atmosphere and the terrain around them have been known to produce ball lightning and other luminous effects, with or without electrical storms. These accounts of course vary greatly. Other witnesses have reported ball lightning appearing over a kitchen stove or wandering down the aisle of an airliner. One report described ball lightning following and engulfing a car, causing the electrical supply to overload and fail. In 1773, two clergy men recalled that they saw a ball of light drop down in their fireplace. Seconds later, it exploded. History is full of such accounts.

Ball lightning can split and recombine and can exhibit large amounts of mechanical energy like carving trenches (e.g. Fitzgerald 1978) as well as blowing holes into the ground. One of the earliest and most destructive occurrences of what is believed to be ball lightning was reported to have taken place during The Great Thunderstorm at Widecombe-in-the-Moor, Devon, England, on October 21, 1638. Four people were killed outright and around 60 were injured when what appeared to have been ball lightning struck a church.

A rather famous anecdote from 1753 suggests ball lightning has violent potential. Professor Georg Richmann, of Saint Petersburg, Russia created a kite flying apparatus similar to that built by Benjamin Franklin the previous year. While attending a meeting of the Academy of Sciences, he heard thunder. The professor ran home with his engraver to capture the event for posterity. While the experiment was underway, ball lightning appeared, collided with Richmann's forehead leaving a large red spot and consequently killing him. His shoes were blown open, parts of his clothes singed, and his friend the engraver was knocked unconscious; the doorframe of the room was split, and the door itself torn off its hinges.

On 30th April 1877, a ball of lightning entered the Golden Temple at Amritsar, India, and exited through a side door. This event was observed by a number of people, and the incident is inscribed on the front wall of Darshani Deodhi. On August 6, 1994 a ball of lightning went through a closed window in Uppsala, Sweden, leaving a circular hole with a diameter of 5 centimeters *in the glass*. The incident was witnessed by residents in the area, and was recorded by a lightning strike tracking system on the Division for Electricity and Lightning Research at Uppsala University.

Many of the sources of information on ball lightning often refer to a questionably related phenomenon known as plasma balls. These floating balls of light often accompany a larger ball of fire that occurs when a lit or recently extinguished match or other material is immediately placed in an ordinary kitchen microwave on high power. These experiments are easily reproduced in home appliances and numerous websites exist with instructions on how to recreate it. Home video clips as well as video of public demonstrations of the occurrence have been posted. The experiments usually involve lighting a match and either microwaving it while lit or blowing out the match and then microwaving it immediately. The plasma balls are usually bright and bluish in color, and roll around the ceiling of the microwave chamber. A buzzing sound is characteristically observed while the plasma balls are present. The effect tends to damage the chamber where the plasma ball(s) have appeared, producing dents in the chamber wall or ceiling, as well as leaving burn marks. Some instructions for the experiment describe covering the lit object with an inverted glass jar, which would contain the flame and "plasma balls" so that they wouldn't damage the microwave oven itself.

Although this phenomenon has been referred to as ball lightning or plasma balls, it is really more of a description of their appearance than what they actually are. It has not been proven that it is actually related to the natural occurrence of ball lightning, or that the balls are made of plasma. No truly scientific explanation currently exists for the phenomenon.

Difficult features of the lightning include its persistence and its near-neutral buoyancy in air. A popular hypothesis is that ball lightning is highly ionized plasma contained by self-generated magnetic fields: a plasmoid. This hypothesis is not initially credible. If the gas is highly ionized, and if it is near thermodynamic equilibrium, then it must be very hot. Since it must be in pressure equilibrium with the surrounding air, it will be much lighter and hence float up rapidly. Magnetic fields, if present, might provide the plasmoid's coherence, but will not reduce this buoyancy. In addition, hot plasma cannot persist for long because of recombination and heat conduction. There may, however, be some novel form of plasma for which the above arguments do not fully apply. For example, plasma may be composed of negative and positive ions, rather than electrons and positive ions. In that case, the recombination may be rather slow even at ambient temperature. One such theory involves positively charged hydrogen and negatively charged nitrites (NO2–) and nitrates (NO3–). In this theory, the role of the ions as seeds for the condensation of water droplets is important. This may also explain certain orb activity as well.

If, however, ball lightning releases energy stored in chemical form, its persistence and neutral buoyancy might be more easily understood. The reaction might proceed slowly due to kinetic or geometric constraints, and the reaction could take place near ambient temperature. One of the first detailed theories of this sort involved the oxidation of nanoparticle networks formed when normal lightning strikes on soil. The coherence of the collection of nanoparticles may be enhanced by vortex motion, like that of a smoke ring. Is ball lightning a known manifestation of an orb?

A proposed explanation for the numerous colors reported for ball lightning is the following known gas phase chemoluminescent reaction. Broadband visible light is emitted from the NO2 as it reverts to a lower energy state. This explanation is supported by the numerous witness accounts of the presence of ozone. Recently, a prominent theory suggests that ball lightning is burning vaporized silicon. When lightning strikes earth's silica-rich soil, the silicon is instantly vaporized, the vapor itself condensing and burning slowly via the oxygen in the surrounding air. A recently published experimental investigation of this effect by evaporating pure silicon with an electric arc reported producing "luminous balls with lifetime in the order of seconds". Singer in his monograph, The Nature of Ball Lightning, published by Plenum Press critiques several classes of theory.

Most theories can match some of the reported properties of ball lightning but not all of them. In addition many of the proposed theories are problematic. Ball lightning theories are distinguished by having the energy either self-contained or with energy being supplied to the ball by an external source. In the latter case much longer life times are possible. The types of theories vary widely. There are electrical discharge theories, spinning electric dipole theory, electro-static Leyden jar theories, nuclear theories, trapped microwave theories, fractal aerogel theories, magnetically-trapped plasma theories, vortex theories, metallic vapor theories, Rydberg matter theories, chemical combustion theories, black hole theories, antimatter theories, optical illusions (e.g. lightning after image on the retina theory etc). But what if that energy source lies in another universe and the orb itself was the mouth of a wormhole?

Back to our problem of proving the existence of orbs (I do apologize for my long-winded tangents). Several investigative groups out there have designed devices for identifying real orbs. One of these devices is called DEVA. DEVA was conceived by Jeff Davis, and designed and built by Erik Smith, and Becky and Ron Cosgrove and details are located at www.GhostGadgets.com . The DEVA (Dust Eliminating Video Apparatus) claims to effectively removes 99% out-of-focus dust contamination from night shot video. In essence, DEVA is a shroud made from a large flower pot and fixed to the lens to isolate it from the effects of dust and flash. It works fairly well, but it is not the only solution to proving the existence of orbs, and all solutions should be employed.

The Synchronous Camera Shoot

This method is relatively straight forward; acquire two identical SLR digital cameras that allow for a remote trigger. Wire both cameras to a common remote trigger and mount them on tripods a few feet apart, but focused on the same area. Leave them in auto focus mode. Take photographs at regular intervals. If you capture an orb in one photo pair, but not the other, you have recorded dust. If you capture an orb in both photographs, in relatively the same location, you have something else entirely!

This is a rather expensive solution if you don't happen to have two team members with the exact same SLR digital cameras. Consequently a cheaper solution can be found and is easy to do, and as most teams have multiple people with digital cameras, try this approach; work with a partner. Point your cameras at the same area. Count to three out loud and both of you take a picture of the same place at once, from two slightly different angles. If you both get an orb in approximately the same location, BINGO!

The Unified Field Plasma Detector

The whole nature of the Orb has perplexed the researchers in the field since they were first photographed. While I am certain the majority of orbs photographed are the result of particulate matter being captured by the flash in the area within four inches of the camera lens (this has been backed up by the shear number of photos I have taken that only show one orb in one photo, while another photo of the same area taken at the same time shows NO orb) my resistance to the urge to fall into one camp (they are all dust) or the other (they are all spirits), and instead, staying firmly on the fence of objectivity is paying off.

The arguments between the two camps have ensued and caused multiple conflicts, and attacks on individuals. Instead of actively trying to find the answer, both camps have assumed the "I am right, you are wrong" stance. I have taken the stance of throwing all of the resources at my disposal to investigate the orb question seriously.

As I have mentioned before, neither side has built a substantial case one way or the other. While I have accumulated some evidence indicating a small fraction of orbs photographed are not dust and may be something quite different, there needs to be proof of what that difference is.

And finally, after all of the years of abstract thought, I was struck with a spasm of lucidity. While watching "Ghost Busters" for the gazillionth time a design materialized in my consciousness and inspired me to build a device to attempt to capture and measure an energy orb, if they do indeed exist.

During the movie, as I laughed at the characters and their antics it dawned on me, that if orbs were energy, they could be measured, and if they could be measured, someone would have to figure out how, and that someone may as well be me.

If orbs were a type of plasma, this could be extremely dangerous, as plasma tends to have a tremendous amount of potential and current, enough to cause my potential annihilation. But, if they were some other form of energy reacting to photon bombardment from a flash, or were visible to the eye as some have reported, then they could be measured. The question was, how?

Since there is no affordable way that I know of to measure multiple energy manifestations, I would have to measure one potential parameter at a time. The first parameter would be electrical. Orbs on video seem to move about, floating in a pattern that would suggest more than air currents. However, could one be captured? In order to capture one from the air, the air would have to be collected and sampled. I looked around the lab and found my trusty portable ShopVac and a light bulb went off in my head. The unit I own is quite capable of sucking the chrome off a trailer hitch, or a proverbial basketball through a garden hose, so I had my collection device. Now I needed a measurement grid. Again, back to the lab. The creative juices evaporated for a moment, until I spied some left over plumbing supplies from an earlier home improvement project. The idea to use PVC pipe struck me between the eyes, so I dug around for a coupling, and a a couple of sections of rigid PVC pipe. I ended up with a long piece of 2 ½ inch PVC scrap and two matching couplings.

Ok, I had my collector, now I needed a grid. I had some aluminum screen laying around (aluminum is an excellent conductor of electricity, third behind gold and copper) so I cut two round pieces that fit over the end of the pipe, leaving a long ¼ inch wide strip leading out from the circle for connection purposes. I then cut the PVC into two sections. I covered the opening of a 30 inch piece of PVC pipe with the aluminum screen and then forced it carefully into a coupling applying PVC cement before connecting them. I then took a ten inch length of PVC and fit the other screen over the opening, and forced it into the other side of the coupling again using PVC cement. This created two grids, isolated from each other, with about a ¼" gap between the screens. I then took my collection tube and fit the vacuum flex hose from the ShopVac to the 30 inch section end, and taped it up to insure an air-tight seal. This would allow me to suck in the air, through the pipe, past the measurement grid.

To measure the potential of whatever I happen to capture, I attached a voltage meter to the grids using the leads I left protruding from the coupling. I soldered the lead wires from the meter to the screen leads and then attached self sticking Velcro® to the tube. I attached the mate to the Velcro® to the meter, and also to a small hand held oscilloscope to observe any frequency the potential may be at, if any. This way I can measure voltage, current, or frequency.

To date, I have captured something on two occasions that had an extremely high potential, but all I know from the experience is I have blown the fuse in the meter twice and registered over 50,000 volts.

Chapter 31
The Scientific Method

"Science is the great antidote to the poison of enthusiasm and superstition."
-Adam Smith-

So where do we go from here? I would like to believe that I have given you, the reader, a greater understanding of the instruments, tools and equipment used today in paranormal investigation. I can only close this with an overview of the Scientific Method from Wikipedia, along with my embedded commentary, which is the law we must follow if our work is to have any serious impact on the field.

The Scientific Method refers to bodies of techniques for investigating phenomena, acquiring new knowledge, or correcting and integrating previous knowledge. To be termed scientific, a method of inquiry must be based on gathering observable, empirical and measurable evidence subject to specific principles of reasoning. A scientific method consists of the collection of data through observation and experimentation, and the formulation and testing of hypotheses.

Although procedures vary from one field of inquiry to another, identifiable features distinguish scientific inquiry from other methodologies of knowledge. Scientific researchers propose hypotheses as explanations of phenomena, and design experimental studies to test these hypotheses. Our study of the paranormal can be no different! These steps must be repeatable in order to dependably predict any future results. Theories that encompass wider domains of inquiry may bind many hypotheses together in a coherent structure. This in turn may help form new hypotheses or place groups of hypotheses into context. ONLY in this manner will the scientific community take our work seriously.

Among other facets shared by the various fields of inquiry is the conviction that the process be objective to reduce a biased interpretation of the results. Another basic expectation is to document, archive and share all data and methodology so they are available for careful scrutiny by other scientists, thereby allowing other researchers the opportunity to verify results by attempting to reproduce them. This practice, called full disclosure, also allows statistical measures of the reliability of these data to be established. Again, we HAVE to do this in order for our work to be taken seriously. And why do we want our work to be taken seriously by science?

So that we may find the answers, grasshopper.

Since Ibn al-Haytham (Alhazen, 965–1039), one of the key figures in developing scientific method, the emphasis has been on seeking truth:

"Truth is sought for its own sake. And those who are engaged upon the quest for anything for its own sake are not interested in other things. Finding the truth is difficult, and the road to it is rough."

I know. I have spent most of my adult life looking for the truth.

Scientific methodology has been practiced in some form or other for over a thousand years. There are difficulties in a universal formula of method, however. As William Whewell (1794–1866) noted in his History of Inductive Science (1837) and in Philosophy of Inductive Science (1840), "invention, sagacity, genius" are required at every step in scientific method. It is not enough to base scientific method on experience alone; multiple steps are needed in scientific method, ranging from our experience to our imagination, back and forth. It also helps to be visionary in one's scope.

In the twentieth century, we have been blessed with a hypothetico-deductive model for the scientific method, and it is pretty easy for all to grasp.

1. Use your experience: Consider the problem and try to make sense of it. Look for previous explanations. If this is a new problem to you, then move to step 2.

2. Form a conjecture: When nothing else is yet known, try to state an explanation, to someone else, or to your notebook. I have found that my notebook always listens.

3. Deduce a prediction from that explanation: If you assume 2 is true, what consequences follow?

4. Test : Look for the opposite of each consequence in order to disprove 2. It is a logical error to seek 3 directly as proof of 2. This error is called affirming the consequent.

This model underlies the scientific revolution. One thousand years ago, Alhazen demonstrated the importance of steps 1 and 4. Galileo (1638) also showed the importance of step 4 (also called simply "Experiment") in *Two New Sciences*. One possible sequence in this model would be 1, 2, 3, 4. If the outcome of 4 holds, and 3 is not yet disproved, you may continue with 3, 4, 1, and so forth; but if the outcome of 4 shows 3 to be false, you will have go back to 2 and try to invent a new 2, deduce a new 3, look for 4, and so forth.

Note that this method can never absolutely verify (prove the truth of) 2. It can only falsify 2. (This is what Einstein meant when he said "No amount of experimentation can ever prove me right, but a single experiment can prove me wrong.")

In the twentieth century, Ludwik Fleck (1896–1961) and others found that we need to consider our experiences with intense scrutiny, because our experience may be (and most likely is) biased, and that we need to be more specific when describing our experiences.

Part of the confusion with the Scientific Method is that there are many ways of outlining the basic method shared by all fields of scientific inquiry. The following set of methodological elements and organization of procedures tends to be more characteristic of natural sciences than social sciences and this is appropriate for our focus. In the social sciences mathematical and statistical methods of verification and hypotheses testing generally tend to be more subjective and less stringent. Nonetheless the cycle of hypothesis, verification and formulation of new hypotheses should resemble the cycle described below.

The essential elements of a scientific method are iterations, recursions, interleavings, and orderings of the following:

Characterizations (observations, definitions, and measurements of the subject of inquiry)

Hypotheses (theoretical, hypothetical explanations of observations and measurements of the subject)

Predictions (reasoning including logical deduction from the hypothesis or theory)

Experiments (tests of all of the above)

Each element of a scientific method is subject to peer review for possible mistakes. THIS IS IMPERATIVE! Read this statement again and memorize it. These activities do not describe all that scientists do (see below) but apply mostly to experimental sciences (e.g., physics, chemistry).

The Scientific Method is not an easy recipe: it requires intelligence, imagination, and creativity. It is also a never ending cycle, constantly developing more useful, accurate and comprehensive models and methods. For example, when Einstein developed the Special and General Theories of Relativity, he did not in any way refute or discount Newton's Principia. On the contrary, if the astronomically large, the vanishingly small, and the extremely fast are reduced out from Einstein's theories, all phenomena that Newton was incapable of observing, it matters not. Newton's equations remain! Einstein's theories are expansions and refinements of Newton's theories, and observations that increase our confidence in them also increase our confidence in Newton's approximations to them.

A linearized, pragmatic scheme of the four points above is sometimes offered as a guideline for proceeding:

1. Define the question

2. Gather information and resources (observe)

3. Form hypothesis

4. Perform experiment and collect data

5. Analyze data

6. Interpret data and draw conclusions that serve as a starting point for new hypothesis

7. Publish results

8. Retest (frequently done by other scientists or peers)

The iterative cycle inherent in this step-by-step methodology goes from point 3 to 6 and back to 3 again.

While this schematic outlines a typical hypothesis/testing method, it should also be noted that a number of philosophers, historians and sociologists of science (perhaps most notably Paul Feyerabend) claim that such descriptions of scientific method have little relation to the ways science is actually practiced. On the other hand, without this foundation, a lot of time is wasted with hit or miss principia. Also, philosophers, historians and sociologists tend to be highly subjective. We need to be highly OBJECTIVE.

Peer review evaluation

Scientific journals use a process of peer review, in which scientists' manuscripts are submitted by editors of scientific journals to (usually one to three) fellow (usually anonymous) scientists familiar with the field for evaluation. The referees may or may not recommend publication, publication with suggested modifications, or, sometimes, publication in another journal. This serves to keep the scientific literature free of unscientific or crackpot work, helps to cut down on obvious errors, and generally otherwise improve the quality of the scientific literature. We need a journal that will reliably fill this need. In its absence, we must modify our focus to fit it in an existing journal based on relevance to that specific field. As if we don't have enough to do!

Documentation and replication

Sometimes experimenters may make systematic errors during their experiments, unconsciously veer from the scientific method (pathological science) for various reasons, or, in rare cases, deliberately falsify their results. Consequently, it is a common practice for other scientists to attempt to repeat the experiments in order to duplicate the results, thus further validating the hypothesis. This practice needs to be deployed in the field of paranormal research.

Archiving

As a result, researchers are expected to practice scientific data archiving in compliance with the policies of government funding agencies and scientific journals. Detailed records of their experimental procedures, raw data, statistical analyses and source code are preserved in order to provide evidence of the effectiveness and integrity of the procedure and assist in reproduction. These procedural records may also assist in the conception of new experiments to test the hypothesis, and may prove useful to engineers who might examine the potential practical applications of a discovery. There are several national databases that archive paranormal investigations and evidence. Few archive actual research in a useable format. Those that do, have no place to put it for public consumption.

Data sharing

When additional information is needed before a study can be reproduced, the author of the study is expected to provide it promptly - although a small charge may apply. If the author refuses to share data, appeals can be made to the journal editors who published the study or to the institution that funded the research. Hording data is a practice that is counter-productive and prolific in the "para" field currently. This gives the field of paranormal research a look of pettiness, selfishness and amateurism that discourages serious considerations by professional scientists. This too must stop for us to move forward.

Limitations

Note that it is not possible for a scientist to record everything that took place in an experiment. He must select the facts he believes to be relevant to the experiment and report them. This may lead, unavoidably, to problems later if some supposedly irrelevant feature is questioned and becomes suddenly relevant. For example, Heinrich Hertz did not report the size of the room used to test Maxwell's equations, which later turned out to account for a small deviation in the results. The problem is that parts of the theory itself need to be assumed in order to select and report the experimental conditions. The observations are hence sometimes described as being 'theory-laden'.

Relationship with mathematics

Science is the process of gathering, comparing, and evaluating proposed models against observables. A model can be a simulation, mathematical or chemical formula, or set of proposed steps. Science is like mathematics in that researchers in both disciplines can clearly distinguish what is known from what is unknown at each stage of discovery. Models, in both science and mathematics, need to be internally consistent and also ought to be falsifiable (capable of disproof). In mathematics, a statement need not yet be proven; at such a stage, that statement would be called a conjecture. But when a statement has attained mathematical proof, that statement gains a kind of immortality which is highly prized by mathematicians, and for which some mathematicians devote their lives. I am in a physics yahoo group where the members constantly argue about the virtues of math, with those who are horrible at it or who understand it the least being its harshest critics. No matter, math and science go together.

Mathematical work and scientific work can inspire each other. For example, the technical concept of time arose in science, and timelessness was a hallmark of a mathematical topic. But today, the Poincaré conjecture has been proven using time as a mathematical concept in which objects can flow.

Nevertheless, the connection between mathematics and reality (and so science to the extent it describes reality) remains obscure. Eugene Wigner's paper, The Unreasonable Effectiveness of Mathematics in the Natural Sciences, is a very well-known account of the issue from a Nobel Prize physicist. In fact, some observers (including some well known mathematicians such as Gregory Chaitin, and others such as Lakoff and Nunez) have suggested that mathematics is the result of practitioner bias and human limitation (including cultural ones), somewhat like the post-modernist view of science. According to George Pólya's work on problem solving, "the construction of mathematical proofs, and heuristics show that mathematical method and scientific method differ in detail, while nevertheless resembling each other in using iterative or recursive steps". This too is a mouthful! But let's explore this in detail.

Mathematical method Scientific method

1 Understanding Characterization from experience and observation

2 Analysis Hypothesis: a proposed explanation

3 Synthesis Deduction: prediction from the hypothesis

4 Review/Extend Test and experiment

In Pólya's view, understanding involves restating unfamiliar definitions in your own words, resorting to geometrical figures, and questioning what we know and do not know already; analysis, which Pólya takes from Pappus, involves free and heuristic construction of plausible arguments, working backward from the goal, and devising a plan for constructing the proof; synthesis is the strict Euclidean exposition of step-by-step details of the proof; review involves reconsidering and re-examining the result and the path taken to it.

I realize this has been a HEAVY reading chapter, but it is one that needed inclusion. While many paranormal investigative groups claim to employ the

Scientific Method, they clearly do not. They need to either stop claiming this and hence looking foolish and ignorant to the scientific community, OR (preferred) practice what they proverbially preach. Only then will our work be taken seriously as a whole by members of the scientific community who can lend vast resources from their disciplines at finding the truth.

This brings our journey full circle. We part here until the next time we meet, when we can fill in more of the blanks we have left behind here by our own mutual discoveries. Until then…great discoveries to you. For there is an old southern saying…"Even a blind hog gets an acorn every once in awhile…"

Afterword

I first met David Rountree in November 2006.

At the time, I had been searching for a group of paranormal researchers and investigators that would fit into my personal stance on the subject. I had been interested in the investigation of the paranormal from an early age, growing up in the era of the Amityville Horror, the offerings of Charles Berlitz, and programs like "In Search Of". Even then, it was the occasional hint of technical detection of the unusual and unexplained that sparked my imagination. It wasn't enough to experience the phenomenon or see the "ghost". I wanted to see documented evidence, but more than that, I wanted to understand it.

Twenty-five years and a couple of engineering degrees later that desire hadn't changed. What had changed, however, was the popularity of the subject. During the 1980s and 1990s, paranormal investigation was considered to be several steps beyond the fringe. Interest in the subject, particularly within technical fields, was discouraged. Part of this was the impression that paranormal investigation had to be based in mysticism and spiritualism. Science frowns on unwarranted assumption, and "ghost hunting" has historically been full of it.

In recent years, that has changed. Interest in the paranormal and investigation of reported paranormal phenomena no longer holds the stigma it once did. While theories may abound as to the reasons, it's clear that the current explosion of paranormal investigation reality programs on television and the internet reflects that popularity. Generally speaking, I have found such shows entertaining and even inspiring. At the same time, they can be enormously frustrating, because of the many liberties taken with the science and improper use of technical instruments and equipment.

Many of the groups depicted in the current programs advertise themselves as "scientific". Most of them (if not all) make the common mistake of equating "technical" with "scientific". The use of equipment alone does not render an investigation scientific. If an instrument is used incorrectly, the data produced by that instrument is worthless. If an investigator doesn't know how an instrument is supposed to be used, what the data means, and how it is related to every other type of data also collected, then the investigator can come to wrong conclusions, however well-intentioned they might be.

Of course, it's not just about proper data collection. It's about how all of that data is interpreted. Investigators often step onto a site with a set of beliefs already set in stone; they are looking to find evidence that validates that belief. It has very little to do with understanding what the data is telling them (or, more often, what it is *not* telling them). The remedy is the Scientific Method, and it is a methodology that takes discipline and training to apply correctly.

In 2006, I was looking for fellow investigators with technical expertise and the scientific mindset. After talking with David at a meeting for a few short minutes, it was quickly apparent that our philosophies were compatible. We were soon spending evenings discussing quantum theory and custom equipment designs. At the heart of every discussion was the belief that a solid paranormal investigation team must have a fundamental technical understanding and must follow the Scientific Method. In the years since, I have had the distinct pleasure of working with David as the Co-Director of the New Jersey Paranormal Resource Group.

This book is the perfect primer for any group wanting to operate under the same core principles. David provides a clear-cut laundry list of what to measure, why it should be measured, and which instruments are the best for the job. Strengths and weaknesses are outlined, and proper data collection methods are stressed. In the process, David explains some of the theoretical reasons for collecting this data, pointing to scientific principle in favor of mysticism. Not just trying to document paranormal phenomena, but to understand it.

In addition, David outlines several of the experiments that he has proposed in recent years. I have had the benefit of discussing these experiments with him at length and analyzing the results first-hand. We conduct these experiments regularly during our investigations in the hopes of generating new and exciting data to shed light on reported paranormal activity.

Perhaps more importantly, these experiments are only part of the scientific process. They are meant to be duplicated, and the results are meant to be shared. They are meant to inspire others to attempt new and perhaps even better experiments. This is what science is all about. As such, this book is not a means to an end, but rather, an invitation.

I hope you accept it.

John Keegan
Co-Director, New Jersey Paranormal Resource Group
(http://www.njprg.com)

About The Author

David M. Rountree

David was born in 1954 in Suffolk, Virginia, an area rich in historic and haunted landmarks. His family originally settled in the Nansemond County area from England in 1735. The Rountree family became one of the prominent families in Southeastern Virginia until 1864, when they lost nearly everything they owned as a result of the Civil War.

He moved to Delray Beach, Florida, in the fall of 1963, where he first became interested in the paranormal. In 1965, his next door next door neighbor, Fred Grosstuck, a retired professor from Joliet University and pattern maker, gave him a book called "Adventures in the Paranormal", essentially a collection of short stories of events from all over the world that were scientifically unexplainable. Fred also introduced him to Fate magazine.

He participated in the exploration of his first "haunted house" at the age of 17 in Boynton Beach, Florida.

He received his B.S.E.E. in 1973 while serving in the Air Force, in microwave technology. In November of 2007 he received his Masters in Electronic Engineering in Digital Signal Processing. He is currently working on his doctorate in physics. David completed several workshops on paranormal investigation in 1976 at the Rhine Research Center at Duke University, and is currently a professional member of that illustrious organization. In 1978 he was certified as an audio engineer. David worked in the entertainment industry as a Technical Director, Lighting Designer and Audio Engineer for over twenty years. He worked for the University of Florida from 1981 until 2001, serving as the Manager of the student technical group Spinal Tech, as well as being the Technical Director of the University of Florida Performing Arts Series. He also served as the Technical Director of the Florida Arts Celebration for four years. During that time period he freelanced for several large production companies in the state of Florida, working a variety of shows ranging from Opera to Rock Concerts across the South Eastern United States. Currently David is Manager of Public Address Communications Technologies and Director of the Audio Research and Development Lab for the third largest public transportation corporation in the nation.

David is a professional member of the American Association for the Advancement of Science, an organization of scientists and professionals who are advancing scientific research. He is also a member of the Audio Engineering Society, an international professional organization dedicate to the standardization of the audio industry. Additionally, David is a member of the International Frequency Sensor Association, which provides a forum for academicians, researchers and engineers from industry to present and discuss the latest research results, experiences and future trends in the area of design and application of different smart sensors with digital, frequency (period), time interval or duty-cycle output.

This organization is essential for developing modern measurement science and technology. He is also a member of The International Executive Guild and is listed in Who's Who International of Information Technology. David is also affiliated with the Institute of Electrical and Electronics Engineers and works directly with audio equipment manufacturers to influence the design of products and implement new technologies.

From 1977 until 2001, he performed many investigations in the area in and around Gainesville, Florida, as a member of a small, highly specialized research team. During this time David experimented with both scientific as well as metaphysical techniques in his study of unexplained occurrences he and his small team encountered. Due to several encounters of a very negative nature from 1985-87, he made the decision to concentrate on the scientific research concerning the phenomena, and not the metaphysical aspects of the events. In 1992 David formed a new organization, Scientific Paranormal Investigative Research Information and Technology (S.P.I.R.I.T.), and began a long and painstaking process of collecting, building and focusing a battery of Hi-Tech instrumentation to concentrate on laboratory and field experimentation to search for the cause of paranormal phenomena. By 1998 his focus of research had narrowed to phenomena specific to "Hauntings".

His primary focus since 1998 has been EVP research, employing his background of audio engineering and psychoacoustics. In 2005 David successfully linked electromagnetic fields as the primary source of EVPs. He continues to gather data to attempt to locate the source of the electromagnetic fields that cause the EVP phenomena.

David is a multifaceted individual with many varied talents: he was on the Renn Fair and Science Fiction - Fantasy Convention circuit for many years (as "Greywolf the Wanderer") working with various vendors selling artwork and Gallo pewter, and eventually promoting a novel he wrote with his wife, Laura, whom he met in 1999, Their novel, "Dark Lord" (ISBN 0-595-14692-9, available from Barnes and Noble and Amazon.com), was published in 2000. David Moved to New Jersey in 2001, and they married in 2003.

Because of their mutual interests in the paranormal, (she was formerly a member of Donna Kent's investigative group and participated in the now infamous Dudleytown investigations) they formed Skylands Paranormal Investigations in April of 2005, and began to work actively in training interested people in investigative methods for no charge. In 2007 they ended their training program and David returned to his original organization, S.P.I.R.I.T. and launched a rigorous new research plan with a small and highly specialized team of scientists to focus on paranormal research specific to haunting phenomena. He began to design new equipment and systems to study findings from field investigations in Florida and New Jersey.

David is the Director of S.P.I.R.I.T., Co-Director of New Jersey Paranormal Resource Group, Co-Founder of New Jersey Paranormal Investigative Coalition, a member of the Rhine Research Center, life member of the New Jersey Ghost Hunter's Society, member of the International Paranormal Investigators, and a member of the International Paranormal Research Association. He supports the World Wide Paranormal Reporting Center.

David's additional areas of research includes investigating the relationship between free air conductance, magnetic fields, radioactive emissions, electromagnetic fields and electrical radiation surrounding paranormal phenomena. He is also experimenting with injecting energy into a paranormal event horizon using Tesla Coil technology in order to observe and record the effects. He continues to measure the effects of massive ion bombardment in a paranormal environment. He is developing a device designed to capture and analyze the phenomena referred to as orbs in order to either prove or dismiss their existence. David is also experimenting with a self designed ITC (Instrumental Trans-Communications) device using electromagnetic field propagation as a medium of cross communication.

David was recently featured on Comcast Newsmakers. He has also been a guest on WNTI FM, and WRNJ AM-FM radio in Hackettstown, NJ, as well as a repeat guest on HSTV Channel 23 in Hackettstown on the show "Science on the Edge" hosted by Dr. Karl Hricko. He has made guest appearances on Web Radio programs such as Ghost Census Radio, The Inner Circle, Magic Mind Radio, The Brian and Baxter Show on Warning Radio, with Royce Holleman on Paranormal Palace Radio, Lights Out Radio hay House Radio with Dr. Eldon Taylor, Paranexus Universe Radio, and more. He is available for speaking engagements for a small honorarium. Current presentations include Introduction to Paranormal

Investigation, Paranormal Research Technology and "Haunted Hackettstown".

Today, Scientific Paranormal Investigative Research Information and Technology is a small dedicated group of scientific researchers based in New Jersey seeking answers to the paranormal questions remaining to be answered. Their research and theories are located on the S.P.I.R.I.T. web site.
http://www.spinvestigations.org

David is also the Co-Director of New Jersey paranormal Resource Group.
http://www.njprg.com

References

The accuracy of material presented in this work was checked at the following online reference sites:

http://www.answers.com/
http://www.britannica.com/
http://encarta.msn.com/
http://www.encyclopedia.com/
http://www.freebase.com/
http://www.halfvalue.com/answers.html
http://www.howstuffworks.com/
http://www.infoplease.com/
http://www.mtnmath.com/faq/meas-qm.html
http://newton.ex.ac.uk/research/qsystems/people/jenkins/mbody/mbody2.html
http://photo.net/
http://www.physics.org/
http://www.quantum-physics.polytechnique.fr/en/
http://spaceweather.com/
http://www.swpc.noaa.gov/
http://www.weather.com/
http://www.wikipedia.org

Bibliography

AES, *The Journal of the Audio Engineering Society*, Monthly Journal, Audio Engineering Society; (2009)

Azzam, R. M. A.; Bashara, N. M., *Ellipsometry and Polarized Light*, North Holland (April 1, 1987)

Barnes, Frank S.; Greenebaum, Ben, *Bioengineering and Biophysical Aspects of Electromagnetic Fields* (Handbook of Biological Effects of Electromagnetic Fields), CRC; 1 edition (October 20, 2006)

Becker, Richard, *Electromagnetic Fields and Interactions* (Blaisdell Book in the Pure and Applied Sciences.), Dover Publications; Unabridged edition (March 1, 1982)

Blackstock, David T., *Fundamentals of Physical Acoustics*, Wiley-Interscience; 1 edition (February 22, 2000)

Bladel, Jean G. Van, *Electromagnetic Fields* (IEEE Press Series on Electromagnetic Wave Theory), Wiley-IEEE Press; 2 edition (June 4, 2007)

Blauert, Jens, *Spatial Hearing - Revised Edition: The Psychophysics of Human Sound Localization*, The MIT Press; Rev Sub edition (October 2, 1996)

Born, Max; Wolf, Emil, *Principles of Optics*, Cambridge University Press; 7th edition (October 13, 1999)

Bothmer, Volker; Daglis, Ioannis A., *Space Weather* (Springer Praxis Books / Environmental Sciences), Springer; 1 edition (November 14, 2006)

Brosseau, Christian, *Fundamentals of polarized light : a statistical optics approach*, Wiley-Interscience (October 15, 1998)

Chen, Francis F., *Introduction to Plasma Physics and Controlled Fusion*, Springer; 2nd edition (May 31, 2006)

Collett, Edward, *Field Guide to Polarization*, SPIE Field Guides vol. FG05, SPIE Publications (September 26, 2005)

Cutnell, John D.; Johnson, Kenneth W., *Physics*, Wiley; 7 edition (March 17, 2006)

Damask, Jay N., *Polarization Optics in Telecommunications*, Springer; 1 edition (November 19, 2004)

Davis, Don; Davis, Carolyn, *Sound System Engineering*, Sams; Carmel, Indiana, U.S.A. (1987)

Davis, Gary; Jones, Ralph, *The Sound Reinforcement Handbook*, Yamaha; 2 edition (January 1, 1988)

Eargle, John M.; Foreman, Chris, *JBL Audio Engineering for Sound Reinforcement*, JBL Pro Audio Publications; (May 1, 2002)

Everest, Alton F., Critical *Listening Skills for Audio Professionals*, Artistpro; 2 edition (June 20, 2006)

Everest, Alton F., *Master Handbook of Acoustics*, McGraw-Hill/TAB Electronics; 4 edition (September 22, 2000)

Fastl, Hugo; Zwicker, Eberhard, *Psychoacoustics: Facts and Models (Springer Series in Information Sciences)*, Springer; 3rd edition (December 28, 2006)

Ford, Kenneth W.; Goldstein, Diane, *The Quantum World: Quantum Physics for Everyone*, Harvard University Press (October 15, 2005)

Freeman, John W., *Storms in Space*, Cambridge University Press; 1st edition (October 15, 2001)

Freidman, Jeffrey P., Plasma Physics and Fusion Energy, Cambridge University Press; 1 edition (August 11, 2008)

French, A.P.; Taylor, Edwin F., *An Introduction to Quantum Physics (Mit Introductory Physics Series)*, CRC; 1 edition (November 30, 1979)

Fridman, Alexander A.; Kennedy, Lawrence A., *Plasma Physics and Engineering*, CRC; 1 edition (April 2004)

Goldstein, Dennis, *Polarized Light*, CRC; 2 edition (June 13, 2003)

Griffiths, David J., *Introduction to Quantum Mechanics*, Benjamin Cummings; 2 edition (April 10, 2004)

Gulick, Lawrence W.; Gescheider, George A.; Frisina, Robert D., *Hearing: Physiological Acoustics, Neural Coding, and Psychoacoustics*, Oxford University Press, USA; 2 edition (April 13, 1989)

Guru, Bhag Singh; Hiziroglu, Hüseyin R., *Electromagnetic Field Theory Fundamentals*, Cambridge University Press; 2 edition (July 23, 2009)

Halliday, David; Resnick, Robert; Walker, Jearl; *Fundamentals of Physics Extended*, Wiley; 8 edition (March 9, 2007)

Hanslmeier, Arnold, *The Sun and Space Weather* (Astrophysics and Space Science Library), Springer; 2nd edition (January 2, 2008)

Harrington, Roger F., *Time-Harmonic Electromagnetic Fields* (IEEE Press Series on Electromagnetic Wave Theory), Wiley-IEEE Press; 2nd edition (August 30, 2001)

Hecht, Eugene, *Optics*, Addison Wesley; 4 edition (August 12, 2001)

Holmes-Siedle, Andrew; Adams, Len, *Handbook of Radiation Effects*, Oxford University Press, USA; 2 edition (March 28, 2002)

Howard, David; Angus, Jamie, *Acoustics and Psychoacoustics*, Focal Press; 3 edition (June 20, 2006)

Kaku, Michio, *Physics of the Impossible: A Scientific Exploration into the World of Phasers, Force Fields, Teleportation, and Time Travel*, Anchor; Reprint edition (April 7, 2009)

Karlsen, Leif, *Secrets of the Viking Navigators: How the Vikings Used their Amazing Sunstones and other Techniques to Cross the Open Ocean*, One Earth Press (February 25, 2003)

Katz, Bob, *Mastering Audio*, Focal Press; 2 edition (October 1, 2007)

Kelby, Scott, *The Digital Photography Book*, Peachpit Press; 1 edition (September 2, 2006)

Kenyon, Tom, *The Ultimate Brain: Psychoacoustic Immersion*, Sounds True, Incorporated; Unabridged edition (June 1, 2005)

Knoll, Glenn F., *Radiation Detection and Measurement*, Wiley; 3 edition (January 5, 2000)

Können, G. P.; Translated by Beerling, G. A., *Polarized Light in Nature*, Cambridge University Press (October 31, 1985)

Kuhn, Karl F., *Basic Physics: A Self-Teaching Guide (Wiley Self-Teaching Guides)*, Wiley; 2 edition (March 1996)

Mann, James; Comarow, Austine Wood, *Paintings in Polarized Light*, Wasabi Publishing; 1 edition (July 1, 2005)

Moldwin, Mark, *An Introduction to Space Weather*, Cambridge University Press; illustrated edition edition (March 3, 2008)

Moore, Brian C.J., *An Introduction to the Psychology of Hearing*, Emerald Group Publishing Ltd; 5 edition (January 24, 2003)

Morse, Philip M.; Ingard, K. Uno, *Theoretical Acoustics*, Princeton University Press (January 1, 1987)

Moser, Paul James, *Electronics and Instrumentation for Audiologists*, Psychology Press; 1 edition (December 23, 2008)

Pressnitzer, Daniel; de Cheveigné, Alain; McAdams, Stephen; Collet, Lionel; *Auditory Signal Processing: Physiology, Psychoacoustics, and Models*, Springer; 1 edition (November 30, 2004)

Pye, David, *Polarised Light in Science and Nature*, Taylor & Francis; 1 edition (February 15, 2001)

Rae, Alastair I. M., *Quantum Physics: A Beginner's Guide*, Oneworld Publications (March 25, 2006)

Scherer, K.; Fichtner, H.; Heber, B.; Mall, U., *Space Weather: The Physics Behind a Slogan* (Lecture Notes in Physics), Springer; 1 edition (February 24, 2005)

Self, Douglas; Brice, Richard; Duncan, Ben; Hood, John Linsley; Sinclair, Ian; Singmin, Andrew; Davis, Don; Patronis, Eugene; Watkinson, John; *Audio Engineering - Know it all*, Newnes (September 30, 2008)

Shadowitz, Albert, *The Electromagnetic Field*, Dover Publications (June 1, 1988)

Shurcliff, William A., *Polarized Light, Production and Use*, Harvard University Press (January 1, 1962)

Stratton, Julius Adams, *Electromagnetic Theory* (IEEE Press Series on Electromagnetic Wave Theory), Wiley-IEEE Press (January 22, 2007)

Talbot-Smith, Michael, *Audio Engineer's Reference Book*, Focal Press; 2 edition (September 2001)

Thompson, Daniel M., *Understanding Audio: Getting the Most Out of Your Project or Professional Recording Studio*, Berklee Press; illustrated edition (February 1, 2005)

Videomaker, *Videomaker Guide to Digital Video and DVD Production*, Focal Press; 3 edition (May 28, 2004)

Wangsness, Roald K., *Electromagnetic Fields*, Wiley; 2 edition (July 24, 1986)

White, Glen D.; Louie, Gary J., *The Audio Dictionary*, University of Washington Press; 3 Rev Exp edition (July 10, 2005)

Young, Hugh D.; Freedman, Roger A., *University Physics with Modern Physics with MasteringPhysics(TM) (12th Edition)* (MasteringPhysics Series), Addison Wesley; 12 edition (April 2, 2007)